THE MAKING OF A LEADER

FRANKLIN D. MURPHY THE KANSAS YEARS

NANCY KELLOGG HARPER

ACKNOWLEDGEMENTS

I am pleased to thank the many colleagues of Franklin Murphy who shared their memories with me. Their names appear in the endnotes to this work or lie waiting in files for another opportunity to speak. Especially, I honor the memory of Robert Vosper, an exceptional individual whose assistance cannot be overstated. He deserves a book of his own.

I am pleased to thank the following University of Kansas academic colleagues for their assistance in this project: William M. Tuttle, Jr., who first suggested that I might investigate the career of Franklin Murphy and whose work as a historian stands as my ideal; members of my dissertation committee, Phillip McKnight, N. Ray Hiner, Jerry D. Bailey, and James Hillesheim. Furthermore, I am pleased to thank Frank Baron, professor of German, for continuous confidence in this project and in my ability to complete it; and John Edgar Tidwell and Ernie Shelby for important civil-rights information.

I am pleased to acknowledge the work of writers and scholars who laid the foundation for this effort, including Clifford Griffin and Michael Fisher, who wrote histories of the University of Kansas, and Heidi Pitts, whose undergraduate research helped guide my work in the civil rights chapter, and to the writers and editors of the *University Daily Kansan*, between 1948 and 1960, whose words provided an invaluable timeline and flesh for uncounted anecdotes.

I am pleased to thank individuals whose technical talents made it possible to finish this book: Paula Courtney and Pam LeRow whose skills allowed me to concentrate on content; Molly Sailors for the book's graphic design; and Rachel Barnes of Jayhawk, Ink who made the publication process easier.

I am pleased to thank the archivists and librarians of the University of Kansas, the University of Kansas School of Medicine, and the University of California at Los Angeles, whose dedication and precision provide the future's key to the past.

And, I am pleased to thank my family, John Parkman Harper and Carrie Harper Wiklund, my children; my uncle, John Congleton Carson, MD; my eight siblings, whose writing skills stand as visible standards and who never asked when will it be finished; my late parents, Robert and Mary Martha Kellogg, who taught me to take responsibility for my beliefs, to look carefully, and to love books; and my husband Jerry L. Harper, my partner in our continuing attempt to live well.

For Jerry

© 2016 by Nancy Kellogg Harper

All rights reserved

Printed in the United States of America

Published by Jayhawk Ink, University of Kansas, Lawrence, Kansas

Graphic design by MollySailors.com

Photographs courtesy of Kenneth Spencer Research Library, University of Kansas Libraries. Reproduced with permission.

Cover portrait: Murphy as dean, 1949. Kenneth Spencer Research Library, University of Kansas Libraries

ISBN 9781611950205

TABLE OF CONTENTS

INTRODUCTION
Learning to Lead   1

CHAPTER ONE
Early Influences: 1916-1947   9

CHAPTER TWO
Medical School Dean: 1948-1951   33

CHAPTER THREE
Chancellor, University of Kansas: 1951-1960   49

CHAPTER FOUR
Art and Books: 1951-1960   65

CHAPTER FIVE
Civil Rights: 1951-1960   107

CHAPTER SIX
Kansas Political Wars: 1951-1960   159

CONCLUSION
The Patterns of Leadership   209

APPENDIX
Franklin Murphy's Positions and Affiliations   223
"The Meaning of University"   227
The Ernie Shelby letter   233

ENDNOTES   237

WORKS CITED   271

INDEX   283

INTRODUCTION

Learning to Lead

An urbane, affable Irishman who reads everything from Rabelais to Runyon, and likes music ranging from Bach to Berlin, Murphy is a genuine whiz at getting the necessary dough-re-mi with which he has performed his wonders.

Bob Considine, 1973

IN THE LATE 1920s, a Chevrolet roadster cost $625, about the same as a baby grand piano or a seven-week cruise to the South Seas and Australia. An electric kitchen range cost $98.50 and a new Crosley Bandbox radio sold for $55. For just one dollar, a serious reader could receive 52 issues of the New York *Herald Tribune*'s supplement, "Books: A Weekly Review of Contemporary Literature."[1]

Teenaged Franklin Murphy's $5 weekly allowance constituted a comparatively impressive amount of money, even though he earned it and used it sparingly. When the Kansas City bookseller told young Murphy that one old, small woodcut (just the size of a page in a book) cost $50, it clearly was not an amount to be taken lightly. After all, had he wished to see reproductions of art, Murphy could have purchased for half as much a two-volume set of *100 Famous Paintings* from Funk and Wagnalls, bound in leather and embossed in gold. The woodcut in question, however, was no reproduction.[2]

Murphy, a Pembroke School student with serious interests in sports and a beginning interest in girls, often walked the seven short blocks from home to downtown Kansas City on Saturdays, just to look around. Cool, even in the summer, the dark downtown canyons lay at the heart of this railroad hub of more than 350,000 people.[3]

One Saturday, as he walked past the downtown Muehlebach Hotel, Murphy stopped to look in the window of Frank Glenn's shop of rare books and prints, on the street level of the hotel. He was intrigued by an old woodcut, filled with furious action; with wild horsemen charging to attack an unseen foe and brandishing a sword, a pike and a scale. Raised on Sir Walter Scott and Tom Swift stories, the teenager saw enormous excitement in the picture in Frank Glenn's window. He was drawn to its minuscule detail, and wanted to know what it meant.[4]

Not until a week later did Franklin Murphy build up nerve to go inside the shop. Having thought about the picture for a week, on this Saturday he went inside to find out more. The owner, Frank Glenn, (the only antiquarian bookseller in Kansas City at the time) was very patient with the young man.[5] The woodcut in the window, Glenn explained, was part of the Four Horsemen of the Apocalypse series by the Renaissance artist, Albrecht Dürer.

A German printmaker, Dürer produced the violent series of woodcuts in 1498 in response to Europe's obsession with the calendar. Many believed that the year 1500 would bring the end of the world. Dürer had interpreted Saint John's revelation of the world's end in fourteen compelling woodcuts illustrating war, famine, death, and hell. According to Bruce Cole, writing in *Art of the Western World*.

The entire image explodes with movement as horses trample people underfoot. Anxiety emanates from every line and form. A bishop falls into a monster's open jaws, while God's destructive forces reclaim the earth and cleanse it of its evil.

Dürer's Apocalypse was intended for the general public and was an immediate success, Cole wrote, bringing the artist fame in Germany, Italy and throughout Europe.[6]

One woodcut print from that famous series lay, in the late 1920s, in front of teenaged Franklin David Murphy, in a dark, musty bookshop in downtown Kansas City, Missouri. He had just been told that it cost $50.

"I'd sure like to buy it," Murphy said, "but I only have $10 at the moment." According to Murphy, more than 60 years later, Frank Glenn had a "second sense" because he made the ultimate purchase so easy. "Look son," the rare-book man said, "if you give me $10 now and come by every month and give me another $10, in a little while it will all be paid."[7]

The deal was struck, and Franklin Murphy walked out with the precious $50 Dürer. That woodcut, the first of many cultural relics that he purchased in the intervening years, set Franklin Murphy on a lifetime path as a collector of fine art and rare books.

In spite of having kept the Dürer, which hung in his Beverly Hills home even on the day of his death in 1994, Murphy's collecting activities rarely served selfish interests. As medical school dean at age 32, as chancellor of two public universities—University of Kansas (KU) and University of California Los Angeles (UCLA)—as head of the Times-Mirror communications empire, and as chairman of the boards of charitable foundations, museums and libraries, Franklin Murphy raised the money that created many opportunities for wide public use of books and art. The first purchase, the Dürer, was kept close by for its sentimental value and for love, Murphy said. What cost $50 in the late 1920s was appraised at $15,000 just before Murphy's death.[8] That appraisal did not displease its owner, a man with practical experience in balancing multi-billion-dollar budgets and in convincing others of the ultimate value of excellence.

The Dürer inaugural purchase and its present value illustrate two sides of Franklin Murphy. On one hand lies the frame of his lifelong *vision*—his goal of excellence: expect the best, whether in people, in resources, in programs, or in library collections. With the same illustration, one sees the leader's vision put into *action*. "If the objective has real value," he said, "you'll find a way to pay for it."[9]

His interests and his skill were obvious to many who watched him work, including International News Service Reporter Bob Considine, who described him as:

> An urbane, affable Irishman who reads everything from Rabelais to Runyon, and likes music ranging from Bach to Berlin, Murphy is a genuine whiz at getting the necessary dough-re-mi with which he has performed his wonders.[10]

Franklin Murphy found a way to pay for an original Dürer—a tangible connection to the Renaissance. It is an appropriate introduction to an individual who led nearly a decade of measurable change at the University of Kansas—nine years that many participants described as a renaissance, an exciting and palpable rebirth—a "glorious rocket ride."[11] That description is also appropriate in that the European Renaissance remained his favorite era, as a collector and enquirer, until his death. "I have always loved the Renaissance," he said. "We—all of us—are still extending what was started then."[12]

Early in 1959, the University of Kansas' Fine Arts Dean Thomas Gorton introduced Murphy to an audience of American contemporary composers. The comparisons he chose reflected his own perception of Murphy: "In the 15th century, he would have been Lorenzo the Magnificent; in the 18th century, a Thomas Jefferson; and in the 20th century, he is the Chancellor of the University of Kansas—Dr. Franklin David Murphy." Gorton's perception, near the end of Murphy's tenure, reflected his years of observing and working with the man who led the university. He was not alone in concluding that Murphy might be described as a Renaissance Man.[13] With this description, observers noted his wide-ranging interests and talents.

But at the beginning, in July 1951, few on the Lawrence campus of the University of Kansas knew the man who had just been named as chancellor-designate. Faculty members didn't know what to think. The humanities and fine-arts faculties were convinced that Franklin Murphy, M.D., dean of the KU School of Medicine, would favor the hard sciences. The scientists were afraid that Franklin Murphy, who was said to like opera, would favor the arts and humanities.[14] All of them soon learned that this polymath wanted nothing less than the very best of everything for the university—and that, in many cases, he could get it.

For many reasons, Murphy seems to have been too good to be true. When the stories one hears make him appear nearly perfect, one must question the anecdotes in an attempt to separate fact from folklore.

A Renaissance man? Lorenzo the Magnificent or Thomas Jefferson? A polymath who wanted the best and could get it? The folklore of Murphy comprises much praise of and few complaints about the man as a leader. The stories suggest that Murphy singlehandedly forced the restaurants and movie theaters in Lawrence to integrate—to change their racially exclusionary policies. He is described as an ethical leader who spoke on controversial issues, such as Senator Joseph McCarthy's Red-baiting and the evil of Orval Faubus, during times of national paranoia when few others took a stand.

In the cultural arena, stories seem to validate his description as a Renaissance man: one who loved rare books and fine art, and who enjoyed reading a dictionary while waiting for appointments. Some say that he deserves credit for having created a library of world renown at KU. Many describe him as charming and a master of persuasion—that he drew outstanding faculty and staff to the university as if he were a magnet.

Anecdotes portray Murphy as a natural politician—of his having been asked to run for President and Governor, and of his having turned down Presidential-cabinet positions. One story relates that President Eisenhower told Murphy that he could be trusted with the duties of the highest political office in the nation. On the other hand, Murphy said that he stood outside politics, and he consistently refused to compete for public office himself. In the final analysis, his skills as a politician may not have sufficed for the impending conflicts with Governor George Docking, which probably caused Murphy to leave Kansas.

Unquestionably, many of his colleagues considered him a leader. "His brilliant talents will continue to champion the cause of education in this country," the faculty senate proclaimed when Murphy resigned from KU in 1960 to become Chancellor of UCLA. "His work here will long be an inspiration to all to enlist in this cause."[15] Do these isolated quotations and common anecdotes merely bolster the mythology of Franklin Murphy or do they represent accurate appraisals? It is easy to become mesmerized by the apparent perfection of the man, by the breadth and depth of his interests, and by his articulate and constant vision of excellence. Personal interviews with Murphy and with those who knew him well help separate fact from fiction, as does an examination of his papers at the University of Kansas. In these, one finds some rust on the shining armor. One finds evidence of confidence that borders on arrogance, of an authoritarian and controlling style, and of an intimidating presence. One sees that he failed to raise the university to the prominence he wished for it. One finds details that separate fact from folklore in the account of Franklin Murphy as a leader.

This work describes Murphy in Kansas with the evidence of his words, his actions, and their results. It explains his actions at the University of Kansas in order to judge his leadership and to separate fact from folklore. It does not follow Murphy's career in Los Angeles, as leader of the University of California at Los Angeles or of the Times Mirror Company, but instead it follows his origins in Kansas, from his birth in 1916 until he left the state in 1960. The book centers on his work at the University of Kansas, as dean of its medical school from 1948-51 and as its Chancellor from 1951-60. During those years, visible and measurable change occurred at the institution: one must ascertain the extent to which Murphy's actions and leadership caused that change.

This record of Murphy's career until 1960 will clarify his actions as a leader, identify some of the influences upon him, and illustrate his style of leadership. Ultimately, one must judge his success or failure as a leader, using the proof that lies not only in tangible evidence of change, but also in the words of the man and of those with whom he worked. Furthermore, the examination of leadership has generated substantial scholarship and has resulted in a range of definitions, each with carefully defined parameters.

This book attempts to see Murphy's career through an Aristotelian concept of change and persuasive leadership. Change occurs, Aristotle wrote, from the interaction of four causes: formal, material, efficient, and final.[16] Very simply, the four may be defined as the leader's vision, the material with which the leader works, the source of movement, and the resulting goal. This work evaluates Murphy's efforts to cause change. Furthermore, it examines Murphy's career in Kansas through the prism of what Mortimer Adler described as Aristotelian qualities of leadership: *ethos, logos, and pathos*—ethics, logic, and passion.[17] "The *ethos* is his moral character," Adler wrote, "the source of his ability to persuade. *The pathos* is his ability to touch feelings, to move people emotionally. The *logos* is his ability to give solid reasons for an action, to move people intellectually."[18] In *Rhetoric* 1:2, Aristotle explained three qualities of persuasion that inspire confidence: good sense, good moral character, and goodwill. All help the leader to persuade his followers. That leader uses three modes of persuasion, he wrote: "The man who is to be in command of them must... be able (1) to reason logically, (2) to understand human character and goodness in their various forms, and (3) to understand the emotions."[19]

While this book evaluates Murphy's leadership style with Aristotelian precepts in mind when they are appropriate, it stands primarily as a record of Murphy's actions.

In carrying its subject through his life until 1960, this book examines influences upon him and patterns in his life. And, it records in detail his work in three arenas: Murphy as the catalyst of change in the KU art museum and library; Murphy's role in efforts to desegregate and integrate the university and the community; and the conflicts between practical politics and Murphy's commitment to a free market-place of ideas. Written as narrative that takes advantage of the words of the participants, as supplied by interviews with Murphy and those who worked with him, this book relies on an examination of correspondence and materials of the University of Kansas Archives. It goes beyond the published research framework laid by the institutional histories of Clifford Griffin and Michael Fisher, and the unpublished manuscript written by Heidi Pitts.[20] And, just as Murphy relied on newspapers, this book draws on the timeline and the points of view of those newspaper reporters and editors who covered Murphy's career in Kansas.

CHAPTER 1

Early Influences

1916 - 1947

Few lifetime honors meant as much to Murphy as his medical-school class standing at the University of Pennsylvania. Tapped as a member of Alpha Omega Alpha, the top medical honorary, he graduated first in his 1941 class.

"I was there with a lot of Ivy League types who had had their undergraduate work at Princeton and Harvard and Yale," he said, with obvious pleasure. *"It pleased me that a little ol' Kansas boy could beat 'em to the wire."*

— Franklin Murphy

THE INFLUENCE of the antiquarian bookseller, Frank Glenn, constituted part of the foundation that formed Murphy's character and interests. More importantly, his family provided lifetime lessons of enormous impact on Murphy's later career. "I was a very fortunate young man," he said often.[1]

Born in Kansas City, Missouri, on January 29, 1916, Franklin David Murphy was the first child of Cordelia Brown Murphy, a concert pianist, and Franklin Edward Murphy, M.D., who for 30 years had practiced medicine in the city. Dr. Murphy had been a founding member of the University of Kansas School of Medicine and served on its faculty until his death. Having met in Berlin, Murphy's parents had established their careers long before marrying.[2] Murphy's mother was 36 and his father was 50 when Franklin, their eldest child, was born.

The Murphy family originated in Ireland, where Franklin's paternal great-grandfather, Patrick Murphy, lived in County Cork. A Roman Catholic, Patrick Murphy was a commissioned broker and a widower when he married a widow, Martha Flanagin, a member of the "Established Church"—the Church of England in Ireland.[3] Both their families vigorously objected to the mixed-religion marriage, even after several years and two children. The young couple emigrated to the United States to escape these familial religious wars. With them came their two natural children, James and Hugh Charles, and Martha's daughter, Mary Elizabeth Paul. After buying a farm in Scott County, Indiana, father Patrick died, as did his son James, leaving Martha Flanagin Murphy to raise Hugh Charles and Mary Elizabeth "without any means at all." She sold the farm to make ends meet.[4]

Franklin's grandfather, Hugh Charles Murphy, worked his way through the Ohio Medical College at Cincinnati (later University of Cincinnati Medical School) and went to practice in Reddington, Indiana. There, according to his grandson's 1956 research, "we find him serving as physician for the poor of Redding Township in June, 1865."[5]

In February, 1866, Hugh Charles Murphy married Martha Jane Cook. The daughter of Silas and Mary Cook, a Quaker couple originally from Pennsylvania, Franklin's grandmother was born in 1844. The first child of Martha Jane and Hugh Charles Murphy became Franklin's father, Franklin Edward, born in November of 1866. The family subsequently moved to Missouri; they lived at Perryville in 1874, at Independence in 1881, and at Kansas City in 1883. Three additional Murphy children followed Franklin Edward: George, Alice, and Lee—who were to be Chancellor Murphy's father and aunts and uncles.

The family lived at 1100 Prospect in Kansas City, in a house built by Dr. Hugh Charles Murphy in 1883. Both the father, Hugh, and son, George, died in 1903—the son succumbed to Bright's Disease.[6] Alice, a talented painter and teacher, had married before her death from cancer in 1912. Although he never knew his Aunt Alice, as he would not be born until four years after her death, Franklin Murphy would feel her influence throughout his life.

Hugh Charles Murphy had been a country doctor. After his son, Franklin Edward, earned degrees in pharmacy and medicine from the University of Pennsylvania, the young man spent several years studying in Germany and Austria.[7] There he met Cordelia Brown, a Kansas City native who was studying piano in Berlin, and who would become Franklin David Murphy's mother.

Cordelia Antoinette Brown was the daughter of Adolphus H. Brown and Tryphosa Beals. Tryphosa's father, David T. Beals, was born in North Abbington, Massachusetts, in 1832, as was his wife, Ruth McCobb. The Beals moved from Massachusetts to Colorado and then to Kansas City, where he was a banker, rancher, and financier. David and Ruth Beals had three daughters, Tryphosa (who later married Welsh Dean Findley), Gertrude (who married Russell Field), and Cordelia (who married Franklin Edward Murphy). This family who would become his aunts and uncles influenced young Franklin more than any other individuals.

A "free spirit often soaring in the clouds and vibrant with enthusiasms,"[8] Cordelia Brown spent four years studying in Germany with the distinguished pianists Henrich Barth and Teresa Carreneo, and performing in concerts in Europe and, after returning to the U.S. in 1905, in this country.[9] She was thirty-five when she married the small and quiet forty-nine-year-old Franklin E. Murphy, in 1915.

After their Kansas City wedding, Dr. and Mrs. Frank Murphy moved into the Murphy family home at 1100 Prospect. Their first child, Franklin David, was born in 1916. Two other children followed: George Edward, born in 1918, and Cordelia, in 1922.[10] During their 1920s and 1930s childhoods, the Murphy children enjoyed the comfort of financial security, the stimulation of a large extended family, and the sensual beauty that surrounded them at home.[11]

A large and sun-filled structure, the Prospect Street house was filled with art, including many original oil paintings by young Franklin's paternal aunt Alice Murphy Gross, whose early death had ended a promising career.[12] Franklin and his siblings grew up surrounded by evidence of Aunt Alice's talent and with stories about her success in the 1903 Paris exhibition, sponsored by the *Societé National des Beaux Arts*, and her friendship with such painters as Mary Cassatt.[13] She had studied in London with the American Impressionist painter William Merritt Chase, who described her work as the most original of his students'.[14]

After declining Chase's offer of a New York scholarship to work with him, Alice Murphy returned to Kansas City where she had earlier opened an art department in the "new and progressive" Manual Training High School and where she continued to give private lessons in drawing and painting [15] Among her students was Mary McAfee Atkins, who, on her death in 1911, bequeathed funds to build an art museum for Kansas City. That bequest combined four years later with funds from the estate of Kansas City *Star* publisher, William Rockhill Nelson, to create the Nelson-Atkins Museum of Art. "One can speculate," wrote Charles Eldredge, curator of the Spencer Museum of Art at the University of Kansas when the Alice Murphy exhibition of thirty-five paintings[16] opened in 1972, "that Alice Murphy had something to do with Mary Atkins' late-flowering interest in art."[17] One need not speculate that Alice Murphy's legacy of beauty in paintings influenced her nephew, Franklin. It is an unquestioned fact that he acknowledged often.[18]

Young Murphy's growing-up world included musical beauty as well. Even though she no longer performed in concert, his mother played the piano in her home every day and would later stand as one of the founders of the Kansas City Philharmonic Orchestra.[19] Her son later wrote that all of her life she was deeply interested in music and in making musical opportunities for young people.[20] Even though he never played a musical instrument[21] and acknowledged no talent in art, he said that he gained from her a tremendous interest in people, music and the arts.[22] Murphy's sister, Cordelia, inherited artistic talent, he said. One of her paintings hung in a place of honor in Murphy's first Kansas City home.[23] As an adult, Murphy's musical interest ranged from boogie-woogie to symphonic classics, but nothing in more than moderate doses, he admitted.[24]

Murphy recalled his mother's genuine interest in people, noting her concern for both the delivery man's family and the friends she met for esoteric discussions of music. For a time, she volunteered to teach music in a neighborhood house for Italian-Americans. She was always tremendously concerned over someone who was ill or in trouble, he said.[25] "Race didn't matter to my mother," he said. "In my family, discrimination and intolerance were just no good."[26] Murphy said that from her he gained great compassion for victims of grinding poverty and privation.[27] In recalling his father's 1936 death, when he and his siblings were in high school and college, Murphy thought first of his mother and of his own need to be responsible, to help make up for her loss.[28]

Much later, a longtime family friend described the adult Franklin Murphy as more like his mother than his father. "Frank's father was a quiet, reserved man," recalled Dr. Thomas G. Orr, Sr., in 1951, "but his mother was a real go-getter."[29]

In 1976, Murphy established the first endowed music professorship in the University of Kansas School of Fine Arts in his mother's honor,[30] prompting Fine Arts Dean James Moeser to write that "this gift is the single most important development in music at the University, for it will help to develop a truly distinguished faculty, the most critical component in building a program of excellence."[31] And, in 1978, Murphy proposed to establish the Cordelia Brown Murphy International Piano Competition.[32]

Described by her son as a "very proper New England-type lady," Cordelia Murphy taught her children always to show respect to their elders, in every way. "In our family," Murphy said, "you never called an older person by their first name, for example." He acknowledged difficulty, even at age 74, in calling acquaintances by their first names and became known later as a chancellor who addressed his elders, whether his secretary or a faculty member, in a formal fashion. His correspondence as chancellor reflected the gentility—as judged by polite words—that he had learned at home, from his mother.

As was the case with many fathers at that time, Dr. Franklin Edward Murphy was wedded to his work and rarely at home.[33] As a member of the KU School of Medicine faculty, Dr. Murphy's medical specialties were diseases of the heart and blood vessels, and much of his time was spent making house calls. Murphy recalled going on rounds, as a child, with his father at the hospital but recalled few other regular father-son activities.[34] Firmly established in his busy profession before fatherhood, Dr. Murphy spent little time with his children.

For cultural events, the Murphy family occasionally drove 40 miles to Lawrence, site of the University of Kansas.[35] Generally, however, such family events remained occasional only. As "my father was an old man by the time I was an adolescent, and because he was away much of the time," Murphy said, "I pretty much raised myself."[36]

While her children were still small and at home, Cordelia Murphy left much of the daily household administration and child care to her mother-in-law, Mary Jane Murphy, who lived at 1100 Prospect with the younger family. Murphy said that his Grandmother Murphy taught him to be practical. She could mold candles and weave cloth. She saw no sense in a big to-do over music and art, he told a reporter in 1949.[37] While this attitude may have created problems for her daughter-in-law, whose life revolved around such interests and who must have felt like a third wheel in the older woman's home, the son/grandson did not recall any problems between the two women.

He did recall his grandmother's practical advice: "Never spend more money than you get," and "There is some good in everybody and it is just as easy to talk about their good points. After all, nobody likes people who say mean things."[38] While his grandmother taught him to do things with his hands, she did not hover over him.[39] Instead, she and Franklin's mother allowed the boy enormous freedom. "Happily," he said, "those were the days when there was no television and very little radio." He spent his free time with athletics and books. "I did a lot of reading," he said. "That was my companion, you see. Books were important in my life early on."[40]

He read Tom Swift and later, adventures by Sir Walter Scott. Murphy's father enjoyed reading and passed along this pleasure to his children by introducing them to a wide range of books.[41] He also shared his love of collecting books. "He was interested in the history of medicine," Murphy said, "and we had some very important first editions around the house."[42] Murphy later donated many of his father's books to the School of Medicine's Clendening History of Medicine Library, which had been endowed in 1946 and grew substantially during Murphy's tenure as dean.[43]

Young Murphy's religious training derived from his mother's Congregational Church influence. His father had been raised essentially as an agnostic, the legacy of his grandparents who left Ireland as a result of the pressure of intense religious feelings on both sides of the family. The immigrant Murphys considered themselves agnostics, and belonged to no church at all. While Murphy later described them as "very religious people, in that the Bible was read daily at breakfast," they deeply resented "professional religion" as it had caused them so many heartaches.[44] They raised their children with the same philosophy and the tradition continued to their grandson, Franklin Murphy's father.

Not at all gruff, Frank Murphy influenced his children in quiet ways.[45] Though small of stature, he had a profound impact on the family.[46] Not only did the elder Murphy impart to his children the need to think for themselves, he also taught them to take responsibility for the results. "It was clear that those boys were raised in a family of stability and with a strong sense of values," said a friend who knew Franklin and his brother, George.[47]

Frank Murphy's comparatively advanced age also influenced his children. His son, Franklin, said that he could not remember ever having questioned the older man's judgment.[48] Though he clearly hoped that both his sons would carry on the family tradition of medicine into its third generation (which both ultimately did), Frank Murphy did not pressure either son into that field but continually, and quietly, presented his work as passionate service. He forced them to think for themselves. Murphy's brother, George, followed the family tradition by earning a bachelor's degree from KU, and a medical degree from the University of Pennsylvania. Like his father and elder brother, George Murphy served on a medical faculty, as Professor of Pathology at Cornell University Medical Center.

"Son, you have just one decision to make," Franklin Murphy remembered his father saying, "If you want to be of primary service, go into medicine. Not otherwise. And remember that primary service means more than just saving human lives."[49]

The decision of a career was left entirely to the young men. Franklin did not make his decision until halfway through college, at which time he chose medicine. During his professional life thereafter, Murphy attempted to follow his father's advice about "primary service:" doctors should participate in civic affairs, his father said, noting that when a doctor declines a civic duty on the grounds of lack of time, he really is running up an alibi for his want of knowledge of such affairs.[50]

In Murphy's case, it was also a matter of curiosity as much as a conscious or unconscious attempt to heed a parent's advice—his interests ranged widely within and without the medical profession. For instance, when he was chancellor of the University of Kansas, Murphy intended to expand the collections of fine books and art. After procuring two small sculptures, following a lengthy series of letters, he then spent an equal amount of time finding and arranging the perfect red granite plinths on which the artwork would be displayed.[51]

Murphy honored his father, in 1977, by establishing the Franklin E. Murphy Distinguished Professorship in Cardiology at the University of Kansas School of Medicine.[52] "In thinking back on my childhood," Murphy said, "I've concluded that this thing called togetherness isn't a necessity. It isn't how much time a parent spends with a child that counts so much as the impact the parent has on a child."[53]

At only one sustained period in his life did Murphy's busy father attend his son's activities—during the high-school student's football career at the old Pembroke School (later combined and called Pembroke- Country Day School).[54] To the boy, the most important thing about the school was the football team on which he played quarterback. He was hurt during his junior year in a game against Lee's Summit, causing a kidney injury which was rather serious for a while.

The next autumn, according to Murphy's memory, he asked for permission to play football again, with little hope of a favorable answer from a doctor father. "Yes, son, if you really want to," his father said. "We will have to get some special pads for you." That season, Franklin Murphy wondered why his busy father came to all the games. Years later, after his father's 1936 death, his mother explained that her husband had been frightened. "He wanted to be on hand if something should happen to you," she said.[55] Fortunately, he played the season without injury and, at the end of his senior year, the five-foot nine-inch Murphy was proud to be elected All Little-Six Conference quarterback.[56]

Even though he remembered the names of few teachers at Pembroke and considered football his highest achievement there, Murphy said he gained much satisfaction from pure learning—mostly from his parents. "I grew up in a family that very early gave me the notion that although you have to prepare yourself to earn a living," he said, "you also have an obligation and an enormous opportunity to explore human knowledge and human beauty."

While he attributed his 19th-century manners to the influence of his "very Proper Bostonian" mother, Murphy could not recall many dinner-table conversations with his parents. Instead, constant intellectual stimulation came from his maternal uncle, Russell Field. Married to his mother's sister Gertrude and father of Murphy's "closer-than-brothers" cousin Lyman, Russell Field constituted an important primary influence on the young man's education.[57] The normal setting was the Field residence, at 3622 Holmes Street, where varying Murphy/Oliver/Field cousins congregated for regular Sunday dinners after church.[58] Cordelia Murphy dropped off the boys at the Westminster Congregational Church, after which they walked, with cousins Gertrude Oliver, and Russell and Lyman Field, to the Field house. The dinners, Murphy said, centered on his Uncle Russell's games, which might begin with "today, boys, we're going to the capitals of the world"[59] and always ended with the announcement of each child's new Word of the Week. From his earliest days, Murphy associated learning with fun—it remained a mental challenge that he loved.[60] His lifelong friendship with cousin Lyman (as family-dinner partners, Boy Scout mates, college-fraternity roommates, and beyond) kept him close to his Uncle Russell and the older man's mental challenges.[61]

Another uncle, Lee Murphy, balanced his nephew's education with practical business training. Childless, Lee Murphy and his wife lived in close proximity to his brother's family and showed special affection for their nephew, Franklin. A tough businessman and "anything but an intellectual," Murphy's uncle Lee had gone to work straight from high school. "He was the ultimate practical person," Murphy said.[62] When Franklin Murphy was about 10 years old, his Uncle Lee had become a division head at Kansas City's Emery-Bird-Thayer department store. With plans for his favorite nephew's future, Lee Murphy made a deal with his brother Frank: "You can have your son for nine months each year," Lee said. "But I want him for three months in the summers."[63] The elder Murphy obviously agreed, for from that young age until he graduated from college, Franklin Murphy spent his summers and school holidays working for and learning from his Uncle Lee. Beginning as a stock boy "in the days before child-labor laws," Murphy said, he advanced to salesperson in the men's furnishings and rug departments at Emery-Bird-Thayer.[64]

From this experience, Murphy gained not only the spending money needed to pay for a $50 Dürer woodcut, but also an invaluable education in administration, business operations, and getting along with people.[65] The boy worked for his uncle throughout his high-school years until his graduation in 1932.[66]

When Franklin Murphy began college at a youthful 16, he had gained a foundation in cultural and intellectual values from his parents and his uncle Russell Field, and experience in the practical world of business and administration from his uncle Lee Murphy. "I was very fortunate to have this bilateral experience," he said.[67]

Undergraduate years at The University of Kansas: 1932-1936

"Everyone thinks Kansas is flat as a billiard table," Murphy said. "As a matter of fact, eastern Kansas is rolling hills. Driving to Lawrence from Kansas City you begin to see the university ten miles away, rearing up high on a hill—Mount Oread. The buildings flow down the sides of this hill into Lawrence. It's absolutely beautiful."[68]

The drive from Kansas City to Lawrence was just as beautiful in September, 1932, as Highway K-10 wound through the dense, green northeastern Kansas hills along Kill Creek, through DeSoto and Eudora. After the first frost, in another month, the roadsides would be filled with pumpkin patches and corn shocks—fields littered with bright orange pumpkins, just waiting for the visiting families and school children from Kansas City and Lawrence to pick among. On a steamy hot September day in 1932, however, the automobile traffic headed one way only, to Lawrence, where the autumn semester of the University of Kansas was set to begin and where sixteen-year-old Franklin Murphy would enroll as a freshman.

No stranger to Lawrence, Murphy had spent many evenings and weekend afternoons in the college town with his parents and cousins. As his father was a long-time faculty member of the KU School of Medicine and as his mother sought out all regional cultural events for her family, Murphy had often attended sports events and cultural events in Lawrence, just 40 miles from Kansas City.

At the University of Kansas, Murphy's constant companion was his best friend and cousin, Lyman Field. Though two years older, Lyman began KU with Franklin in 1932. They both pledged Beta Theta Pi and shared the house with such friends as Clyde Nichols, Blaine Hibbard, Bob Kenyon and J.R. Battenfeld.[69] Franklin and Lyman roomed together in the huge, stone Beta house, just south of 14th Street on Tennessee. In 1935, Murphy's brother George would make it a Beta House trio walking up the hill past Oyler's Shoe Repair and Coe's Drug Store, just through the Beta's back lot, at 14th and Ohio.[70]

On leaving the chancellorship of the same university 28 years later, in 1960, Murphy told the thousands of students who protested his decision to leave that his had not been a job, but "a love affair with KU that began in 1932 when I first walked up the 14th Street hill."[71]

Lyman Field's KU career took him to the heights: captain of the debate team, Mississippi Valley Extemporaneous Speaking Champion, president of Men's Student Council, and organizer of the Progressive Student Government League. "Red Dog" Field was a genuine Big Man on Campus.[72] Heading for a legal career and dreaming of remaking the world—without the human cruelty of Great Depressions—Field led bull sessions that were said to have reached a new peak during 1932-1933.[73] A skilled debater, Lyman argued with gusto. His cousin Franklin is said to have jumped into the thick of it in the Beta house, usually on the opposite side. Murphy said later that these were the nights that gave him a high regard for the bull session as a means of making college students think on their own. Even though he said that he enjoyed the informal bull sessions, Murphy left competitive and public forensics to his cousin—preferring journalism. He was busy, but neither as visible nor as controversial as Lyman, who held decidedly more liberal views than did Franklin. Murphy especially supported his cousin, whose ability to articulate a position, however controversial, made Murphy very proud. While pride in his cousin did not result in moving Murphy to Lyman's political camp, it did result in gentle chiding, in public and in print. Murphy's medium was the *Jayhawker,* which was then published monthly and in which he wrote:

> Among the interesting sidelights of the K.U.-St. Benedict's game was the rather unusual activity on the part of a group of individuals known as the "K" Club, so named because of valiant work and achievement on the field, and in the gymnasium. Their attempt to paddle one of their own group for his refusal to co-operate in matters of dress and equipment aroused no little comment, as regards the group as well as the advisability of paddling generally. The University faculty, in meeting assembled, expressed their feelings in the form of a resolution strongly urging the abolishment of paddling. In the face of a barrage of criticism the "K" Club turned back to the Men's Student Council the official right to preserve certain traditions in relation to the freshmen. This placed the problem squarely on the shoulders of Lyman "Stalin" Field and his proletariat. The matter of traditions is still an unanswered question; we hope not for long.[74]

Murphy also wrote an article in the October 1935 *Jayhawker* with his cousin Lyman Field as the subject. In January, 1935, Field had organized a new student-government organization, The Progressive Student Government League, which battled long-dominant Pachacamac for leadership of the Men's Student Council. In "Dictapators: Dealing With the Purpose and Functions of the M.S.C. and the Program of the New Regime," Murphy described the campaign between the rival parties:

> As far as the students were concerned, the League might have been just another hurriedly constructed political party and the possibilities for another stupid campaign were in

sight. Then began a unique campaign. The Progressive Student Government League, quickly shortened to P.S.G.L., announced their candidates after what they termed an intensive survey by ballot of the male students. Pachacamac's nominations were before the student body soon after and the time was ripe for the usual flow of literary tripe—but the multi-colored handbills were not forthcoming. The Hill awoke one morning to learn that the platforms, as well as the candidates of the rival organizations, were to be presented to the student body by means of formal debate. For the first time in the memory of this writer, the candidates for president of the Men's Student Council explained their stand as well as their party's stand in reference to their respective platforms and aims. The interest in this illuminating discussion was evidenced by the attendance of some nine hundred Kansas men—at least the student electorate at K.U. had been moved to express itself in regard to policy. Instead of endeavoring to stuff student-government down the throats of the students who make it possible, the leaders complimented their respective followings by putting it on the basis of reason.[75]

Murphy wrote that 1,800 men cast their ballots in "one of the closest, yet cleanest elections in recent years" and, when the smoke of battle cleared, Lyman Field had been chosen as president of the Men's Student Council, "...the opinion of this writer," Murphy wrote, "is that the following program of action as outlined by President Field should warrant the serious non-political and courageous actions of the council members, not as representatives of rival political parties but as individuals endeavoring to alleviate and improve irregular and unsatisfactory conditions as pertain to their University."[76]

Field, who always was photographed wearing a vested suit with a golden watch-chain looped across his chest just above the second button,[77] looked serious and striking with his strong jaw, erect posture, and thick and wavy red hair. In a cartoon accompanying the "Dictapator" article, a dapper young man lectures the caricatures of Hitler, Stalin, and Mussolini and says: "Boys, we do it with *forums* at K.U." The dapper young man, who bears a decided resemblance in the drawing to the very popular Prince of Wales, is Lyman Field.[78]

In college, Murphy's *Jayhawker* job remained comparatively minor, but much loved. Forced to choose a major, he said later that he could not decide between English/journalism and a science—the latter to lead naturally to medicine, the family tradition.[79] In the end, the pragmatic decision centered on time. It would take three times as long to do a Ph.D. in English—with its required foreign languages[80]—than would medicine. He chose zoology.

It was not such a difficult choice really. In his junior year, Murphy enrolled in a zoology course under Dr. W. J. Baumgartner, a "lovable, absent-minded, enthusiastic man who encouraged him to write a research paper to present to the Kansas Academy of Science."[81] He joined the KU Zoology Club and was invited to join Sigma Xi, an honorary research society. With his interest in science whetted, Murphy decided to pursue medicine. His father's death at this time cemented the choice. As the eldest son of the family, Murphy immediately felt a new sense of responsibility and became an exceedingly serious student. He graduated on the Dean's Honor Roll with the University of Kansas class of 1936 and looked forward to beginning medical school at the University of Pennsylvania, his father's *alma mater.*

Presidential candidate Alfred M. Landon, a popular Kansas governor and native son, delivered the 1936 commencement address. Murphy remembered nothing of the speech; only that then-Chancellor E. H. Lindley pulled a nationwide faux pas by introducing Landon as the "well-known governor of Indiana" over a national radio network.[82]

The Year Abroad: 1936-37

The young graduate in the KU class of 1936 would not begin medical school just yet. With the urging of his mother and the memory of his father's stories, Murphy accepted a year-long exchange scholarship from the University of Kansas to Goettingen University, one of the most famous and respected German universities, located in a small German college town. His cousin Lyman had spent a wonderful summer in Europe the previous year and his advice surely helped Murphy decide against immediate medical school and in favor of a year abroad.

It was an exciting time for a young man to be completely on his own. In the autumn of 1936, Hitler was in power, having tied the nation together with a network of autobahnen and having eliminated unemployment.[83] In 1936, Hitler had formed the Berlin-Rome Axis and had sent troops into the demilitarized Rhineland, an action that elicited nothing but mumbling objection by the Allies.[84] Mussolini had expanded his Roman Empire the year before by invading Ethiopia, and the Spanish Civil War raged. In spite of these events, Europe did not seem to be on the brink of war, as indeed it was. The public mind seemed caught up in more exciting matters, such as the stories published in the United States of the scandalous relationship between the newly crowned Edward VIII of England and Mrs. Simpson. When the king abdicated for love, in December, 1936, Franklin Murphy was living the student life in central Germany, in Goettingen, fascinated by what was happening in Europe.[85]

As the university's first exchange student in Germany, Murphy felt duty-bound to report about his experiences to Chancellor Lindley. His report mirrors the excitement of this unique experience. Chancellor Lindley provided a contact, Herbert Mueller, a lawyer and former visitor at KU, who arranged for Murphy to experience the Olympic games in Berlin. Murphy reported in a five-page hand-written letter to Lindley:

> I carried away many impressions of the fine athletic performances, the stadiums and buildings that make up the great Reichsportfeld, called by most authorities the finest athletic plant in the world. Here too I received my first impression what we might call the adoration many millions of Germans have for Der Führer. Every afternoon, Hitler, Goring, Goebbles, Hess and all the others would come to the stadium to watch the proceedings. As the cortage would enter the private box, every one rose to their feet. At least 80,000 of the 110,000 people in the stadium would throw their hands, outstretched, into the air and the stadium would be filled with 80,000 voices chanting as one—Heil—Heil —Heil. It was such a new experience that it roused a series of conflicting emotions—wonder—awe—astonishment—foreboding.[86]

Murphy was to have spent his year abroad working in the medical-research laboratory of Professor Hermann Rein, the leading vascular physiologist in the world at that time. However, after about six months, the fellowship ended under unclear circumstances. In a 1990 interview, Murphy remembered that Rein's lab was closed as the result of the professor's anti-Nazi politics. Murphy reported that his mentor had been taken into "protective custody" and Murphy could find no further trace of him.[87] In fact, substantial evidence supports Rein's active involvement in research under the control of the National Socialist government from 1933 onward.[88] His lab was no longer available for teaching duties, and Murphy's connection to it ended.

Murphy said later that the experience of living in Nazi Germany during 1936-37 caused him to neglect the study of human physiology in favor of the political physiology of Europe. He said that he learned never to take free speech for granted. "Stifle the intellectual freedom of our universities," he said, "and you stop the progress of American democracy," he would tell University of Kansas students in his inaugural address, 14 years later.[89]

Until his experience in Nazi Germany, Murphy had rarely considered the American system of education, with its inherent freedom of expression—in fact, he had taken it for granted. But what he saw in 1936 and 1937 made him believe in it with a deep and passionate conviction, he said.[90] He had learned the meaning of freedom of expression through having seen it murdered. He sensed, if he did not see, that America had to take the leadership of the world in education and research and freedom, if not in politics. Those ideals were being blacked out in Europe.[91]

Still shy of his twentieth birthday, with no obligation to attend classes, and without a professor, Murphy struck out on his own Grand Tour.[92] After all, he had not accepted the fellowship merely to study medicine, but also for an opportunity to live in another culture, in another part of the world. "I'd have to frankly admit that the medical and the scientific experience was almost secondary," he said years later, describing the year that changed his whole outlook on life.[93] That change developed as Murphy spent the following months travelling through Europe, where he visited art galleries and historic churches in Florence, Rome, and Paris, listened to music, and talked.[94]

Lyman Field had written in the May, 1936, *Jayhawker* about his own trip abroad the previous summer and had devised three types of college-student travelers:

> The wild riotous type who drink(s) up all the rare old wines, liquers, beer, champagnes and (who goes) to 32 Rue Blocedel, Paris; or the lorgnetted devotee of art type, who (spends) hours amid the treasures of the Louvre, the Pinotels, the Pitti Palace, the British Museum amid gasps of ecstatic delight; and the gay Richard Halliburton type - romancers of romance— swimming the Hellespont, or even the English Channel, or crawling thru the sewers of Paris for the sheer hell-of-it.[95]

As a student abroad, Murphy fit the "devotee of art type," without the lorgnette: no Hellspont swims or Marathon runs, no memory of drinking tours through European wine cellars. He simply wandered— "a mind-stretching, eye-opening experience for a provincial little Midwestern boy who had never been anywhere," he said.[96] To have grown up in a house filled with his aunt's paintings from Europe and to have heard so many stories of his parents' travels, Murphy recalled the joy of his peripatetic year. "To go to Europe and see the great museums and the great public buildings and cathedrals right face-to-face, rather than through a book, was a very, very mind-stretching experience," he said. "And, from that day on, I've always had an intense interest in art"[97] and especially the Renaissance.

Was Franklin Murphy a *leader* at 21, after his year in Europe and before medical school? Would he have been singled out as a man who had the potential to appear later on an important short list for President of the United States? Would those who knew him have suggested, at this time, that Murphy would lead two important universities? Probably not. At most, he appeared to be a bright and enthusiastic young man, with many family connections, who would be a fine physician in Kansas City. Murphy was not the central figure in his high school or even in his college. Only in medical school did he come into his own.

Always, when he pointed to the 1936-1937 time in Germany as the year that changed his outlook on life, Murphy referred to the beginning of his interest in art. Why would simply seeing great art in person make such a difference to an individual who had grown up surrounded by art and by people who were interested in it? Why would this year be seminal in such a memorable way? The answer is clear: this was the first time that Franklin Murphy was alone.

His father had died just a short time before. In Europe, Murphy had no mother, no grandmother, no brother George, or sister Cordie. Perhaps most important of all, there was no cousin Lyman: Although older than Franklin, the cousins both graduated in 1936. Throughout college, Murphy stood happily in his cousin's shadow. Lyman Field was simply perfect: handsome, visible, courageous, popular, important. He had thick hair and his dapper suits fit him magnificently. Franklin Murphy did not have thick hair, even then. Every one of those interviewed who knew the two young men in college responded in the same way. They speak first of Lyman, the Big Man on Campus, and then of Franklin, who few say they knew as well.[98]

At KU, young Murphy loved to write and could not decide easily between journalism and medicine for a career. Yet, in every published article by Franklin Murphy at KU, Lyman Field stands at the center. Murphy simply reflected his light. Field was the champion debater who led the bull sessions that taught Murphy so much about thinking for oneself. Franklin Murphy was an exceptionally fortunate young man in his family ties and close friendship with Lyman Field. Had they not spent their childhoods together, the less-slim, less-visible, less-popular Murphy might have withered in Field's light. The year abroad forced Murphy to rely upon *himself* for the first time. From 1937 on, Franklin Murphy radiated his own light. And, Lyman Field remained his "as close as a brother" friend until Murphy's death.

Medical School, Marriage, and Army Research: 1937-1946

Back in the United States, Franklin Murphy entered The University of Pennsylvania School of Medicine in 1937.[99] He helped pay board and room by serving as treasurer of Nu Sigma Nu, the medical fraternity, but otherwise spent four years studying. Later, he recalled having wise-cracked to a professor that nobody had learned anything about the kidneys since Bright. "If you think so," the professor responded, "go into the subject and write a paper on it."[100] Murphy did just that, perhaps in memory of his Uncle George, who had died of Bright's Disease in 1903. His work won the university prize for a paper on medical history and set him on a new interest—the same history of medicine that his father had loved came to Franklin Murphy on his own terms.

At Christmas time during the semester before medical-school graduation, Murphy made a life decision that equaled his choice of a career: he married Judith Joyce Harris.[101] Born in Kansas City, she was the daughter of P. Stephen Harris, owner of the Lucky Tiger Manufacturing company, and Judith Welsh Harris, whose grandfather Hanna had founded the early-day Burnham, Hanna, Munger mercantile firm. The company manufactured Lucky Tiger Hair Tonic, a fact that generated years of Murphy quips about the connection between hair tonic and medicine, according to Charles W. Graham. One wonders if Murphy's receding hairline generated any quips about the potential use of his father-in-law's product.

A Kansas City girl, Judy Harris had attended only one school from kindergarten through high-school graduation, The Barstow School in Kansas City. A senior at Vassar College in the 1938-39 school year, she was in Kansas City attending the pre-wedding parties of a friend when another friend, Gertrude Field, set her up with a blind date. The date was to be Gertrude Field's cousin, Franklin Murphy, a sophomore in medical school who also was at home for the week. Murphy remembered his cousin's conversation well:

"Oh, heck, Gertrude," he said over the telephone. "I don't want to go out to dinner, least of all on a blind date."

"Don't fool yourself, this is an attractive girl."

"Well, Gertrude, I'll do it, not because I believe you," he said, "but we are cousins and I guess you're in a jam."[102]

After the dinner, Murphy apparently agreed with his cousin's assessment of Judy Harris.[103] They discovered that not only were their colleges in relative proximity, but also that their families lived just three blocks apart in Kansas City and that their parents were acquaintances.[104] During the months that followed, Judy occasionally went to New York and met Franklin Murphy there, who offered "the only entertainment he could afford—a picture show followed by a soda at a drug store."[105]

The next year, 1939, with a B. A. in history from Vassar College, Judy Harris returned to Kansas City where she spent her time as a volunteer. She joined the Junior League, served as an art-museum docent, drove for a well-baby clinic, and participated in a singing group.[106] The couple married in December, 1940, in Kansas City and spent their honeymoon on the train to Philadelphia, where Murphy would spend his final semester of medical school.

Tapped as a member of Alpha Omega Alpha, the top medical honorary, he graduated first in his 1941 class.[107] Few lifetime honors meant as much to Murphy as his medical-school class standing. "I was there with a lot of Ivy League types who had had their undergraduate work at Princeton and Harvard and Yale," he said, with obvious pleasure. "It pleased me that a little ol' Kansas boy could beat 'em to the wire."[108] Throughout his later life, Murphy referred often to this honor, to the importance of standing up proudly for "things Kansan," and to the excellence of the University of Pennsylvania. The medical-school experience would become central to his vision of excellence for the University of Kansas—and later, for the University of California at Los Angeles.

Twenty five years old when he graduated from medical school in 1942,[109] he began a postgraduate internship in internal medicine and cardiology at the University of Pennsylvania Hospital at Philadelphia—his first choice.[110] He also held a fellowship in cardiology and research.[111] As the United States had entered World War II during his final year of medical school, he found more and more of the senior physicians being called up and as a result, his internship and residency carried more responsibility than normal.[112] After a year of internship, he was made resident physician at the hospital and for two years took over the teaching assignments of older doctors, many of whom had been sent to Assain, in India, where the University of Pennsylvania staffed the 20th General Hospital.[113]

After having written a "hurry-up research project" on penicillin, Murphy was loaned to the National Research Council, which placed him on a team of three doctors working on the new wonder drug.[114] The team's goal was to test penicillin's effectiveness with various diseases and to determine the proper dosages for each. Working with research speed unknown except in wartime, the team reported its findings to military doctors, who immediately used the new drug with sick and wounded soldiers and sailors.[115]

With the penicillin work completed in 1944, Murphy joined the tropical-disease research unit of the Army Medical Corps as a captain and went to Memphis to test synthetic drugs for malaria.[116] A debilitating enemy of American forces in the South Pacific, malaria historically had been treated with quinine, a natural drug obtained by distilling the bark of the cinchona tree.[117] Unfortunately, most of the world's cinchona trees grew in Asia and the East Indies, areas controlled by the Japanese.[118] The development of synthetic quinine— Atabrine[119] —became a high priority. Murphy worked with great caution, since the drug was a powerful agent whose effect on humans was unknown and dangerous. The work, which was completed "just at VE Day time,"[120] resulted in valuable knowledge—the synthetic quinine remained standard medical treatment,[121] for which he received the Army Commendation Ribbon.[122]

After the war ended in Europe and the military focus shifted to Japan, Murphy was ordered to Atlanta to organize the cardiology section of the evacuation hospitals under construction in the Philippines. "We expected huge casualties from the invasion of Japan," he explained, "and they were to be sent to these hospitals."[123] The weekend before he was to leave for the Philippines, he said, "Judy came down to Atlanta to see me off, and they dropped the bomb on Hiroshima."[124] The war had ended.

During the war, although extremely busy with penicillin and malaria research, Murphy did not concentrate on that interest alone. Always proud of his Midwest background, Murphy had paid close attention to his colleagues' geographical origins. Through the years of research in Philadelphia and Memphis, he noted that while many of the most able medical minds had come originally from the Midwest, they invariably chose to stay in the eastern universities and research institutions when the war ended. For one who reveled in beating out the Ivy League as first in his med-school class, Murphy deplored the brain drain of talent that strengthened the eastern schools and weakened the institutions from which so many had come. "Why must they come East for medical school?" he asked himself.[125] Furthermore, if they needed graduate work or wanted to study a speciality, they usually went east. He remembered debates and bull sessions with other doctors during the war years and consciously began to consider why the Midwest had been unable to hold the most skilled.[126]

Murphy also began to calculate available research funds and to identify the institutions that received the grants and contracts. Without too much effort, he discovered that the Middle Atlantic and New England states, with less than half the nation's population, captured at least 70 percent of the $100 million available annually in this country for research.[127] While Murphy knew that his home region should receive a fair share of the money, he also knew that the region would first have to provide facilities for research.

In any science, teaching and research cannot be separated. If he were to think of ways to generate research money, Murphy needed also to think about teaching, particularly as it occurred in medical schools. He watched trends and pondered his own training, coming to the conclusion that it could be improved. For example, third-year students traditionally trained in out-patient clinics, and fourth-year students learned in the hospitals, with bedside clinical study.[128]

Murphy believed that the pattern should be reversed. After all, he explained later, during out-patient work a doctor sees a patient for only about 15 minutes and must diagnose and prescribe in that space of time. Although this kind of work required mature judgment, it typically occurred during the third year, when the student had not developed sufficient judgment to handle diagnosis. Hospital clinical study should come before out-patient work, he said, because in hospitals the patients are available for much longer periods of time. Doctors and students have time and facilities for longer study and better treatment. The new trend that Murphy pondered would give the third-year students more appropriate work to help them learn to observe, and the fourth-year students, with more experience and judgment, would take on the out-patient work.[129] He would have an opportunity to consider the ideal solution soon.

The Murphys Return to Kansas City: 1946

When Murphy's military commitment ended in 1946, he resigned his position at the University of Pennsylvania and moved to Kansas City, because his roots lay deep there and because he wanted to play with a few ideas there, he said.[130] "This, one of the most important decisions of his life, might have been stimulated by the hunch that eventually he would have the opportunity to demonstrate his ideas of what medical education in the Midwest could be," according to one observer.[131] Perhaps the decision was more personal and immediate—like millions of young couples at the end of the war, Franklin and Judy Murphy may have sought close family ties. For whatever reason, Franklin and Judy Murphy went home. The family had grown during the war to include daughters Judith Joyce and Martha Alice. They bought a house in Johnson County, Kansas, at 6723 Tomahawk Road, and helped their children become acquainted with the Kansas City family.

Without question, Murphy returned to Kansas City as a physician with a bright future. His brother George had finished medical school by this time, so the family tradition was solidly in place. He joined the private practice of Dr. Lawrence Steffen and Dr. Graham Asher,[132] specializing in cardiology and internal medicine.[133] In the mornings, he taught at the University of Kansas School of Medicine, saying that he wanted to help expand the start that KU had made in cancer and viral-disease research.[134] He wanted to help provide the courses and research projects that would keep post-graduates at home and attract research funds to them. And, as the grandson of a small-town country doctor, he knew that in spite of increasing specialization, the general practitioner still stood as the primary deliverer of medical care. Because of specialization, he knew that the general-practice doctor would become more and more scarce, especially in rural communities. He wanted to help train those doctors.[135]

Soon after returning to Kansas City, Murphy began to talk about his ideas with his physician colleagues. In 1946, leaders were older men—ideas from a typical thirty-year-old would have been tolerated, at best, but probably not taken seriously. However, he was taken seriously by the group of men who had watched his progress throughout his life and who had worked with and admired his father. Even though Kansas City was a major regional center, its financial leaders comprised a small group. The Murphy and Field families had always been part of that group.

Most of those colleagues who listened—but who had not known him since childhood—might have been surprised to learn that he was merely thirty. He certainly did not appear to be that young. His hairline was receding and what remained had thinned prematurely; even as a teenager, his neck had really never met the chin at a right angle and certainly did not now; and his wide-cut trousers, high waistline, and 5'9" frame combined to hide youth in a physical package of indeterminate age. Nothing on his wide face detracted from the dominant brown eyes. Perhaps his appearance was a blessing for one who would be chosen to lead important institutions so soon in the future.

"Of average height, balding, Dr. Franklin Murphy, Dean of the University of Kansas Medical School, is inconspicuous in a crowd," according to the cutline under his photograph in the *Kansas City Star* just two years later. "But when he speaks, people turn to listen."[136]

"It is an invigorating mental experience to talk to Dr. Murphy," according to an observer at the time. "He stimulates the students in his classes, and he has that quality of personality that (is stimulated) through the doings of others. It is the quality of leadership."[137]

Now, in 1947, as a Kansas City physician and junior member of the medical school faculty, Murphy found a sympathetic group of colleagues who often talked about the school and the possibilities for it. What had been vague ideas, explored in Philadelphia and Memphis bull sessions, now were growing into concrete plans. In 1947, Deane Malott, Chancellor of the University of Kansas, supplied the means to carry them to the next level. Murphy said later that Malott called together a group of six or eight young medical faculty members. "I would like to form a committee of younger people to look at this medical school for me," Malott told them. "Tell me what is wrong and tell me how we can improve it."[138] Malott said that the medical school dean, Dr. Harry Wahl, had suggested the idea. The group chose Murphy as chairman and he guided them into consideration of his vision, which had, after all, been taking shape for several years.[139] These "Young Turks," as Murphy always described them, included Paul Shaeffer in surgery, Herb Miller in pediatrics, Bob Stowel in pathology, and a few others. Before many meetings, the group agreed that they had been thinking along the same lines as had Murphy.[140]

They reached a number of conclusions, including the basics of Murphy's vision for change. In practical terms, the committee reported the need for more money for facility expansion and day-to-day operations. Furthermore, it concluded that the school deserved a full-time dean as well as a full-time director of the hospital. Dr. Wahl not only filled these positions, but also taught as professor of pathology. The Young Turks recommended that Wahl be allowed to retire as dean and to spend his time teaching, as they knew he wished.[141]

Murphy wrote the recommendations of the committee and delivered the report to Chancellor Malott in Lawrence. "Here's the recommendation," he said, "and thank you very much." A week later,

Malott telephoned Murphy in Kansas City. "I accept the whole thing, without modification," he said. "Where we'll get the money for the new buildings, I don't know. I accept the fact that there (needs to be) a new dean." Malott explained that he had asked several of the older faculty members, including Dr. Wahl, for suggestions of who the new dean should be.[142]

"They were unanimous that you should be the new dean," Malott said to Murphy, who was stunned into silence. "That's ridiculous," Murphy responded. "I'm 32 years old, for God's sake. I'm a kid and I have no administrative experience."

"They all say that you are the one to do it," the chancellor said. "You are well-trained, you have a good background, and you are articulate." Murphy said he would think about it.[143] He thought about it and then went to Lawrence to speak to Malott in person. Malott knew that Murphy was very hesitant to take the job, and he listened as Murphy explained that he had spent his entire life planning and working to practice medicine. "I like the laying on of the hands," Murphy said. "I like dealing with people, and I don't know that I want to sit in an office and move paper around."[144]

In what Murphy later described as an effective seduction, Malott convinced him to take the deanship temporarily, for a minimum of three years. "During that time you can try to get some of these things done," Malott argued, speaking of the "Young Turks'" report, "and simultaneously go on the search for a dean." The seduction worked. "Well, what the hell," Murphy replied. "It's still medicine and I can always go back."[145]

CHAPTER 2

Medical School Dean

1948-1951

> "The health plan became the agricultural group's own plan in a very real way," Murphy wrote. "From all the Legislature could hear, everyone in Kansas was for it, and it sailed." A barrage of well-timed editorials from his friends of the press tied the package nicely. "One of the very few legislators who opposed it," Murphy said, "amusingly enough, was an undertaker." The bill creating the Kansas Rural Health Plan passed the Legislature in late January and Governor Frank Carlson signed it on February 18, 1949, just six months after Murphy had become dean and less than one year after his appointment had been announced. It was a nice thirty-third birthday gift.
>
> Franklin Murphy

MANY PEOPLE WHO read the February 28, 1948, announcement of Murphy's appointment as dean must have been surprised that KU's Chancellor Malott had named a relatively unknown physician to lead the medical school.[1] However, there was little surprise among those who had listened to Murphy's ideas when he first returned to Kansas City. "Watch this fellow," one doctor said. "He has horse sense along with a rare mind. Things are going to happen."[2] Many of his colleagues probably were looking for someone like him anyway, because it was common knowledge that Dean Wahl wanted to become head of the department of pathology. Dr. Wahl had served since 1924 and he, too, wanted to see a younger man take over.[3]

When Dean Wahl began, only one unit stood on the 15-acre site at 39th and Rainbow Boulevard in Kansas City. Eight units were added under his direction and construction of a new surgical building was underway. The center comprised 400 patient beds,[4] admitted 80 new medical students each year[5] and graduated 70. This was the operation that Franklin Murphy would begin to lead on July 1, 1948. His $9,600 salary as dean would cut his income in half but that was not a consideration, he said.[6] While he might not have recognized it consciously, this was precisely the opportunity he had been waiting for. He had celebrated his thirty-second birthday one month before.

Though he had hemmed and hawed with Chancellor Malott, Murphy's vision for the medical school was clear to him. Quite simply, he envisioned a medical school that would *deserve* equal standing with the best in the country. It would provide the exceptional post-graduate study that would keep the best physicians at home, would draw others, and would generate the research grants that such study required. Moreover, he envisioned a system of group study, comprising teams of doctors from the university who would go out into the state, holding clinics in any field of medicine that the doctors needed. He knew that they needed to keep in close touch with clinical medicine, and he felt certain that the new and improved University of Kansas School of Medicine could provide the means.[7]

In order to accomplish these goals, the facilities on Rainbow Boulevard would need extensive expansion and Murphy intended to follow the plans laid out by Dean Wahl, with a few additions.[8] Most importantly, the plans showed the need for a substantial infusion of cash. To accomplish any of it, especially the cash part, Murphy would need to learn to administer, he said, "whatever that means."[9] In March, 1948, he introduced his patients to a medical partner, moved his office to the hospital, and started learning to "administer." He would not actually become dean for another four months. Before long, he found himself absolutely fascinated. "This was not just pushing papers around," he said. "This is the whole business of people: dealing with people, identifying them, motivating them, having some dreams ... some ideas."[10]

Murphy learned that a successful administrator must be a politician. He had no intention of running for office—of being a professional politician, then or ever.[11] However, he knew that he would need to work closely with politicians. To do that, he had to understand their world, their procedures, their methods, and their personal interests. He turned to more experienced colleagues for advice, beginning with the school's politically astute business administrator, Charles B. Newell, and Dr. J. H. Haddon Peck, of St. Francis, Kansas, then president-elect of the Kansas Medical Society.[12] They told him to concentrate on persuading legislators.[13]

Without question, Franklin Murphy could hold his own in debate.[14] And, though he was equally adept at attacking the logic of those with whom he disagreed, he had developed the style of gathering others' ideas before suggesting any of his own. In fact, he seldom put forward any of his own ideas when he first began the medical-school effort. "I am the employee of the 1,900,000 people of Kansas," he said. "I want to see what they need from the medical school."[15]

Although he denied having contrived this information-gathering style of persuasion, he did acknowledge that he used such "it's your idea, not mine" methods successfully.[16] Translated into current motivational buzzwords, Murphy's style allowed his audiences to "own" the idea—"to become invested" in his point of view. He would have rejected those terms as thoroughly manipulative, even though he became a master at it with the people of Kansas, with legislators, with potential donors, and with his own faculty and students. "The job," he said, "is to convince them to share your vision of whatever it is you want to do. That's critical, in that they'll work their tail off if they believe subconsciously that they participated in the decision. They'll work very, very hard to make it come true."[17]

Murphy acknowledged that the team leader in such situations must be willing to share credit when a project succeeds. "The leader," Murphy said, "has to be shrewd enough and self-confident enough to share credit. Pour the credit on. There's usually enough credit to go around for everybody. If (the leader) is someone who holds to himself and talks about 'I did this,' and 'I did that,' then he isn't going to get a lot of cooperation. But, if it's 'we,' then you've got loyalty. You've got people willing to go beyond the call of duty. You've chosen them well and they're motivated and rewarded and then you can just sit back and they'll do your work for you," he concluded. "They're the ones that make a hero of you."[18]

Murphy put his information-gathering style into practice quickly, beginning with a series of personal visits around the state, even before taking over as dean. Persistently and without fanfare, he went to dozens of communities—making speeches to service groups, Farm Bureau meetings, and women's clubs. He met with community officials, and always with legislators, on their home grounds. He explained later that he was a good listener who liked "chewing the fat with local people after the meetings."[19]

In doing all of this, he launched a leadership style that became standard operating procedure throughout his career. Very early, Murphy the "non-politician" figured out how to get things done. According to men of long experience on the Kansas scene, he came to the job with what appeared to be natural political instincts. In action, the "innocent" Murphy amazed them.[20]

Wherever he went in the state during these information-gathering months, Murphy introduced himself to the individuals who controlled the flow of information to the public—in 1948, before television, the most powerful gatekeepers were newspaper editors. He turned early to the *Kansas City Star*, whose editorial staff influenced many of the small-town editors. Alvin McCoy and Lacy Haines at the *Star* were especially helpful, he said.[21] McCoy would later serve on the Kansas Board of Regents. Always, Murphy attempted to develop personal connections with local newspaper publishers and editors, and kept in closer touch with them than with any other group. These new friends all over the state became Murphy's front line in many of his later efforts. In fact, many were not new friends at all but were friends from college whose families owned newspapers and on whom he would depend throughout his Kansas years.[22]

His newspaper contacts also helped him begin to reach the most important group—Kansas' doctors. In mid-April of 1948 before taking over the dean's job, he was the subject of a long interview in the *Kansas City Star*. Murphy's invitation appeared as a direct quotation in the final paragraph, clearly visible above the fold on the first page of the society section: "By the way," he told the reporter, "I wish you would say for me that I want to meet every doctor in Kansas; every one of them! I want to learn their needs, what they are thinking on medical questions, and know them as individuals."[23] In his pre-dean travels, Murphy met hundreds of them. In meetings with county medical societies and with individual physicians, he listened and gathered ideas for improving health care. And, in all this listening—to legislators, mayors, editors,

Rotarians, farmers, housewives, and physicians—Murphy heard a clear message: Kansas's greatest medical need was to secure doctors for small towns.

Later, in an article that he wrote for *Saturday Evening Post,* Murphy condensed the statewide crisis into one illustration:

> On a June day in 1944, in the little Southwestern Kansas town of Minneola, death closed the long and useful career of a country doctor, the only physician in a trading area of 2,000 people. At his funeral the local minister remarked that because of the doctor's passing, "the community sustained a great loss." A conventional phrase, the statement carried in this instance more than the usual depth of meaning. For the seriousness of Minneola's loss became increasingly apparent as, year after year, efforts to bring a new doctor into the town failed. A number of people died without the care of an attending physician, and one bitter, blizzardy night the minister himself felt the sharp truth of his own words when, with a daughter near death from hemorrhage, he was forced to drive twenty miles over icy roads and through snowdrifts to reach medical care in another town.[24]

"...Minneola's six years without a physician was not a unique situation," Murphy wrote. "It can be paralleled by many other small towns in rural America."[25]

During the years of Depression and war, large numbers of people moved away from rural America, migrating toward the coasts and the jobs in fields and factories. After the war, few of those who had left, for whatever reason, returned. The result had left at least seventy Kansas towns with no doctor at all as the old physicians died and the young did not return to the home town after the war. In dozens of other communities, the one aging doctor had hoped to retire years before, and, in spite of the American Medical Association's assertion that the nation enjoyed a surplus of physicians,[26] at least 20 percent of those counted as active doctors in Kansas were seventy or older—usually too old to carry a full load of medical work.[27]

"It is perfectly true that doctors were relatively more numerous around the turn of the century than they are today," Murphy wrote, responding to older critics who longed for the mythical old days when there was a family doctor at every crossroads, one who could do everything with his own hands, and who charged very little for what he did. In fact, in 1909, the U.S. average was one doctor for every 568 persons, as compared to one for every 760 in 1949. Wellington, Ohio, in fact, had had five physicians for its eighty-seven inhabitants at the turn of the century.

"What our elders forget, or perhaps never realized, " Murphy said, "is that the plentiful supply of physicians in those days had been achieved at the expense of quality, the very situation we are seeking to avoid today." While thousands of those family doctors were excellent physicians, far too many were not, he said. "The bald truth is that as recently as forty years ago America was suffering ... from an appalling overproduction of undereducated and incompetent M.D.s."[28]

With the expansion westward in the 19th century, doctors were trained in dozens of proprietary schools and diploma mills. "Many of them took in boys without even a high-school education and turned them loose on an unwary and uncritical public after a year or two of the sketchiest kind of instruction," he wrote. "Anatomy lessons were often given without benefit of a human body for dissection, and some of the 'laboratories' consisted of a box of assorted bones and a basket of dirty test tubes."[29]

After being exposed, evaluated, and rated by the Carnegie Foundation for the Advancement of Teaching in its 1910 Flexner Report, about half of these schools were forced to close or to merge with stronger institutions. In twelve years, the number of medical schools fell from 155 to 80, with a resulting paucity of new doctors. Medical school enrollment in 1906 had been 25,204; by 1920, it was 13,798.[30] The Flexner Report was good for the country in that it resulted in better-trained physicians, but it marked the beginning of the doctor shortage.[31] A large number of the closed schools had been located in the Middle West and the South. Their graduates became many of the country doctors who, in 1948, were dying and not being replaced.[32]

In spite of the movement to the coasts, the population of Kansas had increased 25 percent since the turn of the century, but the number of practicing physicians had decreased 30 percent.[33] In actual numbers, that meant the alarming loss of nearly sixty doctors every year, leaving ten Kansas counties without any medical care.[34] While the School of Medicine had graduated 92 new physicians in 1943, class size had dropped to 56 in 1948—far too few, Murphy knew.[35] Even if he could manage to average the total, he also knew enough about his new job to realize that if every one of the average seventy doctors who would graduate annually chose to practice in rural Kansas, it still would riot be enough. Later, he wrote of four ways that the nation could increase its number of doctors:

1. Build new medical schools where none existed—the most expensive option.[36]
2. Expand existing schools to accommodate more students—almost as expensive as beginning from scratch;
3. Work harder to help existing students finish their studies, instead of dropping out or flunking out, as was the case with 15 percent of those admitted; or
4. Accelerate the curriculum, telescoping four years into three, thereby turning out more graduates in a given span of time.[37]

Kansas did not need to consider the first option: its medical school had been in operation and highly rated since the turn of the century. While the third and fourth options could be incorporated, to some degree, in whichever plan he devised, Murphy especially rejected suggestions to accelerate the curriculum, citing the nation's experience during World War II, when physicians were trained too quickly, in Murphy's opinion. "Too often," he wrote about wartime accelerated medical studies, "the doctors produced by that speeded-up educational assembly line proved to be inadequately trained. Certain facts or skills were not bolted down tightly enough. There were too many poorly soldered connections and places where the informational oil hadn't penetrated."[38] Clearly, the KU School of Medicine had only one choice—expansion. The facilities needed to train at least twenty additional doctors every year would cost $4 million, more than the Kansas Legislature had ever allocated for construction to any institution at one time.[39]

Contrary to what many believed, expansion of medical education was much more costly and complex than expansion of a college. For the latter, one merely needed to pay for lecture halls, additional faculty and their offices, student housing, and books for the library. While an expanded medical school needed all of these, it also required much more. For example, only part of the teaching followed the lecture-in-a-classroom method. Much medical education occurred in an expensive laboratory, where a professor worked with a small number of students, and at a hospital bedside, where the student learned by observing and treating actual patients.

"For the third-year class," Murphy wrote, "the medical-school hospital should have at least eight teaching beds per student, in order to provide each student with an average of three new cases each week. The out-patient department should be well-enough patronized to permit each fourth-year student to see three new cases every day."[40] One sees with this example that Murphy very quickly had changed to the third- and fourth-year rotation that he had preferred years earlier.

So, when he considered expanding the KU School of Medicine, Murphy knew that he was talking about more faculty, more labs, and more hospital rooms. If the school admitted 80 students and graduated 70 after four years study, and if the hospital needed eight patient beds for each third-year student, then clearly the 400-bed medical-center hospital was already 160 beds short—even for those currently enrolled. And, if he were to help resolve the doctor-shortage crisis, Murphy knew that he must admit and graduate more than 80. Even without considering the higher-than-liberal-arts salaries for the new medical faculty that expansion would demand, it was an expensive proposition—$4 million, at least.

Concentrating on talking with *young* doctors in his early travels, Murphy asked why they would not consider rural practice. The answers were simple. They had come out of medical schools in debt and could not afford the $15,000 to set themselves up in practice with an office building and modern equipment. And, they did not want to isolate themselves in small towns, away from the new trends in medicine.[41]

By the time that Murphy actually became dean, on July 1, 1948, he had devised a plan. Although no one in all of the 48 states had ever proposed such a far-reaching partnership, it was an obvious solution for him.[42] In order to solve the medical school's cash-for-construction problem, Murphy needed to find a way to convince the legislators and Board of Regents, who held the purse strings, that the state would benefit from such a hefty investment. He rarely dealt in platitudes when selling an idea. Instead, he *quantified* the potential benefits. Murphy also appealed to the listener's higher standards—almost all of his speeches, then and later, urged his listeners to consider the moral choice. For physicians already in practice, moral duty demanded that they begin to resolve the problem themselves—to lead the effort. Murphy helped them recognize "their own" idea and organized a growth fund into which they could and did contribute.[43]

Clearly the doctor shortage constituted a moral dilemma for both Murphy and the state. As the new dean, he said that he often received letters from towns seeking medical help.[44] Just as often came letters from qualified Kansas boys who wanted to become doctors and practice in Kansas. "It was not easy to tell Bill Jones that our facilities permitted us to take only eighty freshmen," he wrote, "and he was No. 81. Rejecting good potential medical students in the face of an obvious need for more doctors seems to me to be morally, socially and economically wrong."[45]

The resulting plan derived from all sides of his character. Franklin Murphy the visionary saw a unified medical service for the entire state of Kansas, led by the state's only school of medicine. Murphy the ethical leader saw his moral duty. Murphy the astute administrator saw a way to generate the money needed to expand the school's facility and reputation.

His solution became the Kansas Rural Health Plan—The Kansas Plan—the idea that raised him to national prominence within six months of becoming dean. It just clicked. Murphy tied the building program, which the legislature did not want, with his ideas for expansion of rural health care,[46] which they loved, as soon as they realized how many of their constituents supported it. The plan that Murphy developed was "what the people wanted," he said. "The whole business of administration is in the first instance and in the last instance 'people' related. Now, obviously, you've got to have a vision of what you are going to do with the organization. If you are running an automobile company, you've got to have a vision of what kind of vehicles you want to create and if they've got something to do with what people want," he said. "The vision is the leader's. So it's two things, the ability to identify the vision and the ability to get the people motivated."[47]

The Kansas Rural Health Plan

The Kansas Rural Health Plan had three main features, which Murphy outlined in the *Saturday Evening Post* article:

(1) It called for expanding the faculty, hospital and laboratories at the University of Kansas Medical Center ... to permit us to take in 100 instead of 80 freshmen, and thus to increase the output of medical graduates by 25 percent.
(2) It sought to help rural communities plan the kind of 'medical workshop'—office, examining rooms, small diagnostic X-ray room and small clinical laboratory—that we knew would attract good doctors. These were facilities our students and young graduates had told us they would like to have, but could not afford to buy in one lump sum.

We felt that a town could, as a community project, build and equip such a workshop, which the incoming doctor could then rent or purchase out of current income at little or no interest.

(3) It provided for a broadening of our postgraduate-education program, both the short refresher courses held at the Medical Center and the 'circuit courses' of lectures given in towns throughout the state. This feature was designed to keep rural physicians in constant touch with new developments in diagnosis and treatment. Fear of becoming medically isolated and turning into mere 'pill rollers' had deterred many young doctors from taking practices in remote parts of the state. Point 3 aimed at banishing such isolation.[48]

The chancellor and Board of Regents supported Murphy's efforts, even though the medical center price tag surely would cut into legislative appropriations for other higher-education projects. But trying to get $4 million from the Legislature was a big order,[49] for the total cost would amount to $3,862,000.[50]

The men whose advice Murphy had sought early were some of the most influential men in Kansas politics. They had told him to expect the most resistance from legislators from rural districts, even though the plan would most help farm communities. Murphy and medical-society president Peck countered by approaching the Farm Bureau's board, which, with many of the members who Murphy had visited with early and long, became active lobbyists for the plan—especially with recalcitrant rural lawmakers.[51] Ultimately, two of the legislature's strongest farm members, Lawrence Blythe, of White City, and John McNair, of Jetmore, sponsored the bill.[52]

"The health plan became the agricultural group's own plan in a very real way," Murphy wrote. "From all the Legislature could hear, everyone in Kansas was for it, and it sailed."[53] A barrage of well-timed editorials from his friends of the press tied the package nicely. "One of the very few legislators who opposed it," Murphy said, "amusingly enough, was an undertaker." The bill creating the Kansas Rural Health Plan passed the Legislature in late January and Governor Frank Carlson signed it on February 18, 1949, just six months after Murphy had become dean and less than one year after his appointment had been announced. It was a nice thirty-third birthday gift.

In fact, the Kansas Plan had been put in place before most people knew what was happening.[54] Later Murphy would explain, with some regret, that he had "learned on the job" about persuasion and only later would refine his preferred style of sharing the glory. "I'm afraid," he said, recalling those days, "there was a little too much of I when I first got started, but it didn't last long. There were a lot of things that wouldn't have been done had I not done them. I felt a sense of urgency to get some things done."[55] Mostly by talking to the right people at the right time, Murphy had convinced the economy-minded legislature to appropriate $3,862,000. That money, combined with $750,000 in federal matching grants, was used to build a medical sciences building ($1,000,000) and a nurses' home and women's residence hall ($450,000.) The nurses' building supported another element of The Kansas Plan: providing trained nurses to rural areas to care for mothers, new babies, convalescents, and infirm old people. The funds also allowed construction of a chest diseases building, a psychiatry building, a service structure, and additional floors on several existing buildings.

Newspapers all over the country printed articles about The Kansas Plan. The *Milwaukee Journal* on Sep. 26, 1949, wrote that "the University of Kansas Medical Center becomes the first hospital in the nation to install permanent television equipment for instructional purposes."

> Dr. Franklin D. Murphy, dean of the university's medical school, said the television project will enable students to get a clear, close-up view of operations on 5 by 7 foot screens in the lecture rooms. Reproduction at first will be in black and white, but school heads are contemplating color adaptations when these become practical.
>
> Under present conditions, medical student's view of an operation is greatly limited by doctors, nurses and technicians crowded around the operation table. The student hears the lecture, but sees little of the actual operation.[56]

With the Kansas Plan, Murphy also learned how to raise money. He needed to finance a $500,000 student center to include dining and recreation rooms.[57] Using a method that would come in handy later with the KU basketball stadium/armory, Murphy combined in one building necessary functions with those that might be considered luxuries. Vital but non-teaching requirements went into a building with an auditorium—space for doctors from across the state to gather for post-graduate study. Then he went "big-game hunting" after foundation and philanthropic funds to pay for it.[58] After having tapped

$150,000 from an eastern foundation that required a local match, Murphy turned to his team of Kansas City friends, including George Davis, Joyce Hall, Roy Roberts, and Arthur Mag. That group raised the matching funds in twenty minutes over dinner.[59] The same foundation pledged $400,000 over a ten-year period for research projects. He generated grants from the Public Health Service, National Foundation for Infantile Paralysis, Atomic Energy Commission, American Cancer Society, and American Heart Association. One K.U. alumnus gave the income from 1,000 acres, and the mother of his late Beta brother, Dr. J.R. Battenfeld, Jr., agreed to construct the auditorium in her son's memory. With a $10,000 gift of the Kansas Medical Society, Murphy had paid for the Student Center.[60] Before his deanship ended in 1951, private and foundation gifts to the School of Medicine had increased annually from $200,000 to $700,000.[61]

"I guess I still don't know anything about politics," said an apparently nonplussed Murphy: "I like people and I like to talk things over with them. I've had good advice from men who know more about politics than I do."[62] He had learned how to be a politician and how to raise money, and would become even better at both. He also learned valuable lessons about team building. The editors and legislators with whom he had worked became valuable allies on the Murphy team. If they were not on his team, he made sure that they understood his position. And hundreds of farmers and housewives whom he had met across the state were on his team as well. He genuinely liked people, as he said so often. Months after the Kansas Plan had been secured, Murphy continued to correspond with friends he made in and out of the Legislature. Farmers wrote to him about crop conditions in their parts of the state, and Murphy related what he had heard about crops and farm problems in his trips around the country.[63]

The results of Murphy's work on the Kansas Plan were speedy and tangible. By December, 1950, the KU School of Medicine had admitted 100 new students to its new facilities, where 80 had been the limit. Those potential doctors helped comprise the 638 students enrolled at the medical center—it now trained doctors, nurses, occupational therapists, physical therapists, medical laboratory technicians, X-ray technicians, and hospital dieticians.[64]

Within two years, 252 new or newly located doctors had begun practice in Kansas, 67 of whom set up practice in towns with fewer than 2,500 people.[65] Across the state, small clinics and health centers popped up "faster than new post offices in the hey-day of the New Deal,"[66] and even Minneola, the town that suffered six years without a doctor, had one. And, by 1957, every single community or county of 1,000 people in the state had a doctor in residence.[67] The percentage of KU medical graduates who remained in Kansas to practice had jumped from 33 percent to 55 percent. The KU Medical Center consistently graduated 100 new physicians every year and its postgraduate educational program was "the best attended in the nation." "We have been uniquely fortunate," Murphy said. "Everybody is pulling together. That's what makes the Kansas Plan work!"[68]

Murphy the non-politician became a hero indeed. Soon after *LOOK Magazine* featured him in its millions-circulation weekly, The U.S. Junior Chamber of Commerce named him one of America's Ten Outstanding Young Men of the Year.[69] *Life, Reader's Digest*, and *Saturday Evening Post* followed with major articles on his work.

He learned that a leader who wished to put a new idea in place not only must listen and gather information, but also must explain the idea clearly. His colleagues across the nation recognized the truth and value of Murphy's articulate message. After having been invited to serve as vice president of the Association of American Medical Colleges at his first meeting, Murphy equally promptly became chairman of its public-information committee.[70] In September, October and November of 1950, he made 23 speeches and attended 36 other meetings all over the country. As a member of the Medical Advisory Board of the Veterans Administration, he addressed Washington, D.C., audiences four times a year. In addition, he became active in the American College of Physicians and served on the Kansas Council for Rhodes Scholarships. In his spare time, during the first year and a half of his deanship, Murphy also served on the Board of the Kansas City Philharmonic Orchestra, the Kansas City Conservatory of Music, and the Midwest Research Institute.[71]

Franklin Murphy is Chosen as University of Kansas Chancellor: 1951

During the two and one-half years of Murphy's tenure as dean of the KU Medical School, he had not forgotten that this was to be a temporary position—that Chancellor Malott had asked him not only to take on the task, but also to find an outstanding candidate for the future. He had been told on taking the deanship that he might return to private practice when he had found and trained a successor. Standing policy allowed the dean to name his successor.[72]

A likely candidate seemed to be Clarke Wescoe, a Cornell University pharmacology professor whom Murphy had hired for the KU Medical Center's faculty. Murphy did not consider his own work complete and was not ready to turn it over to anyone, but he had kept his eye on Wescoe as a suitable replacement when the time came.[73] It came sooner than he expected. Early in 1951, the university's chancellor, Deane Malott, announced that he would resign as of September, to lead Cornell University. Malott wanted Murphy to succeed him as chancellor, and made that very clear to his Medical School dean.

As a result of Murphy's success with the Kansas Plan, many others in the state made it equally clear that he was their choice as well. However, in this search, the public procedures proved to be a bit more formal than his selection as dean. Early in 1951, a special Board of Regents committee began a search process that "scoured the country" for the best candidate.[74] Walter S. Fees led the Regents' committee to select a new chancellor.[75] The only problem cited with Murphy's candidacy lay in his *alma mater*. Having graduated from the University of Kansas, he was perceived by some as perhaps too close to home. "He is exactly the man the school needs," said Governor Ed Arn, before Murphy was chosen, "but precedence lies against him. It seems to be a must in education circles to look every place except on your own campus for a president. And this is a bit silly."[76] The Board of Regents realized, however, that another precedent had been set earlier that eased their choice of homegrown Murphy. After all, the departing chancellor, Deane Malott, also had graduated from KU. He had returned to his *alma mater* as chancellor in 1939 after serving as assistant dean of the Harvard Business School.

Students at the university fought to have a voice in the selection process, according to Robert Dunwell, a 1950s student-government activist.[77] His group was allowed to interview and screen the candidates. "A fantastic gentleman," Dunwell said of Murphy, his group's unanimous choice. The selection process also involved committees of alumni and deans. Both groups gave Murphy high recommendations.[78]

In spite of the public search procedures, the selection committees, and the newspapers' assurances that none of the members had been urged to choose one candidate over others, the facts seem to fit a sole-candidate search.[79] Regardless of other candidates' strengths, Franklin Murphy was a very popular candidate among all groups. Murphy remembered the process, not as a formal search, but as "another seduction" led by Deane Malott and the Kansas Board of Regents.[80]

He had no intention of applying, formally or not, for the just-announced chancellorship opening, he said. However, as he was leaving for a two-day meeting out of town, Murphy received a call from a member of the Board of Regents, asking for a meeting with him on his return. "I had a premonition," he said later, but was not prepared for the blunt suggestion, made without any preliminaries, at the meeting in Topeka. "We want you to succeed Malott as Chancellor of the University," he was told. "Well, you must be crazy," the 35-year-old Murphy replied to Regents Oscar Stouffer and Lester McCoy.[81] He explained that he had made a deal with Malott that would allow him to go back to the practice of medicine when he had found and trained a successor. "I've found him; he's in place," Murphy said of Wescoe. "Maybe he needs another year of getting acquainted with people in the state, but he's the guy."[82]

The Regents made it clear that they did not want Murphy to return to private practice, but instead to succeed Malott as chancellor. "You've got to do this," one said. "We need you." He described it later as a "strong-arm job."[83] He also described this experience as his second seduction away from medicine and into administration. The first time was like any other seduction, he said, in which the ardent seducer makes promises: "Just one time," he said, mimicking the logic. "Just once—that's all I'm asking. What harm is that going to do?"[84]

"Well," Murphy said, "I'd been seduced once and the second seduction wasn't all that difficult."[85]

In part, he did not fight it because he had discovered that he really enjoyed the creative challenge of administration. He did not fight it, but "did know that that was the ultimate crossroads," he said.[86] Franklin Murphy never did return to the practice of medicine. Instead, on July 2, 1951, home-grown and Ph.D-less, thirty-five-year-old Franklin Murphy was tapped to be the ninth chancellor of the University of Kansas.[87] Even though the salary would be raised from $13,500 to $15,000 and even though the chancellor would have use of the hilltop residence without charge,[88] he could have made substantially more income had he not yielded. In fact, he said that he had been seduced by the challenge—by the prospect of fun.[89]

In making the announcement, Regent Fees noted that the nine members had chosen Murphy unanimously: "The committee feels it has made a wise choice," he said, "and is fortunate in getting a chancellor who has the qualifications, ability and popularity of Dean Murphy."[90] With modesty, Murphy commented on his appointment: "Naturally," he said, "I am pleased to be named chancellor."[91] With humility and in a private letter, he acknowledged his debt to Deane Malott, his administrative mentor. "I shall never forget," Murphy wrote to Malott, "that my opportunity to move along in the academic world was initiated almost single-handedly by yourself, in an action which took considerable courage on your part. ... In many senses of the word, I am your creation."[92]

CHAPTER 3

Chancellor, University of Kansas
1951

> *It must be our aim to demonstrate that human effort of lasting value is achieved only when the razor sharp tools of the intellect are fashioned and used by those whose primary concern is the common problems of mankind.*
>
> Franklin D. Murphy, Inaugural Address

IN 1951, women were called "girls," wore skirts on college campuses, even in the coldest weather, and rarely questioned the required 10:30 p.m. closing hours. Male students were called "boys," in spite of their role in the war just six years past and in the Korean conflict that dominated the news. Seoul had been captured by the North Koreans and General Douglas MacArthur had been relieved of his command by President Harry Truman. 1951 saw the founding of NATO, the Kefauver investigations into organized crime, and the passage of the 22nd Amendment to the United States Constitution that limited presidents to two elected terms in office. It was the year of Juan Peron's election in Argentina, and Bogart and Hepburn's cinematic journey in *The African Queen.* Jersey Joe Wolcott won the heavyweight boxing title, Conrad Richter won the Pulitzer Prize for *The Town*, the final novel in his trilogy, and J.D. Salinger completed *Catcher in the Rye*. In science, 1951 was the year of the first transistorized hearing aide, the first saleable electricity produced by atomic energy, the first 33-LP record, and the first trans-continental television hookup.[1]

In the Middle West, 1951 was the Year of The Flood. All along the Mississippi River tributaries—from the Missouri, the Kansas, the Arkansas—everything backed up during that 1951 summer. Thousands of people spent days and nights on their own river banks, frantically filling sand bags to keep the rising waters from their homes. On June 21, the Flood of 1951 had pushed the Kansas River out of its banks, cutting off the roads to Kansas City and swallowing the northern part of Lawrence. In its fury, the river changed its course.

One could stand on the south bank, near the barbed-wire factory, and watch the power surging toward the southeast all the way to the limestone escarpment 10 miles away. Not merely a wide river, this was liquid iron that changed everything in its path. One chunk of land on the north bank, formerly just across the bridge, was swept away— four full blocks of businesses and the land they stood on went into the river's gorge to be seen no more. All of North Lawrence was under water. On July 2, the river had been raging at 18 feet above flood stage for 12 days.[2] That was the same day that the Kansas Board of Regents announced in Topeka their selection of Franklin Murphy as Deane Malott's successor as Chancellor of the University of Kansas.

At five feet, nine inches in height and 160 pounds, Franklin Murphy appeared older than his 35 years. Photographs show his receding hairline and balding crown, his occasional hats, and his ever-present cigarette. If he wore glasses during the 1950s, he did not wear them for photographs. News reports describe a man of "medium height and build, intelligent and wholesome in appearance, friendly in manner, tending toward baldness, erudite, a good public speaker, and possessed of apparent unlimited energy."[3]

Although not commanding in appearance, Murphy's *modus operandi* reflected the respect he held for others. After the announcement ceremony and press conference in Topeka, for example, Murphy negotiated his black Buick[4] through the flooded roads to Lawrence in order to pay respects to his fellow faculty members, his prospective office staff, and his former teachers, including John Ise.[5]

As her husband listened to the advice of his former teachers and launched into the work of turning his vision into action during that post-flood summer, Judy Murphy supervised the family's move to Lawrence.[6] She brought to the white, verandaed hilltop home on campus the couple's four young children (Judith Joyce 9, Martha Alice 8, Carolyn Louise 2, and Franklin Lee 1) and years of experience as a hostess. The house lent itself well to the functions she would host in it during the nine years to come, set as it was, large and sun-filled, at the manicured corner of the campus on the edge of the hill. Since July 2, when Murphy's appointment had been announced, the Murphys had visited the unfurnished home often, allowing the children to explore it and its grounds.[7] "Our two oldest daughters, who are nine and eight, are delighted," Murphy told a reporter. "They have learned that they will each have a room instead of sharing a bedroom as in the past."[8]

Judy Murphy looked forward to having her husband closer to home. His KU office would be a short three-minute walk from the residence. Knowing that he had not been a "desk dean" at the Medical Center, she doubted that he would curtail his constant travels as chancellor.[9] In fact, his peripatetic working style led Judy Murphy to describe herself as one who sits on the roadside "watching the Murphys go by."[10] While her husband assured her that the new position would keep him home more often, Judy Murphy could not expect much change based on the evidence of the 1951 summer months.

Except for a family vacation, the chancellor-elect used the two months before taking over the leadership of the university as if the ceremony had occurred already. Flood or not, Murphy was ready to get going. His office staff churned out correspondence in spite of his chancellor-designate status. In fact, Murphy had already built his office team, with Raymond Nichols running the office until the September 17th inauguration. Dean of the Graduate School John Nelson would serve as Interim Chancellor during the summer months.[11] Miss Rublee, Murphy's secretary, was never addressed by any other name, according to Murphy and Nichols. In fact, some of the principals in the office, with whom she worked daily, reported that her name was Mae when in fact it was Dorcas.

Ray Nichols held it all together between the chancellors—as he held it together so often before and later. Serving as Assistant to the Chancellor and, later, Secretary of the University, Nichols had been a journalism student in the late 1920s and left for one year only. He seemed to know everything and became Murphy's right hand. After 45 years at the University, in 1973, Nichols became its Chancellor himself.

It *was* a tiny staff: Nichols, Miss Rublee, and one part-time typist. At the busiest time of Murphy's tenure, it was not much larger. Within a year, George Baxter Smith, formerly Dean of the School of Education, joined the administrative team and during the next nine years, Rublee hired young women to bring the maximum office support to three part-time typists. Together, the secretaries managed the paperwork of the university and its chancellor. He dictated and they produced a mound of letters every day, in an era of manual typewriters and carbon paper, and without photocopies, computers, or FAX machines.

Nichols began the work immediately. "Dr. Murphy will be in town on September 1," he wrote, "and will be in touch as soon as he arrives." Nichols dealt with the details and Murphy dealt with projects that would solidify future support for the university. He worked on expanding the support team on which the realization of his vision relied. Quickly, the efforts appeared promising, especially with Murphy's August appointment to the Board of Directors of the Hallmark Card Company, whose founder Joyce Hall had been and would remain a powerful ally, especially in Murphy's later friendships with Dwight Eisenhower and Winston Churchill. With the experience of 25 years at the University of Kansas, Ray Nichols understood the importance of such board memberships: "The more he is tied up in that way," he wrote to Malott, "the better."[12] Within two months, Murphy would also hold a trusteeship of the Midwest Research Institute, a board he had served during his deanship.

Other important connections solidified quickly. On September 9th, for example, Murphy wrote to Dr. Donald Young, General Director of the Russell Sage Foundation, inviting him to attend the inaugural ceremonies. "As you might have surmised," he wrote, "gritting my teeth, partly closing my eyes to my well-known deficiencies, I have jumped into the waters of general education."[13] The men had met on a train between New York City and Ithaca at the instigation of Deane

Malott and to the substantial future benefit of the University of Kansas. "I simply wanted you to know," Murphy continued, "that as I step into the job here with its many hidden traps along the way, I will from time to time be thinking of our brief conversations in which you perhaps unwittingly sounded a few notes that were not without influence in my ultimate decision." Young responded on the 17th after having been away from his office for two weeks and noted Murphy's "uneasiness about taking the job" expressed on the train trip. "I am entirely sincere when I say that your election as chancellor strikes me as one of the two or three most suitable elections to university leadership in recent years."[14]

When the family moved into the "White House" on the August 29-30 weekend, summer had returned in full force.[15] It was the hottest end of August on record, after the wettest summer. In two weeks, 6,282 students would arrive to watch Franklin Murphy's inauguration as chancellor. He began officially on September 1, 1951.

Dr. Franklin Murphy would replace Deane Malott. Unfortunately, few faculty knew Murphy well and speculation raged. The initial faculty uncertainty split along lines by disciplines. The humanities and fine-arts faculties were convinced that Franklin Murphy, M.D., Dean of the K.U. School of Medicine, would favor the hard sciences. The scientists were afraid that Murphy, who was said to like opera, would favor the arts and humanities.[16]

In fact, Murphy did like opera—he and Mrs. Murphy regularly invited friends to join them in their four reserved box seats. Frank Burge recalled an exciting evening as the Murphy's opera guests. Only on the job a short time as the new director of the Kansas Union, Burge received a 3:00 p.m. phone call from the chancellor inviting him and his wife to use the suddenly free tickets for that evening.

"Got a tux?" Murphy asked thirty-three-year-old Burge. "Call Glad and tell her to wear an ankle-length dress. Judy and I will pick you up at five." After dinner at the River Club, the Murphys and Burges went to the opera and sat in a box over the stage. Around the wall Burge could see President and Mrs. Truman in their opera box: "Jud, let's give these kids a treat," Murphy said to his wife. At *entre acte*, he greeted his friends, President and Mrs. Truman, and introduced them: "Mr. President," Murphy said, "This is Frank Burge. He was an artillery commander at the Battle of the Bulge." Burge recalled that Truman enjoyed talking about his own artillery experience, in World War I. "After three light notices," Burge said, "Truman was still telling artillery stories—punctuating each story by punching my chest with his fingers. Chancellor Murphy loved it."[17]

Murphy wanted a simple ceremony for the September 17th inauguration, noting that even though some of his colleagues might be disappointed not to wear academic regalia, simplicity seemed more fitting in light of the war in Korea and "so shortly following the devastating flood."[18] He asked purposely that the inauguration take place during the traditional convocation, that the only speakers be himself and Lester McCoy, chairman of the Board of Regents, and that the event be followed by a buffet luncheon at the Memorial Union. The Murphy-planned event centered on his message, not on ritual, and on Kansas, not on a prominent out-of-state speaker. After he and Governor Ed Arn led the suited procession in the sunshine from Strong Hall across the street to Hoch Auditorium, Murphy received the university seal from McCoy and spoke, for the first time as chancellor, to the 4,400 students, faculty, and state officials who had packed into the 3,500-seat hall.[19]

"I stand before you, quite unable to lay bare the depth and breadth of my feeling," said Murphy, the son of a University of Kansas faculty member and an alumnus himself. "Suffice it to say, I humbly accept your charge with a full recognition of the honor and trust it implies and with equal cognizance of the heavy responsibilities which it imposes."[20] In the inaugural address that followed, Murphy laid out his philosophy of education in a catalogue of principles that reflected all of the experience and lessons of his 35 years.[21] Those who heard the speech in person or as broadcast on the radio and those who read of it in newspapers across the state learned the tenets of Chancellor Murphy's philosophy—principles that he would repeat often during the nine years to come.[22]

Citing the "inextricably interwoven" history of Kansas and its university, he told of the pioneer settlers who quickly built their churches and their schools as soon as they were settled. "To them the spiritual and moral went hand in hand with the cultivation of the intellect," he said, explaining the common task ahead of validating their belief. "It must be our aim to demonstrate that human effort of lasting value is achieved only when the razor sharp tools of the intellect are fashioned and used by those whose primary concern is the common problems of mankind."[23] His speech called for complete freedom of expression without fear of reprisal:

> The university must provide a moral and intellectual climate in which men are free to continue their search for truth. Character assassination by innuendo and half-truth, with careless regard

for the facts, if encouraged, inevitably will lead to a paralysis of free thought just as debilitating to American democracy as the conduct of those who would utilize American institutions to overthrow and subvert these same institutions. Stifle the intellectual freedom of our universities and you stop the progress of American democracy.

Any influence which has as its avowed purpose the ultimate elimination of the personal rights of individual people must and will be rooted out with dispatch and vigor.

"Nothing is more certain in this life than change," he said, reflecting his training as a scientist and his Aristotelian mindset. "Society, like man, never stands still. Our concern must not be with the foolish denial of the inevitability of change, but rather with means to channel its forces in those directions which permit progress in a free society." The new chancellor urged all listeners to accept the obligations of educated leadership in taking on and resolving the problems of the world:

It should be the aim of our public servants to encourage individual enterprise, not deny it. Otherwise one day we shall discover that the source from which this nation has drawn its strength will have been enfeebled beyond repair. Our graduating men and women must clearly recognize and be capable of assuming their personal obligations, which a true democracy imposes on its citizens.

Murphy laid out an argument for a proper perspective on the whipping post of the day, collegiate athletics:

At this point I must note that the country is presently showing great concern over the softness and immorality of our youth. Editorial writers, educators, congressmen and just plain fathers and mothers unwilling to put the blame where it really belongs, turn to the nearest relatively impersonal whipping posts and in this generation discover it to be intercollegiate athletics. In 1951, just six years after our youth has concluded a savage war, not of its own making—in 1951, when in every quarter appears a mounting toll of broken homes, in 1951, when the questions 'what's in it for me? motivates too many of our leaders in public and private life—yes, in 1951, the best explanation for the moral confusion of our youth (we are told) is the so-called hypocrisy engendered by our present system of intercollegiate athletics. I leave it to you to decide who is hypocritical about what. Can we not put first things first![24]

Still, he acknowledged that a determined and coordinated effort must be made to curb excessive emphasis on college athletics. In calling for a proper balance, Murphy said that he hoped such an effort would meet with "support as vigorous as the emotional attacks which almost daily entertain a public needing something to divert it from the really fundamental and apparently insoluble problems which bear upon society with such urgency."[25] To the other state institutions of higher education, Murphy promised friendliness "with the possible exception of our athletic contests," he said, generating the only audience laughter of the day."

Above all, the inaugural speech exhorted its audience to accept its responsibility for excellence. "This generation," he said, "has a crucial date with destiny. It is the terrible yet exciting responsibility of the University of Kansas to prepare men and women so that they may bring to this meeting wisdom, courage, vision and understanding. We will not fail," he said on closing. "We dare not fail."[26]

Franklin Murphy's Vision

Thirty-five years old when he was hired to lead the University of Kansas, Franklin Murphy brought to the challenge a clear and unwavering vision of excellence that developed from his family, his schooling and self-education, and his experience. The lessons that he learned as a very young man solidified into the vision he would follow throughout his life. It was not a pattern of experiences, but a pattern of *expectations*. It was a personal vision.

Stated succinctly, Murphy's vision for the University of Kansas encompassed all of the qualities that he considered perfect for any great university and for the cultivation of an educated man: "that he has been challenged to think, has been put into intellectual ferment, has acquired the makings of a sound and purposeful philosophy of life." In the final analysis, he said, "these are the true fruits of a university experience."

To enjoy such fruits, the student must also enjoy the finest faculty and the most exceptional resources in libraries and laboratories. Jerry Waugh, a friend who knew him well, asked Murphy to describe his hopes for sports at the University of Kansas: "I want KU to have the best sports program in the country," the new chancellor replied, "just as I want the chemistry department to have the best equipment and best faculty."[27] Murphy's vision encompassed all of it and more. Clearly, he intended to boost KU up to the top ranks of American universities, alongside such schools as the University of Michigan, the University of Pennsylvania, and the University of California at Berkeley.[28]

For Murphy, the vision of a great university stood clearly in his mind. He articulated it most fully in a commencement speech to the graduates of the University of Pennsylvania, on June 15, 1955. Penn, his medical school *alma mater*, represented *the* ideal that he sought for the University of Kansas.[29] The speech appears in its entirety as an appendix to this book, standing as an illustration of his writing and storytelling skills, his understanding of history, and his ability to organize and explain an idea in a speech. With it, one may judge Murphy's use of persuasion—with logic, ethics, and passion. Most importantly, the speech at Penn articulated his vision for the university—for any university—and underlies his actions throughout his tenure at the University of Kansas.

"The Meaning of University" began with a history lesson. Murphy described the differences between the formal medieval university and the "essentially personal and unorganized" methods of higher education of Greece, Rome, Egypt, the Near East, and the Orient. The soil from which the medieval European university sprang was black indeed, he said, as "the lamp of learning seemed to have been permanently extinguished" in Europe during the Dark Ages. In the 12th century it became "a great flame," he said. "It was as though a subterranean fire had been burning through several hundred years of darkness, which had developed such intensity that its appearance, when it came, was explosive."

He described the dangers that young men faced as they travelled to sit at the feet of masters in Paris, Bologna, Oxford, Padua, Prague and the other university towns. "To defend themselves from religious and civil tyranny, masters and scholars banded together," Murphy said, "in corporations, or universities, and thus the immediate ancestor of the modern university came into being." He spoke of the intellectual ferment of open debate and of the enormous power of the universities that resulted. "The basic strand which ties any modern university, worthy of bearing the designation, to early university tradition is the ferment of the 'free market-place of ideas'," he said. "A strong case can be made for the view that the best yardstick with which to measure the real freedom of a people is the freedom which exists in their market places of ideas, their universities."

The crucial need today, he said, is the *educated* mind that can be fashioned, tempered and toughened only in the crucible of free and open discussion.

> The market place, where ideas are traded, has always been and continues to be under assault. Would-be tyrants try to close its doors. Some trained but misguided and intolerant minds foul it with their denial of human dignity and with their conspiratorial and clandestine efforts to destroy it. Such persons do not deserve admission to it. But to confuse these evil efforts with non-conformity is both stupid and dangerous, leading to a denial of our national birthright, our constitution and the whole movement of western civilization for a thousand years.

The free market place supports the nation, Murphy said, through research and investigation, and through the curiosity of men and women who merely seek to know. "We must agree with Milton when he writes in *Areopagitica*," he said, "'Though all the winds of doctrine were let loose to play upon the earth, so Truth be in the field, we do ingloriously, by licensing and prohibiting, to misdoubt her strength. Let her and Falsehood grapple; whoever knew Truth put to the worse in a free and open encounter?'"

"Your first obligation," he told the graduates, "is to help guarantee that the market place of ideas will, in your time, remain free and therefore productive so that man may continue to proceed through reason as well as through faith."[30] In writing these words, as he did, Franklin Murphy set out the standards he held for the University of Kansas. Here, he revealed the depth of his reverence for the Renaissance. Here, he laid out his vision for the university as the guardian of reason.

The Lessons Learned by Murphy's Career at KU

Without question, the world of higher education has changed since 1960 when Murphy left Kansas. To some degree, the methods Murphy used cannot be replicated. The most obvious difference lies in hiring practices. The only public objection to Franklin Murphy's candidacy as a potential chancellor of the University of Kansas in 1951 related to his home-grown status. As dean of the KU School of Medicine, he was a candidate from inside the institution. Furthermore, he was a KU graduate. Though stated, it was a weak objection and carried little weight. When Murphy was chosen for his first leadership position, as dean of the KU School of Medicine in 1948, he met with no search committee and did not even apply for the job. He was 32 years old, had absolutely no administrative experience, and had never raised money for a cause beyond the Kansas City Symphony Society. He had earned an M.D. and had published, but had earned no Ph.D. It is doubtful that Franklin Murphy's leadership gifts would have been given a voice had he been constrained by the infinitely more fair, but much less flexible, hiring procedures in place today. "I can't believe they hired me," he agreed. "I didn't really have any qualifications."[31]

Decades later, the tradition to choose a leader from outside the institution remains and has solidified, but that is the only element of the search process that remains the same. In every other respect, times have changed. Today, leaders of higher education are asked to be generalists but are required to be specialists. As generalists, they must guide increasingly differing constituencies, pleasing all, all of the time. As specialists, candidates are expected to have excelled in at least three often-contradictory careers.

First, they must cram into as few years as possible an outstanding and traditional academic career, launched with the requisite Ph.D., followed by national offices in professional associations, and resulting in an impressive curriculum vita outlining their published research accomplishments. In addition to the academic credentials, the university leader now must have demonstrated a successful career as a chief executive officer, the magical title that means running a multi-million dollar enterprise with sufficient agility to dance through myriad regulatory hoops without tripping. And, the most important experience required of the current university leader lies in the very specific skill of fundraising.

It is true, the hiring procedures have changed for the educational leader. One is no longer "seduced" into taking a great job as Murphy described. No leader can select a team member who lacks a terminal degree simply because they both like books, as was the case when Murphy hired library director Bob Vosper. No longer can one search the world for the most promising candidate and simply hire that person, sight-unseen and with no search committee, as did Bob Vosper with Alexandra Mason. Even Clarke Wescoe, who succeeded Murphy as chancellor in 1960, was appointed after a three-day search-and-evaluation process.

Today's educational leaders must hire with procedures infinitely more fair, but also more driven by a rather mechanical and impersonal process. Today, one might well be chosen on the basis of administrative skills, which might have nothing to do with leadership. The process drives the selection, not the person or his or her vision. In an age that seems desperately to need leaders of uncommon ability, we perhaps concentrate on procedural and administrative trees instead of on the visionary forest. An individual of exceptional promise but without requisite credentials rarely has a chance.

On the other hand, the former methods fitted very different times. When Murphy began as chancellor, the civil rights movement was only a dream. While he played a role in integrating the university and the community, that was neither his primary goal nor a national priority. A tiny minority of the university's students were non-Caucasian and the melting-pot theory that would blend all races into an Anglo-Saxon mold was rarely questioned. And, even though one sees evidence of its beginnings during the late 1950s, the women's movement was far in the future.

Very few government regulations intruded on Murphy's personal leadership during the 1950s. As the Board of Regents' policy prohibited the use of federal-government funds for dormitory or classroom construction, the chancellor dealt with the federal government in the construction of only one building—the Field House—and that only because he chose to designate it as an armory in order to obtain federally controlled steel. Federal rules intruded primarily during the Korean War, when draft-board requirements determined a students' status and when GI Bill students' $50-a-month allocations depended upon university record keeping. As he used few federal funds, he faced little outside interference from non-state agencies. The State of Kansas had set a forty-four-hour working week for its employees, but beyond that regulation, each division set its own personnel rules. In fact, the library wrote its own rules of vacations and working hours. When Murphy left, in spite of having required John Ise and 'Phog' Allen to retire at the mandatory age, he could not protect the employees with a pension plan for their retirement. The Association of Research Libraries constituted the primary accrediting agency that evaluated the university during the 1950s. Murphy and his American Association of Universities colleagues approved the beginnings of national accreditation for higher education, but he warned that it might become more than a collegial standards-raiser and take on a life, and unwanted power, of its own.

Higher education in the 1950s was collegial, indeed. The individuals who led the universities knew each other well and relied upon each other. Murphy became active in all of the national and international associations of higher-education leaders. Young and articulate, he made a national impression quickly on his older colleagues. He did not need to work his way up a leadership ladder. He did not need to begin as an associate vice chancellor and make his way slowly. Higher education was much smaller in the 1950s and much more personal. The same was true locally. At the University of Kansas, Murphy came into a community of about 440 faculty members and no vice chancellors. He and three other men—at most— comprised the administration: Ray Nichols, George Baxter Smith, and Keith Lawton. At the beginning, one of these men, or perhaps Tom Yoe, wrote the news releases. The first public-relations plan, aside from that in Murphy's head, appeared in 1958 with James Gunn, who taught until his retirement in the English Department, and who is a world-renowned writer of science fiction. What is now the Office of University Relations was then one person.

One must attempt to judge the buying power of a dollar in different ways. In 1960, a pound of coffee cost fifty-five cents[32] and one could travel by train, round-trip, from Lawrence to Los Angeles for $87.00. The chancellor's $22,000 salary amounted to a comparative fortune, especially when professional librarians were hired for $4,260 a year. Although costs are always relative over time, the differences are interesting.

In the 1951-60 decade, a leader used far fewer media to influence public opinion than today. In those days, "the press" meant printing presses —newspapers. A few newspaper editors who enjoyed multi-county circulation could speak to the entire state. As television was in its infancy, the power of print journalism was much greater than today.

The communication and business technology of today was non-existent. It was much more difficult to communicate. For example, the chancellor's secretary, Dorcas Rublee, typed his voluminous correspondence on a manual typewriter and made the ubiquitous copies with carbon paper. When Robert Talmadge sent copies of 15 letters each week to Bob Vosper in England, a typist re-typed each letter as a copy. If Miss Rublee made an error in typing a letter with eight copies, she methodically corrected the error on eight carbon copies. No white out. No strips of correction paper. She could not type one perfect letter and make photocopies, as that process had not been invented. Certainly, she could not type the letter on a computerized word-processor and personalize each copy with the touch of a button.

If the chancellor wished to contact an angry legislator or a prospective donor, he had three choices: make a personal visit, dictate a letter for Miss Rublee to type and mail, or make a telephone call. Only during the latter years of his tenure does one find much evidence of Murphy having relied on the telephone over the letter, though undoubtedly, he spent hours on the phone every day. Even if they had imagined the future availability of FAX machines and Internet, they might not have considered such technology particularly necessary. After all, the US Postal Service delivered letters across the state on the following day, to the East Coast in two days, and, by airmail, to England or Rome in three.

As Murphy relied upon personal appearances and on the power of print journalism to carry his message, he had the leisure to craft the words as he wished. Without the immediacy of television news reporters feeding a 24/7 news cycle, he usually had time to reflect upon the response he would give to a question or to an issue. Today, the leader's impact—and reputation —in any arena must live or die without such reflection. Whether considered or not, a leader's response to a live television microphone now sends one's message instantaneously around the world. Perhaps it is not surprising that so few are willing to speak out on controversial issues.

Certainly, none of the leaders of higher education in Kansas since has attempted to become a statewide leader as was Murphy. He exemplified higher education in Kansas. Even though he and James McCain worked together, and even though they generally included the presidents of the smaller Regents schools, Franklin Murphy spoke for higher education in the state. In Kansas during 1950s, students could choose one of three avenues to higher education: the Regents' institutions, two municipal universities, and private colleges. Although KU and Kansas State operated extension offices in the western part of the state, for practical purposes the state was untouched west and south of Hays. (Only years later did community colleges come onto the scene to give all students a close-to-home option beyond high school.) In spite of some differences of opinion, the Regents schools generally stuck together during the 1950s, and Murphy was their unquestioned leader. Today, the Regents colleges and universities and the community colleges, all supported by taxpayers, not only actively compete for students, but also send their separate squads of lobbyists to the Regents and to the legislature to fight for funds against their own brethren—all of whom must share the public purse.

Times have changed. A leader in 2016 higher education faces very different challenges than did Franklin Murphy at the University of

Kansas between 1951 and 1960. But perhaps those who are responsible for guiding the patterns and decisions of young lives today could learn a lesson from the past, from Franklin Murphy.

Here, Murphy's leadership skills center on three areas: his impact as chancellor in the arts and libraries at KU, his impact on civil rights at the university and in Lawrence, and his methods of dealing with Kansas politics.

CHAPTER 4

Art and Books
1951-1960

*He thought it happier to be dead,
To die for Beauty, than live for bread.*

Ralph Waldo Emerson

Man shall not live by bread alone.

Franklin D. Murphy

THE GERMAN SCULPTOR Tilmann Riemenschneider lived between 1460 and 1531—at the same time as Michelangelo Buonarotti carved and painted in Florence and Rome. Both were born just a few years after Johann Gutenberg launched the Renaissance with movable type and both lived in the ferment following Martin Luther's religious revolution in 1517. While Riemenschneider, like Luther, opposed the Church, his work in stone and wood continued to center on religious themes.[1] The Renaissance in art moved from Italy northward and Riemenschneider reflected more the High Gothic period, just before the German Renaissance.[2] In 1499, a few years before his countryman Albrecht Dürer struck the Apocalypse series of woodcuts, Riemenschneider carved a block of linden wood into a lovely, pensive, 47-inch-tall *Madonna and Child.*

Franklin Murphy loved the Dürer that he had purchased as a teenager from his friend, the rare-book dealer Frank Glenn. They had remained in close touch ever since. Glenn was still in his book-and-art filled shop in Kansas City's Muehlebach Hotel, and Murphy now served as chancellor of the University of Kansas. Murphy knew of Riemenschneider's brilliance and now, in 1952, he wanted that *Madonna and Child* for his university. He did not want a copy of a copy: he wanted excellence. As did Ralph Waldo Emerson, Murphy believed that life is not life without beauty. Writing to Dr. Burzle, Murphy's enthusiasm was obvious: "A Riemenschneider? Wow! Let's get it."[3]

The University of Kansas' Spencer Museum of Art advertises its collection in a brochure, printed on appropriately heavy stock, noting the hours for viewing and illustrated by a few of the very best items in its collection.[4] A 1990s brochure included seven such treasures: a wooden carving of a Bodhisattva from the Chinese Sung Dynasty; a large *Madonna and Saints* by Zenale of the Renaissance; the marvelous, symbol-filled Pre-Raphaelite *La Pia de' Tolommei* by Dante Gabriel Rossetti; *The Ballad of the Jealous Lover* by Kansas Citian Thomas Hart Benton, a huge fluid canvas of color and movement; a woodcut by German Expressionist Franz Marc, a Weegee photograph of social contrast, *The Critic,* and Tilmann Riemenschneider's 15th century woodcarving, *Madonna and Child.*

Murphy had secured the Riemenschneider in 1952, his second year as chancellor, as a purchased gift in memory of Professor Harry C. Thurnau through the estate of Myrtle Elliott Thurnau.[5] It remains one of the university's most-prized treasures.

Four of the seven masterpieces highlighted in the museum's 1990s brochure came to the collection as a result of Franklin Murphy's love of art and of his skill at paying for it. "If you want something badly enough," he said, "you'll find a way to pay for it."[6] For example, he encouraged art history faculty member Marilyn Stokstad to track down a purchase while in Barcelona. He wrote to her on July 9, 1959:

> "Dear Marilyn:
> When Ed Maser was in Barcelona he found a place which he describes as "the best photo place in Spain." I could not read his writing, but it is something like the "The Auchiniv Mas." He said he found there an archive of 450,000 negatives of Spanish art. The director stated that photographs could be obtained at 50 cents apiece. I have been able to scratch together $3,000 for the purchase..."

When he wanted a piece of art or a collection of books or a new university building, Murphy found the money—generally by matching the need to an individual who would be pleased to pay for it. On Murphy's death in 1994, the *Los Angeles Times* chose this skill of matching people and projects as his greatest legacy.

> An urbane, affable Irishman who reads everything from Rabelais to Runyon, and likes music ranging from Bach to Berlin, Murphy is a genuine whiz at getting the necessary dough-re-mi with which he has performed his wonders.[7]

Franklin Murphy learned how to do that in Kansas. Before his first year as chancellor ended, he had laid the groundwork for private giving—the Greater University Fund—that would supply the "more than bread alone" art and books on which his vision relied.

A treasure of art or print carries with it a precise record of its heritage—its provenance—to authenticate and prove its origin. Beyond the bare bones of that record one may flesh out stories of each stage in its life. As ownership changes, more stories emerge—of who first knew of its availability, of who approached the owner, of who generated the money. These are the stories of living collections in the University of Kansas libraries and art museum that centered, at first, on the Renaissance, Murphy's favorite period. In the library, for instance, Murphy's careful suggestions generated the money that would provide $10,000 annually for the Summerfield Renaissance Collection. And, in the museum, his efforts helped capture Riemenschneider's *Madonna and Child*.

The Summerfield Renaissance Collection derived from the estate of Solon E. Summerfield, a Lawrence native, a graduate of the University of Kansas and its School of Law, and a New York City businessman. Solon Summerfield's grandfather, Abraham, emigrated from Prussia in 1850. His wife and children settled with him in 1860 in Lawrence and nearby Eudora, Kansas. There, the family led a vibrant Jewish community with successful careers in medicine, law, railroads, mining, manufacturing, and university teaching. On Solon's death in 1947, his estate amounted $10 million, according to historian, David M. Katzman.[8] Solon Summerfield had begun to support the University of Kansas as early as 1929 when he gave $5,000 to help the university launch a fund-raising campaign. In the same year, he donated $20,000 to provide annual scholarships.[9] After the donor's death, the funds were handled by the chairman of the estate's foundation, William Felstiner, a man who traveled to Lawrence occasionally to check on the scholarships.[10]

"I think Mr. Summerfield would have liked to have done something more," he said to Murphy, shortly after the latter had become chancellor, "but I've come out here before and nobody seems very interested in anything but the scholarships."[11] That's when Murphy began to talk to him about the library, he said. It started modestly but allowed the university to purchase books, especially of the Renaissance period. "Happily, he was a man who was humanistically oriented, too," Murphy said.[12] Within a short time, Murphy had convinced Felstiner to commit $10,000 annually for ten years for the purpose of building a Renaissance collection for the library. The first purchase happened to be the first travel book, the tale of a German going to Jerusalem, which the university purchased for $250. "The same book sold recently for $250,000," Murphy said, years later.

In 1957, the Summerfield Foundation launched a scholarship program for men in the creative arts, at Murphy's urging. "I am convinced that it is just in these supercharged scientific times," Murphy wrote to Felstiner in thanks for the funds, "that we must especially nurture the creative arts such as music, painting, etc., for I firmly believe that 'man does not live by bread alone'."[13] The Summerfield grants would help the university immeasurably in the years to come. In 1957 alone, the foundation's support amounted to $115,723.05.[14] Almost always, the funds for books and art centered on the Renaissance, which pleased Murphy.

"A book to me is a living force which dissolves the chains that bind me and permits me to live richly in the past, the present and the future—in all parts of the world and with all kinds of people," Murphy wrote. "Without access to books we all would be as insects without antenna or aircraft without radar. I am sure it is true that without Gutenberg, the Renaissance of learning, of beauty and of political freedom would be impossible."[15]

Franklin Murphy loved the Renaissance for its intellectual and artistic ferment and he enriched the university's holdings of that period. But with equal fervor, he loved the Great Plains, his native region. He referred to it over and over as the "trans-Mississippi West," and he held high expectations for it.[16] He explained it in a 1956 speech to regional leaders in higher education:

> The potential of ever-greater development of the total human being stands immediately before us. (We must have) an ever-greater dedication to an understanding of our cultural heritage (to know the) real significance of the immortal phrase, "Man cannot live by bread alone."
>
> These are the matters which must continue to attract increasing educational interest and exploitation if this area is to make its most effective contribution to the growth of our country and our culture. Music, literature—the history of our development—man's interest in and capacity to describe his environment by way of the brush or the chisel—the gathering together and utilization of the basic books and manuscripts which describe man's intellectual and cultural achievements from the earliest times—such matters are central to this necessary and continuing cultural expansion.[17]

His vision for the university involved bringing to the Great Plains books, art, faculty, students, and ideas that represent the best that the world has to offer. But equally importantly, Murphy wanted the university to reflect the indigenous greatness of the region. In art, for example, he wanted the university to own work of the regional triad of painters—Grant Wood, John Steuart Curry, and Thomas Hart Benton—artists who "signify the American tradition of painting," he said.[18] And, before he left in 1960, Murphy's work had paid off.

One-third of the triad, the small Grant Wood painting, *Near Sundown,* came to the university in 1959 as a "life interest" gift from its owner, George Cukor of Beverly Hills, California.[19] KU's art museum director, Edward A. Maser, wrote to Cukor's representative outlining the details and wishing "Mr. Cukor a long, happy life!"[20] Chancellor Murphy expressed his delight in a letter to Cukor a few days later: "I want you to know how deeply grateful we are that you would give serious consideration to making this gift to the University of Kansas and its Museum of Art," Murphy wrote.

> Grant Wood sprang, after all, from the soil of the Midwest and it is our great hope through the years to bring together important materials of the so-called regionalist trio of Benton, Wood and Curry here at the University of Kansas. The prospect of your gift, therefore, comes as great good news, for such an acquisition would make for us an enormous step forward in this regionalist project.[21]

The University of Kansas' primary acquisition of John Steuart Curry's work is an oil sketch of the artist's very controversial mural in the Kansas Capitol. It depicts the "abolitionist John Brown against a background of Kansas symbols—a tornado, sunflowers, and Conestoga wagons on the Santa Fe Trail. Brown, larger than life, rouses his men to action with a Bible in his left hand and a 'Beecher's Bible' (a Sharps rifle) in his right."[22] Murphy must have known that few subjects could be more perfect for the University of Kansas Museum of Art in Lawrence. In 1956, the university sponsored a Curry exhibition that unveiled the Kansas Capitol murals, with Murphy as patron and with the governor as honored guest. In 1957, Murphy took "advantage of an appropriate situation" and convinced Mrs. John Steuart Curry to donate "all of the oil sketches, plus an oil painting, a water color and a crayon" sketch.[23]

The Thomas Hart Benton painting, *The Ballad of the Jealous Lover of Lone Green Valley,* carries a more personal provenance. Murphy and the artist were good friends, especially through Murphy's "closer than a brother" cousin, Lyman Field. Benton's family had come to the west long before the Murphys. His great grand-uncle Senator Thomas Hart Benton had come to Missouri as early as 1815, served as a U.S. Senator from that state from 1821-51, and played an enormous role in its development from the fur-trading days; and the senator's daughter, Jessie Benton Fremont was the wife of the Oregon Trail's explorer and the first Republican candidate for the presidency, John Charles Fremont.[24]

With the great success of the John Steuart Curry exhibition, the art museum hung a Thomas Hart Benton retrospective exhibit in April, 1958. Murphy and the art museum's director Ed Maser often discussed the "opportunity the exhibition gives us of studying his work with the object in mind of acquiring one of his paintings," Maser wrote.[25] Murphy had chosen *Jealous Lover* and Maser concurred.[26] In May, 1958, Murphy wrote to his friend, Tom Benton, explaining his longtime wish to have a Benton in the university's museum in perpetuity. But a problem existed in "the present political climate," he wrote, referring to the ugly gubernatorial race between George Docking and Clyde Reed. "We are unable to use state funds for objects of art. However, from time to time we do manage to scramble together a few dollars here and there," he wrote. He told Benton about the Curry gift of the previous year, asked if the artist would consider selling "*Jealous Lover*," and, if so, "how much I would have to go out and raise."[27]

The deal was struck to everyone's benefit. Benton's payments were spread over a number of years, which suited both the artist and Murphy's budget, and the university obtained one of the centerpiece paintings of its collection. The "trans-Mississippi West" triad was in place. In 1978, curator Charles Eldredge wrote a description of the Helen Foresman Spencer Museum of Art's permanent collection. From more than 25,000 items in the collection, he selected 350 to represent the finest for the publication, Of those 350, nearly one-third came to the university between 1951 and 1960—the years of Franklin Murphy's chancellorship. Eight of the items described in the published book came to it as gifts from Dr. and Mrs. Franklin Murphy—all masks from Oceania or New Zealand.[28] In the years that followed Eldredge's 1978 publication, long after the Murphys had left Lawrence to live in Los Angeles, they donated much more to the cultural life of the university and the community: the Franklin Murphy Library of Art and Architecture, the Murphy Travel Fund for faculty members in art history, at least five boxes of art books each year "just for the shelves,"[29] The Judith Harris Murphy Courtyard at Murphy Hall, the Cordelia Brown Murphy Professorship of Piano, and the Edna St. Vincent Millay Collection.

In 1980, Murphy returned to KU to dedicate the new Murphy Library of Art History at the Spencer Museum of Art. Murphy said his contributions to the library "reflect my deep and abiding interest in the University of Kansas per se ... and my interest in the two things of higher interest wherever I have been—art and books. To bring them both together in a productive way is the best of both worlds."

Thanking Helen Foresman Spencer, whose initial gift from the Kenneth A. and Helen F. Spencer Foundation built the museum, Murphy said, "We have at long last completed what I think, perhaps not in numbers but in quality, is as fine a resource as can be found anywhere in the country."[30]

Upon retirement, he devoted most of his time to these cultural endeavors—as trustee or board member of the Los Angeles County Museum, the Ahmanson Foundation, the J. Paul Getty Museum, the Huntington Library, the Samuel H. Kress Foundation, and the National Gallery of Art.[31] He served on the latter board for 27 years, according to Margaret Leslie Davis, in her excellent biography of Murphy, *The Culture Broker: Franklin D. Murphy and the Transformation of Los Angeles*. She compiled the comprehensive list of Murphy's lifetime positions and affiliations, which appears in the Appendix of this volume.[32] "More than any other single figure," according to Del Shankel, speaking in 1987 as acting executive vice-chancellor, "it was Franklin Murphy, KU chancellor throughout the 1950s, who established a pattern of unequivocal support for an arts partnership between campus and community."[33] He wrote with interest, knowledge and conviction, as is illustrated in this June 1, 1959 letter to Edward A. Maser, director of the Art Museum:

Dear Ed:
It seems to me that we should be thinking of late 19th and 20th Century sculpture, at least for one of the two pieces (for the outdoor sculpture garden). I think, of course, of such names as Barlach, Koike, Maillol, Lehmburck, Rodin, Brancusi, Lipschitz, etc. I am sure that bronze is the medium, since we must constantly consider vandalism, etc. If stone, I think it should be hard stone, and of course wood would be impossible. I shall also be keeping my eyes open in New York.

Murphy believed that an educated person should appreciate all the arts, and articulated the belief in many, many speeches always using the Biblical phrase: "Man does not live by bread alone."[34] Murphy really lived those words, according to George Baxter Smith. "He went to any long-hair concerts and really liked it."[35] When Kansas was attempting to bring in a professional baseball team, which became the Royals, Murphy told the audience of sports leaders, "It's ok to have a baseball team, but until you have a symphony, you're not a first-class city."[36]

As one who sought excellence in everything, Murphy widely supported the arts at the University of Kansas (often insisting that his name not appear as benefactor).[37] The Ahmanson Foundation established, as of 1980, the Murphy Lectureship in Art, and the Cordelia Brown Murphy Chair in Music to honor his mother, the Franklin E. Murphy Professorship in Cardiology to honor his father. The Judith Harris Murphy Professorship in Art History honors Dr. Murphy's wife. Established in 1978, it is the first of its kind in the department of art history. The Murphys were longtime friends of Helen Spencer, and the professorship was stimulated by the creation of the Helen Foresman Spencer Museum of Art.

Franklin Murphy and the Renaissance of the University of Kansas Library

Called "the man of the century for the University of Kansas,"[38] Murphy's appreciation of the cultural arts may be seen most clearly in his work with the library. He loved and valued books:

> ...for me the book is a many splendored thing, having as many facets as the most beautifully cut diamond. A book can be appreciated for its beauty, the information contained therein, as an historical artifact, and the way to become personally acquainted with the greatest and most fertile minds in recorded history...
>
> Books should go into university collections for all of the above reasons and one should not apologize for acquiring books for any of the above reasons.[39]

Murphy's love of books was not an affectation. "For me, may I say that from my earliest days, reading has been my greatest source of satisfaction," he wrote to an enquirer in 1958. "In fact, I have always conceived of the book as something with its own personality and true life and vitality. True it is that with books we accumulate facts. The printed page permits us to expand our understanding of the world in which we live today and the horizons to which we might look tomorrow. By way of the book we gain an insight into the subconscious and emotional life of the greatest figures in human history as well as ordinary people like you and me.[40]

He collected books himself, a passion that would continue throughout his life. With the early example of his father and with notes from Frank Glenn over the years, Murphy built personal collections of Winston Churchill, Sean O'Casey, and Edna St. Vincent Millay. He donated the last to the University, writing to Robert Vosper, the director of libraries: "I intend to present my collection of Edna St. Vincent Millay to the University of Kansas Library through the Kansas University Endowment Association. ... I would not wish to have any newspaper publicity about this gift..."[41]

That his interest in books and art constituted a passion is clear in his correspondence. After a New York City visit with George Matthew Adams, in 1954, Murphy wrote: "I want to thank you very much indeed for the splendid opportunity I had to visit and have lunch with you. I am still somewhat dazzled at viewing the Hern material, followed by our exploration of your treasures in your safe. What a wonderfully satisfying experience the acquisition of this magnificent collection of books must have been," Murphy wrote. "And of course you know how much I envy you the beautiful little Rodin. ..."[42]

Murphy did not spend all of his reading time about rare books from the Renaissance. "He keeps abreast of current thought and events by reading magazines and newspapers," according to an article about Murphy "and through such books as Jimmy Byrnes's *Speaking Frankly*, and Rebecca West's *The Meaning of Treason*. He reads also an art magazine and offsets it with a propensity for buying, every now and again, a 25-cent murder mystery book with a lurid cover. His reading table also holds *The Black Rose*, by Thomas B. Costain. On his bookshelf is, among other sets, the *Complete Works of Benjamin Franklin*.[43]

Although not the library's director, Murphy has been described as the catalyst for what Alexandra Mason, a rare-book librarian during the later Murphy years, described as a nine-year rocket ride. "It was simply the most fun," she said, "that anyone could imagine.[44]

It can't have looked like fun in 1951 when Murphy became chancellor and when the University of Kansas library holdings stood at a weak 407,000 volumes, placing it in a dismal fifth place among the Big Six Midwestern institutions.[45] It held no national ranking at all. In fact, the library's weakness was not merely an inside-the-institution embarrassment. Early in 1951, the national Association of Research Libraries had barely allowed KU to maintain its membership: The accreditors voted and kept KU in its powerful fold only by the slimmest of margins.[46] All that changed quickly. In 1955, the same national association ranked Watson Library at the University of Kansas eighth in the nation in number of volumes added during 1954, with its 60,416 acquisitions that year. To be ranked eighth out of all accredited university libraries put KU in weighty company, with only Illinois, Harvard, California, Cornell, UCLA, Columbia and Minnesota beating it out for the annual prize.[47] During the nine years with Murphy as chancellor, the University of Kansas library holdings more than doubled—to 920,000 volumes.[48]

But Franklin Murphy was not interested only in numbers of books: he wanted the best. In books, in art, in people—in life—Murphy would not settle for second rate. "We must have here in the Great Plains, as well as elsewhere in the country, the original documents—books and manuscripts—that are primary records of our cultural and intellectual heritage," he said. "Our libraries cannot accept second-class status by virtue of possessing only utilitarian copies of copies."[49] Franklin Murphy would not work to fund a library of digests: "Whether of an article, a book, an opera, or a philosophy," according to Jacques Barzun, "the digest anticipates collective judgment by eliminating what is unexpected and difficult."[50]

To make any of it happen, Murphy had to find the perfect person to direct the libraries. He needed a "grand acquisitor" whose ideas matched his own.[51] That would not occur, formally, until Murphy had been in office one full year. In the meantime, he needed to understand the library program—the "heart of the university"[52]—as it was before the renaissance that he intended to lead. To do that, one must go back to early 1951, when Franklin Murphy was dean of the University of Kansas School of Medicine, busier than most, and not especially well-informed about Watson Library, the primary library on the Lawrence campus.[53]

The Library, 1951

At the beginning of 1951, the University of Kansas library was in a dreadful state. While every university division at the time felt the GI Bill students' influx as in a flood following a drought, the university library was in particular need of support.[54] Its director, Charles W. Baker, was a "sweet, gentle old man, but he'd had no money and no authority."[55] Baker had exhausted himself as one of few trained librarians on the staff during the '30s and '40s. By 1948, the money began to flow, but he had been frugal for too long to deal with it. In his 1950-51 Report to the University Senate's Library Committee, Baker noted the difficulties of handling a twice-as-large book-buying budget (for 1948-51) with only one addition to the professional staff. Lacking support from Chancellor Malott, the Regents and the legislature, Baker had merely maintained the services and basic holdings in a status-quo pattern.[56] Unfortunately, Mr. Baker's status quo had been set in 1929.[57] For the most part, the new acquisition money just sat there, as it was not matched with funds to catalog the volumes. "We don't need any more books," he is reported to have said, in exhaustion and desperation.[58] If Baker did not want any new books, he certainly did not intend to allow any of the old ones to get away. He paid close attention to faculty members who were leaving KU for other positions, said John Glinka, who joined the library staff in 1948. One of those teachers had checked out 200 books that had not been returned. Baker and the sheriff met him at the train, just as he was leaving, went through his belongings and retrieved the books.[59]

Some post-war renovations to Watson Library eased the strain slightly, as did a small "Extra Fund." Set up to allow the purchase of research collections, the fund was allocated rigidly, at a set time once a year, and therefore was unusable in the unpredictable and competitive rare-book market. Ultimately used to purchase periodicals, the "Extra Fund" allowed the first sizable additions to the library's holding since 1945.[60]

In that year, a book-collector's treasure of 65,000 items arrived unexpectedly in Lawrence with its eccentric owner, Ralph N. Ellis, Jr. Representing one of the "classical cases of galloping bibliomania,"[61] the astounding Ellis Collection of ornithological material had completely filled two railway freight cars. The Ellis Collection, which until the 1950s constituted the largest and most valuable research tool in the university's libraries, was not obtained by administrative design, but rather through the misfortune of its owner and the years-before kindness of Professor E. Raymond Hall, Director of the Natural History Museum at K.U.[62] Obtaining the Ellis Collection was a happy accident for the university library. In 1949, it comprised fully one-third of all the volumes added to K.U.'s holdings since 1929.[63]

In spite of its weaknesses, the library reflected some very real strengths, especially through the work of a few faculty members who had carefully supervised the acquisition of books even in times of financial stringency. Frank Melvin, in history, and Richard Howey, in economics, single-handedly built collections of great value, according to Ambrose Saricks, one of the pre-Murphy professors who was attracted to KU for its Melvin-begun collection in the history of the French Revolution.[64] Still, he said, Lawrence was just a "typical frontier town, with no traffic and no noise" when he arrived in 1950 from Madison, Wisconsin, and the university "was by no means in the first rank." The library, Saricks said, was even worse.[65]

Just as the Great Flood of 1951 buffeted unanchored items along its edges, the great flood of veterans had caught the university library without an anchor. As if it were a flimsy and leaderless boat, with neither sails nor weight in its centerboard, the library was barely staying afloat on the edges of the flood. The strongest academic departments were those that did not rely on the library, Saricks said.[66] Faculty members in those disciplines that relied on a strong library decided to act.

After 17 investigative meetings, a Special Committee of the College of Liberal Arts and Sciences published its Report on the University Library in March, 1951 —just about the time that Chancellor Malott was beginning to seduce Murphy into considering the chancellorship. Members included W.H. Shoemaker (chairman), Max Dresden, Francis Heller, Richard Howey, James Seaver and James Wortham.[67] Though written in gentle non-accusatory language and with obvious understanding of the causes of the library's malaise, the report reflected a library in chaos.

Seeming to grasp for any positive note in the introduction, the LAS Committee members wrote that the "reading room facilities compare most favorably with those of other institutions in this region."[68] From that faint praise onward, the report chronicled disasters great and small. In size of holdings and rate of growth, for example, K.U. ranked (at best) forty-fourth among fifty-three colleges and universities judged nationally.[69]

The holdings and collections were so weak, in fact, that in early 1951, the university nearly failed to receive sufficient votes in the Association of Research Libraries to remain a member.[70] In number of staff, professional training and salaries, the LAS Report noted, "comparisons do not favor us, not even with other institutions under our State Board of Regents."[71] Noting that KU's 31 library staff members include only 17 who "qualify as trained,"[72] it reported that "seven of every nine man-hours worked at the University Library are handled by sub-professional or student help."[73] In March, 1951, when the report was produced, most of the staffers were "superannuated faculty wives"[74] or students. The committee's recommendations reflected its obvious individual and collective frustrations. The 22 remedial changes suggested to the library administration may be categorized as reflecting six major problems, followed by the committee's recommendation:[75]

1. Lack of communication between library and faculty, *(Recommendation: Do not cancel book orders without notifying the department that ordered the book).*
2. Failure to follow through on previous suggestions, *(Recommendation: Institute new order card systems. Set library rules and observe them).*
3. Lack of understanding of a library's role in a research university, especially in service to students, *(Recommendation: Disseminate instructions to library*

users) and in service to faculty, *(Recommendation: Notify any borrower when a previously unavailable item has become available and disseminate information on new books).* [76]

4. Need for total re-organization and institution of modern procedures, *(Recommendation: Record, in the central card catalog, the location of books in...branch units of the Library)*[77]
5. Lack of imagination, *(Recommendation: Actively invite, encourage and secure gifts for the Library).*[78]
6. Protectiveness, *(Recommendation: Permit screened and designated proxies to sign for faculty books, and extend stack privileges to all graduate students and in exceptional cases, to qualified seniors).*[79]

It all seems so basic now, but in an anti-intellectual climate nationally, and without strong leadership locally, money for and interest in libraries was not a high priority.[80] The LAS Committee's aim was clear—to change the direction of the university library, through the College of Liberal Arts and Sciences, through the chancellor, or through pressure and active assistance from individual faculty members.

Reminding its colleagues that, in the humanities and social sciences, the library is its laboratory and its equipment, the committee wrote: "We who teach at the University of Kansas owe to this institution more than the performance of mere schoolmasters' tasks. The place of this university in academic circles hinges on the research activities of its faculty as much as on the caliber of its graduates...."[81]

One route to reform seemed to be through the chancellor. However, shortly after the LAS Report was issued, the university announced a change in leadership.

On the LAS Library Committee at the University of Kansas, in early 1951, one member could speak with authority about the chancellor-to-come: R. S. Howey of the Economics Department had been Murphy's undergraduate professor at the university in the mid-1930s.[82] Howey assured his colleagues that the new chancellor liked all of it—especially books, that he liked people most of all, and that the university library would improve dramatically under Murphy's leadership.[83]

Professor Howey, as he was always addressed by the younger Chancellor Murphy, would become as close to being a library staff member as was possible. Few days passed during the next decade that the economics scholar was not seen in Watson Library, checking through the card catalog.[84] He was a valued bibliophile whose advice was followed and whose scholarly treasure hunts paid enormous dividends to the University Library.

In writing its aims for the library, early in 1951, the LAS Committee had written to Chancellor Malott. The plea, however, took root with his successor. "The University Library should be thought of as a true laboratory of the mind," they urged, "and its collections as tools essential to learning and research. The Library of the University of Kansas should be devoted to the needs of scholarly research no less than to the demands of undergraduate reading. "Internal management of the Library should aim at freeing the senior staff members of the burden of routine administration," they continued, "thus enabling them to keep the Library in closest harmony with the teaching faculty, the statewide reservoir of good-will, and the ever-changing world of books and book-dealers. The ambitions of a growing university call imperatively for boldness and vision in library planning as in the teaching field."[85]

The LAS Committee members didn't need to wait long for action. They learned quickly that Franklin Murphy was a dedicated bookman and agreed with them entirely. Often reminding his audiences that "man cannot live by bread alone," [86] Murphy rarely missed an opportunity to emphasize the integral role of libraries in a society's progress: "... libraries...have both an intellectual and a cultural responsibility," he said to a regional audience after becoming chancellor: "With vigor and with a cooperative spirit, they must accumulate books and journals that are essential tools for research in many fields." [87]

For the university library, Murphy's greatest opportunity lay in its near-*tabula rasa* state.[88] Murphy needed a man to match his vision; a man he could trust to create an excellent library in Kansas. But first, he needed to consolidate his strength. As the search for a new director would be conducted by the University Senate's Library Committee, the new Chancellor worked quickly to form that group into one that reflected his vision of library-as-university-heart. To do so, he drew from the LAS Committee that had spoken so forthrightly earlier in the year. In the past, the seven-member committee had been chaired by C.M. Baker, as Director of Libraries. Immediately, the Chancellor urged Baker to retire early, to vacate the directorship as of July, 1952.[89] At that time, Murphy expected to have hired a new director. In the meantime, the University Senate Library Committee was increased to nine members, two of whom (Wortham and Shoemaker) had served on the LAS Committee. Wortham, not Director Baker, was appointed Chairman—and thereby, head of the search committee.[90] It was one of the first, but not the final, examples of Murphy's controlling hand. More than a few described him as an authoritarian administrator.[91]

A Man to Match Murphy's Vision: Robert Vosper

Moving very quickly, the Library Director Search Committee, with James Wortham as chair, began the process of matching a man to Chancellor Murphy's vision. In language strikingly similar to Murphy's speeches, letters and unpublished conversations, the announcement went out in December, 1951, on Department of English Language and Literature letterhead:

> The University of Kansas is seeking a new Director of Libraries, who will take office on July 1st, 1952, when the present Director retires.
>
> The University desires a library that will be an increasingly prominent focus of academic activity. It hopes that, under a vigorous and imaginative leadership, new services and facilities will be added to those now in being.
>
> The qualifications of a person fitted to provide such leadership cannot of course be exactly specified, but the following points seem to indicate the ideal:
>
> 1. A vital conception of the function of a university library as a center of teaching and research, and the ability to imagine new and better ways to realize that function.
> 2. The capacity to appreciate the highest excellence in books, so that volumes that possess real distinction and foster an appreciation of the best, as great paintings do in the field of art, may be added to the University's libraries.
> 3. Professional training and experience in library science, or other evidence of a competent comprehension of the functions of a university library.
> 4. A high level of training in an esteemed academic discipline, preferably indicated by a Ph.D. or other research degree.
> 5. The administrative capacity necessary to handle a large staff with efficiency.

6. An understanding of public relations—with the students, with the faculty, with the alumni, and with that portion of the public which is likely to take an interest in a university library: in other words, the ability to represent the University and its library before the public.
7. The power to discover desirable materials and to secure them for the University.

It should be clearly understood that the University will consider great potentialities, wherever found, quite as seriously as ability which has been already demonstrated.[92]

The announcement was written, to some degree, with a candidate in mind. Wortham, who had come to KU from the University of California at Los Angeles to head the English Department, was aware of a young librarian there—Robert Vosper, who would be Acting Director of Libraries at UCLA until the summer of 1952. Wortham contacted Vosper, asking him to apply. Vosper's initial response was decidedly negative: "Why would I leave Los Angeles and go to Lawrence, Kansas, which I had never heard of or seen," he asked.[93] The Californian's answer became a challenge. At KU lay an opportunity, Wortham told him, to build a library in tandem with a powerful and bibliophilic chancellor. An unparalleled opportunity, the Kansas position deserved Vosper's application, Wortham said. "At least," he told Vosper, "you could be polite and apply."[94]

With a B. A. and an M.A. (honors) in Classical Languages from the University of Oregon, Vosper had earned a Certificate in Librarianship from the University of California, Berkeley, in 1940. After working in reference at Berkeley and Stanford, Vosper moved to UCLA in 1944 as Assistant Librarian. In 1950, the 37-year-old had been appointed Acting Librarian, UCLA and Acting Director of the prestigious William Andrews Clark Memorial Library, during the sabbatical absence of Lawrence C. Powell, Librarian and Director.[95] Married with four children, Vosper had served on the boards of state and national professional associations, and the UCLA chapter of Phi Beta Kappa. A prolific scholar, he also produced several articles each year. Moreover, Vosper not only collected books himself, but also had joined three Los Angeles clubs for bibliophiles, historians and printers.[96]

On paper, Vosper appeared to match Murphy's energy. Certainly his description of the UCLA effort reinforced Wortham's predictions:

"We have developed here, I think," Vosper wrote of UCLA "a wide reputation for having a strong and imaginative staff, a well-ordered house, an effective program of service and of good relations with faculty, students, and community."[97]

While other candidates applied for the position, none generated the volume of correspondence that passed between Wortham, for the search committee, and the "hundred or so" referents writing to support Robert Vosper's candidacy.[98] Generally two pages in length and consistently effusive in praise, the responses to Wortham's inquiry read like eulogies. Indeed, they were just that for his Southern California associates among booksellers, faculty and library staff. Every one of them noted the decided loss to UCLA should Vosper choose Kansas.[99] From Lawrence Clark Powell, UCLA Librarian and Vosper's immediate superior, came a note of caution. "I can assure you," he wrote, "that if you want to secure him, you had better not draw out your inquiry much longer, for fear someone else will move in and enlist his interest. ...he is increasingly known in the national picture, and will undoubtedly be sought after all through his professional career."[100]

After six weeks of voluminous reference-checking correspondence, Wortham invited Vosper to visit the campus for an interview on February 29, 1951. Although in truth "completely skeptical," Vosper replied that he would be happy to meet for an interview and expected to fly into Kansas City and then catch the Santa Fe direct rail line to Lawrence. "If I miss that," he wrote to Wortham, "I suppose there is a bus service."[101] Like many others, Vosper did not believe entirely that Kansas had progressed beyond stagecoaches. "I'd never been in that part of the world before except going over by plane or train," he said.[102] While not spoken out of arrogance, Vosper's statement reflected the bi-coastal attitude about Kansas that Franklin Murphy intended to change.

In Vosper, Murphy appeared to have found a man of youthful vigor, of imagination, with proven experience in administration, and with an apparently identical vision of a library's role in a great university. And, he had earned a fine reputation nationally as a scholar and professional librarian. "Of course I was looking for a man who could run a major library program," Murphy said. "But most of all, I intended to hire a man who loves books"[103] Active membership in three book-discussion clubs in the midst of a meteoric career and an active family life was a good sign. Chancellor Murphy saved his job applicant a bus trip and a train ride—he drove to Kansas City to meet Robert Vosper.[104]

Each man realized immediately that he had found an intellectual brother—a brother of the mind.[105] "He and I talked," Murphy said later, "and I knew in an instant that he was the man I wanted."[106] And Vosper agreed: "We chatted on the way to Lawrence from Kansas City. He was interested in books and ...we got on swimmingly," he said. [107] The two bookmen were so close,[108] according to library professionals who watched them work together, that they *were* like brothers.[109] "The library didn't have any strength alone," according to John Glinka, who later became acting director, "but with those two working together, it was about the strongest department on campus. Certainly we felt that it was."[110]

"Not being a chancellor who stayed in his office, Dr. Murphy was in and out all the time," Alexandra Mason said. "What a pair those two were!"[111]

They might have been intellectual brothers, but one would not mistake Bob Vosper for Murphy—they did not look alike physically at all. Bob Vosper resembled a young version of Mr. Chips or John Dewey. About five-feet-nine-inches tall, he wore wire-rimmed glasses and a bow tie, smoked a pipe, and sported a trim, soft-brown mustache that matched his thinning hair. He was lean of frame and absolutely crisp in his browns and greens during the most-steamy Kansas summers—even without air conditioning, which was unknown at the university in 1952.[112] In winter, he often wore a three-piece suit or a buttoned sweater beneath his ever-present suit coat. Three years older than Murphy, Vosper was 39 in the spring of 1952 when he came to Lawrence to interview for the position of director of libraries.

Franklin Murphy could not be described as lean and wiry—he was fleshier, rounder. Their heights matched as did the amount of hair remaining to these young men. Murphy's slightly padded bones produced an image not lean, but always "bandbox."[113] In photographs of the period, one sees Murphy always wearing light-colored suits with an old-school striped tie. "He had penetrating eyes," said Frank Burge, who saw him often. "Franklin Murphy was one of the biggest men I've ever seen—for one who wasn't especially tall."[114]

During Vosper's initial visit, at the end of February, 1952, the two men talked of their dreams for the ideal library program. They also talked about what it would cost. Vosper wanted to double the current $100,000 acquisition budget; Murphy was more realistic. He confidently promised a fifty percent expansion for the coming year, as a minimum below which it would never fall.[115] Vosper also wanted an additional $25,000 for new positions (top administrators would later be hired for $5,000 and $6,000). Murphy explained that Vosper's proposals would constitute seven percent of the university's total budget, an amount he was pleased to expend, he said later, because the library is symbolic of a university's stature.[116] And, the two men discussed their potential working relationship. They agreed that the director of libraries must act independently, but that they could have quite a lot of fun as a team. Vosper wrote to Murphy immediately after the visit:

> I went to Lawrence somewhat skeptical; I left so full of enthusiasm that I cannot forbear reporting immediately that, if a vigorous library program can be funded along the lines you and I discussed, I would consider it a great honor to direct such a program for the University of Kansas. This would offer one of the most challenging opportunities in the field of university libraries in the country.
>
> I am convinced that you and your colleagues deserve, in fact, require, a forward-looking program of the kind I envision, rather than a low level or parsimonious program. I say this not only because of the present state of library service at Lawrence; I say it particularly because of the uncommonly strong body of informed, eager, and enlightened opinion on library matters displayed by your faculty, and of course by yourself. Anything short of a vigorous and imaginative library renaissance would, I am sure, be a disappointment.[117]

To James Wortham, the chairman of the search committee, Vosper wrote the following day: "I can say heartily that I am very very enthusiastic about the situation at Lawrence and that if the Chancellor is able to provide the kind of financial support which he and I discussed, I'd be only excited by an opportunity to come ..."[118]

The Murphy/Vosper team that became formal a few days later was launched by the two bookmen. With Robert Vosper building an incomparable staff and finding the books, and with Franklin Murphy building connections and finding the money, the University of Kansas Library entered its renaissance—its nine-year "glorious rocket ride."[119]

"Hiring Bob Vosper was the best thing I ever did for the library," Murphy said, after years of reflection. "Even with unlimited money I couldn't be the librarian. It was wonderful to have somebody who was just like a brother intellectually putting this together."[120] Many, including Murphy, described Bob Vosper as the chancellor's "greatest contribution to the library."[121]

"Ray -
Excellent and wonderful idea—Will save us money in the long run—will you tell Vosper to go forward at once and let's find the money somewhere."

Franklin Murphy to Ray Nichols,
  Handwritten note on Robert Vosper to Murphy,
  letter, Nov.21, 1956.

Murphy and Vosper: A Leadership Team in Action

A space rocket must propel itself instantly if it is to break out of the earth's gravitational pull and reach its goal. There can be no faltering in its initial expenditure of energy—its first few minutes will spell success or failure. Although the early 1950s were before Sputnik and before the days when everyone knew about rocket thrust and watched each launch with anxiety, Robert Vosper and Franklin Murphy seemed to have understood the analogy. If they were to break the hold of lethargy, they seemed to know that the first year of a new director of libraries would require visible energy unseen at the university before. Many would see the books; few would see how they were funded. No one who watched it could have been disappointed at the energy in that first-year's launch.

Between September 15, 1952, and the same date one year later, the Murphy and Vosper team had found $51,000 to buy 30,000 books that filled two houses, a barn, and a shed and that constituted the astounding Fitzpatrick Collection; had launched a series of statewide speeches and newsletters to inform the public of the university, its books and libraries; had begun to purchase the nearly 30,000 volumes of the Crerar Collection in economics; had put together an impressive exhibit on the evils of censorship; had opened the first-ever undergraduate reading room; had hired a full contingent of professional staff members; had held the first of an annual lecture series; had instituted an embryonic fund for private gifts; and had enjoyed themselves thoroughly.

Murphy had hoped that Robert Vosper could begin on July 1, but moved the date in order to allow the Californian to finish his work there and take his family on a Yosemite vacation. The official starting date, for salary purposes, was set at September 1, 1952 but Murphy characteristically played with the funds when he told Vosper that the Regents would not pay moving expenses. "In other words," he wrote, "I can begin your salary two weeks ahead of the time your official duties are to be taken on, which would represent an amount of about $365 toward the expense of your move."[122]

During the summer, before Vosper began, Murphy continued his own acquisitional play on behalf of the library, purchasing a 1603 edition of Dürer's *Opera* (for $270)[123] and, through his bookseller friend, Frank Glenn, $1,400 worth of books from the Hernandez library.[124] While Murphy took his family on a month-long vacation in the East,[125] Vosper, in the mountains, had been hard at work since accepting the position in April.[126] He had negotiated with the chancellor, in several letters, for additional personnel and for a doubled book-buying budget. In his first post-acceptance letter, Vosper laid out a plan that "may seem impatient," he wrote, "but I feel that several library operations must be pushed forward at once, and they all interact."[127] He intended to begin the search for two key administrators, he wrote, and Murphy replied, explaining the procedure for hiring, which methods illustrate one of many differences between 1952 and now:

"When you determine the individuals," Murphy explained, "I would appreciate receiving a short statement of their training, background, age, etc., as well as the details of employment which you propose, such as salary, starting period, etc. I will then send you my approval and that of the Board of Regents. Upon receipt of this memo, you may then officially offer them the position. On receipt of a note from you as to their acceptance, I shall then proceed to send them the official forms of employment which they should fill out and return to me."[128]

He reminded Vosper that his own moving expenses should be "considered one of these exceptional circumstances" and that any new personnel could not expect similar benefits. As for Vosper's move to Kansas, Murphy wrote "no one's enthusiasm is greater than mine."[129] Murphy was enthusiastic indeed, for his new team-member had written that the first need is for books: "The University . . . had suffered a long book drought," Vosper wrote. "With a few notable exceptions, the collections lacked distinction: in many cases, they were even below the level of bare utility."[130]

"Bob Vosper had an insatiable appetite for books,"[131] according to Ray Nichols, who paid attention to the budget. Vosper also had mentioned a plan that was close to the chancellor's heart—the "immediate and urgent need for the development of a vigorous and informed library public service program."[132] Those words must have proved to Murphy that he had chosen the right man. According to Vosper, the feeling was mutual. In a later interview, Vosper explained his initial impression of Murphy: "He read books," Vosper said. "Latin books."

Years later, Franklin Murphy acknowledged apparent patterns in his life. His friendship and working relationship with Robert Vosper stood as the quintessential example of one such pattern: share the vision with all, but share complete trust with few. The two men worked so well together that Murphy not only trusted Vosper completely, but also he gave absolute free rein to his new director of libraries.[133] "I took the job because of Franklin," Vosper said. "It was clear that he and I had a meeting of the minds on books and libraries. His agreement was to let me run the whole library system. Furthermore, he was busy becoming Chancellor and running the university, so he gave me a pretty free hand."[134]

One of Vosper's first actions, however, as director of libraries, was to ask Murphy's permission to designate Mr. C. M. Baker—his sweet, gentle, exhausted predecessor—as "University Bibliographer" for the remaining short time of his tenure. "I hope that this meets with your favor," Vosper wrote.[135]

The two men agreed on many things, but their management styles were not as similar. Both knew how to build a staff of loyal workers, but they went about it in different ways. Murphy fit the project to the individual. When he needed a supporter (whether the parent of an angry student or a legislator) he spoke and wrote with charm and courtly prose. Unfailingly, he treated his elders with respect. But as a 36-year-old chancellor in 1952, he was also authoritarian and brusque, qualities that he seemed to need in order to stand his ground and to effect the change he intended.

Murphy acknowledged that he *was* a demanding individual—in a quiet way, he said in 1992, during his mellowed seventies. "I've learned over time not to yell at people. But yes, they all know that I want... the best."[136] Both of the men who worked most closely with him report that Murphy never shouted or lost his temper, but others remember differently.[137] Vosper, for example, said that one could hear him all the way down the corridor of Strong Hall. "I would go over there," he said, "and Murphy would be shouting in the telephone. Impatient. A very demanding person who could be very tough on people who couldn't live up to his expectations. That's Franklin."[138] Clearly, Murphy's style was no secret. "He was fairly intimidating," according to a colleague, "because he was so brilliant and so powerful. You knew when he was losing patience because his voice would get loud."[139]

Assistant Professor Ambrose Saricks said that he got no sense of an open-door policy to Murphy's office. "He was not very approachable," he said. Later, however, Saricks was surprised by a call from the chancellor who asked the French scholar's advice about a purchase of Marquis de Sade materials. "Mostly," Saricks said, "I was surprised that he was interested enough to ask my advice."[140]

Historian Clifford Griffin wrote that Murphy was, to that time, "the University's liveliest and most provocative—though not always best-loved—chief executive."[141] Immediately on assuming the office, for example, he flexed his muscle successfully with the faculty senate—not only in re-ordering its search committee for the director of libraries, but also in by-passing its budget committee. Henceforward, his office would approve expenditures.[142] Murphy "struck another blow for administrative autocracy" over a College vs. School of Education disagreement and resultant Faculty Senate Advisory Committee investigation.[143] The chancellor decided that the partially completed investigation should be an administrative matter, not a faculty matter, and added, according to the Senate minutes, that if "he felt that the advice of the Senate would be valuable, he would ask for it."[144] The senators sat silent, "timid—as usual—before Murphy's assertiveness."[145]

Most assistant professors had few dealings with the chancellor, but one who did recalled a brusque Murphy indeed. In the spring of 1956, Calder Pickett was the faculty adviser of a journalism society that published a humor magazine called *The Sour Owl*. In an effort to make a little more money, the group published one issue lampooning a number of administrators, including Murphy. "It wasn't very funny, that Sour Owl," Pickett wrote, "but it sold well for about two hours." The administrators didn't like it at all. "We heard the riot act" from Murphy, Pickett said. "I was an assistant professor, 'way down in the economic pits, and the future looked bleak."[146]

A few years later, Pickett had occasion to see Murphy in a milder light—as a lover of art. In 1959, Pickett wrote an article about the John Steuart Curry mural at the Kansas Capitol—an oil sketch of which had recently become part of the University Museum of Art's collection. Murphy read Pickett's description of the controversy that the mural caused and "insisted that I publish the names of the people who had made life miserable for the Kansas artist."[147]

As director of libraries, Robert Vosper also could be brusque—but only mildly so.[148] Murphy was Irish, Vosper explained, "and I'm not."[149] He rarely raised his voice, but always made his point. "Madam," he said to one employee who asked to work fewer hours than the required

44 each week, "if you want to play golf on Thursday afternoon, I suggest you get a faculty job."[150] Alexandra Mason recalled only one chastisement from Vosper, her boss. When she had handled an annoyed reader very undiplomatically, he told her: "I backed you up, of course, but don't ever do it again."[151] Never a "weakly administrator who doesn't dare say what must be said," Vosper was, for Mason, the ideal boss. "And, I never did that again," she said.

John Glinka, who began and ended his library career in the KU library, reported that Vosper asked all employees to report the number of overtime hours they had amassed during the time before he became director.[152] Very democratic in an age when such was atypical, "he'd ask you to do something," Glinka said, "and you absolutely wanted to do it—through a sense of unity with him."[153]

Neither Franklin Murphy nor Robert Vosper recalled a loud or heated dispute between them. They were a team of two. Most of the library employees agreed that it worked very well. "Chancellor Murphy and Bob Vosper ran the show," according to Mason, "but Mr. Vosper let us all feel part of it. We were all in it together."[154] She described a typical day, working until midnight without noticing the time. "I was living a life of complete joy with my rare books," she said, "which, thanks to Vosper and Murphy and the rest of the team, just kept rolling in. It was the most exciting time imaginable."[155] The books rolled in because Vosper had taken the chancellor at his word: "Do whatever you want," Murphy said that he told Vosper. "I will find the money."[156] The money came from lots of sources. In one month, for example, Murphy convinced the Board of Regents to fund a $51,000 collection of books and a month later, he paid for a $40,000 collection with "bits and pieces here and there," he said, "and by parasitizing a budget here and shifting funds there. Where there's a will, there's a way."[157]

Sometimes Murphy raised money by shifting funds and other times by approaching the right person for the project. Just as had been the case when he raised money privately for the KU Medical Center, as its dean, "I made speeches in every corner of the state of Kansas," he said. "I was in Topeka and I was talking to the newspaper guys."[158] Whether he was convincing the Boeing Company's Earl Schaefer to support the science building with money, or whether he needed $3,000 quickly to capture 6,000 slides of Spanish art, Franklin Murphy raised the money—by himself. "You're the one that has to make the pitch," he said. "They want to see the number one man. You don't send a boy to do a man's work."[159] He explained that the staff would figure out who should be a target and would pull together all the research, such as a target's connection to the university and whether "they have children or grandchildren or uncles or aunts or whatever. But the pitch has to come from the boss," Murphy said.[160]

In fund-raising activities, Murphy might have left many of the details to his staff, but he fed constant reminders to them. "Dear Irvin," he wrote to Irvin Youngberg, the executive secretary of the KU Endowment Association, for example, "It is extremely important that we keep them [a particular alumnus and his wife] involved in the life of the University. He is the kind of person who, I think, would love to represent the University at inaugurations, for he loves his academic costume."[161]

When something interested Murphy, he paid very close attention, especially if it concerned donations to the university. Throughout his tenure, he was very interested in the Solon E. Summerfield Foundation, which had proved to be a generous and reliable source of money for unusual projects. In 1955, for example, its president William Felstiner agreed to provide $10,000 annually for the Summerfield Collection of Renaissance and Early Modern European Works—15th - 17th century books printed in continental Europe.[162]

Vosper handed the Summerfield present to Joseph Rubinstein, who had been hired in 1953 to lead the library's rare book division—a man who "had books in his blood" and many friends in the trade.[163] Rubinstein also had degrees from the University of California in medieval history and librarianship. His impact on the library led Alexandra Mason to describe him, with Murphy and Vosper, as "the third member of the missionary group bringing the Gospel of the Book to the Great American Desert."[164] Rubinstein, who was "fearfully learned,"[165] taught in the Western Civilization Program—for which he supplied his *own* John Calvin translation[166]—and also taught a graduate course in bibliography.

Rubinstein's friends were booksellers and collectors all over the United States and Europe, and they kept him supplied with tips about available books. With the Summerfield funds in mind, Vosper sent him to Europe in late 1957 on a three-month book-buying trip. He returned with 4,000 volumes, 2,500 of which would launch the Summerfield Renaissance Collection. While in Europe on his first buying trip (the first ever by a KU librarian), Rubinstein learned about a collection of Renaissance works that was offered through a New York City dealer.[167] The collection comprised 2,000 books, mainly Spanish of the 16th and 17th century, which had been owned by Sir William Stirling-Maxwell and stored in his Keir Castle in Scotland since 1878. The most important group of books in the collection was of Cervantes.

An ideal addition to KU's Summerfield Collection, the collection cost $75,000. Rubinstein bought it.

As it contained many original works of Cervantes, the collection's purchase was announced formally at KU's 25th Annual Cervantes Day celebration on April 26, 1958.[168] Murphy, who paid close attention to detail concerning donors, was not entirely pleased with the resultant publicity. The collection that Vosper continued to refer to as "Stirling-Maxwell" materials had been funded by the Solon Summerfield Foundation, Murphy told him, using words as stern as one sees from the chancellor to his director of libraries. "In the publicity... for the Sterling [*sic*]-Maxwell library purchase," he wrote to Vosper, "let me remind you *again* that full credit should go to the Summerfield bequest, to the Endowment Association and to the Greater University Fund."[169] In December, 1958, Murphy wrote again: "I am enclosing a copy of the latest 'Students and Libraries.' In the part under 'Special Collections' we fail to make note of the Summerfield collection of Renaissance materials. Furthermore, we refer to the Stirling-Maxwell collection as such, when as a matter of fact it was bought with Summerfield funds and the rationale to get the funds was that it would make a significant addition to the Summerfield collection. The more we highlight this as one collection, the greater the possibility of getting continuing support for the Summerfield Foundation."[170]

Moreover, Murphy wanted external press coverage to reflect the gift's importance, as is illustrated in the first letter to Vosper about the Stirling-Maxwell purchase, in February, 1958: "Toward the end of March," he wrote, "I wish you would call me so that we can see if the Kansas City *Star* would be willing to do a Sunday feature on the K.U. Library, with special emphasis on this Renaissance project."[171] He did not suggest that Vosper call Tom Yoe or Jim Gunn, who wrote the news releases for the university. Vosper was to remind Murphy to call his friend Alvin McCoy at the *Star*. For Murphy, fund raising and public relations went hand in hand.

Murphy and Vosper agreed on the value of public relations for success of all their fund-raising projects—whether for political or vocal support, or for books and art. For the library, they jointly instituted a number of activities to tell its story—on campus, in the Lawrence community, among Kansas voters and bibliophiles, and in the wider bibliophilic profession. In large measure, all of the activities served an educational function more than a public-relations function—but the latter could not be overlooked. The goal of such activities for both men was as multiple as their audiences: generate understanding of the need for a strong library and an excellent university; generate private funds to purchase books; find collections and make vocal friends for the program. In April 1953, for example, they launched the Annual Lectureship in Books and Bibliography, which "proposes to focus the attention of the University family and the people of this region on the basic importance of books and the fine art of printing in the lives of men," Murphy said.[172]

The first lecture featured Elmer Adler, Emeritus Professor of Graphic Arts at Princeton University. "The complex history of civilized men's deeds and thoughts and hopes has been preserved and transmitted to all of us through books," Murphy said in announcing it.[173] Following Adler's lecture, Murphy hosted a dinner for about 20 book-lovers and potential donors. To them, Murphy promised that "your companions at the dinner will all be people interested in books and in book collecting, so there should be ample and pleasant opportunity for the kind of bookish talk that we all enjoy and find insufficient opportunity for."[174] It was not an idle promise as Murphy did not invite any spouses, but sent specifically to the man or woman addressed. Two were women.

Vosper described the lecture and dinner in an article in UCLA's *Hoja Volante,* noting that the event drew book collectors as far away as Denver and Ponca City, Oklahoma. At the small dinner, he wrote, "with our Chancellor as host and Elmer Adler as high priest, we talked so much of books that a new book collector's club was born. In good tradition it was christened the Jotham Meeker Club, after the first printer of the area."[175] Its members would expand the library's holding and funds measurably.

Vosper also spread the word of the library with a new publication, *Books and Libraries at the University of Kansas*, a thrice-annual treasure trove of details to which Murphy contributed often, as did faculty members.[176] Distributed widely to all of the staff's national and international friends and colleagues, *Books and Libraries* served as an informal and readable textbook for scholar-adventurers in the rare-book arena. It was educational in the extreme, and Vosper and Rubinstein were the teachers. Rubinstein, for example, described his 1957 European book-buying trip in the February 1958, *B&L,* noting the best and worst bookshops for finding the treasures he sought, including "of course, Blackwells on the Broad (Oxford), which provides a warehouse and a lavish tea. Before one gets to the warehouse one has to pass the trial-by-basement, by means of a tough skull and a flashlight."[177]

In *Books and Libraries,* one finds regularly such advice about where in the world to find what, as well as scholarly histories of new books obtained—and when and where the reader might find them in the library. While it was an educational tool, *Books and Libraries* served an important public relations function. Its readers far and wide could see the depth of interest and scholarship of the librarians at the University of Kansas. And, those who were close could attend the lectures and exhibits, could enter the book-collecting competition, or could read the books that *B&L* announced.

While not considered a public-relations tool, the library's in-house newsletters, *Jayhawk Biblio-Tracks* (which became *The Gamut* in September 1954), helped Vosper solidify the fast-growing library team. These illustrate the more human face of the library, reporting on staff members' accomplishments and of covered-dish suppers on Saturday nights at Potter's Lake, at the Vosper home, and at the library—after hours, in the undergraduate reading room. Vosper's wife, Loraine—"Mary Martin with bobbed hair, vivacious and outgoing"— often presided over these staff events.[178] Even in these mimeographed, informal publications, one sees Vosper's emphasis on the university as educator. When Vosper helped form the Midwest Inter-Library Center, for example, he wrote detailed articles so that his staff might understand the history and the value of MILC, as well as the procedures needed to make the innovative book-sharing consortium work.[179] Not only did MILC expand a member-library's holdings through this first inter-library loan agreement, but also it cleared shelf space. Thousands of seldom-used books were shipped on loan to Chicago for storage. John Nugent headed the MILC effort for KU and wrote about the first shipment to MILC of 300 boxes, in May 1953.[180]

Murphy's public-relations activities ranged widely, but generally relied on personal correspondence and speeches. He wrote his own speeches and edited them carefully, in his own bold handwriting.[181] One often finds evidence of paragraphs or ideas from others' speeches that caught his eye and that he marked for potential future use. Without exception, his written drafts for speeches reflect what he later described as an attempt at Aristotelian simplicity.[182] In front of an audience, Murphy seems to have rarely used the notes he had prepared.[183] "When I'm on my feet," he told Nichols, "those grey cells start to work for me and I just talk."[184] With few exceptions, he used his favorite phrase to describe excellence in books, art, and music—"man cannot live by bread alone" and whenever possible, "stuck in" the glories of the "trans-Mississippi West."[185] He loved words and used his face and his arms and his voice to drive home their message.[186]

The words he chose made an impact on those who read or heard them, if one is to credit the comments of a few of his friends in high places. From President Eisenhower, to whom Murphy had sent the copy of a speech, he learned in 1957: "I agree thoroughly with all you say, and I like so much the language you used, you may possibly find me guilty of borrowing a phrase or so for the speeches I plan to make before the end of the year."[187] Former President Harry Truman asked Murphy to speak at his 71st birthday celebration in 1955. Murphy received a lot of criticism from Kansas Republicans for having lent his name to a Democrat, but he enjoyed Truman and brushed off the complaints. Obviously, Truman liked Murphy. "I don't know when I have enjoyed a speech or appreciated its contents any more than I did yours the other night at the birthday dinner," Truman wrote. "I hope you will send me a copy of it and that you will autograph the original and allow me to place it in the archives of the library when it is built."[188]

Robert Vosper's speeches tended to involve fewer grand gestures and more Latin phrases. A writer of notable talent, he crafted his speeches with the eyes of an artist (he described Highway K-10 as "a country lane lined with hedge apples and sumach... all yellow, red, and light green as fall creeps into Kansas") and the training of a classicist.[189] And, he delivered lots of speeches. In the month of May 1953, for example, Vosper gave eight speeches—only one of which duplicated another.[190] On campus, in that thirty-one-day period, he spoke to Pi Kappa Lambda and the faculty club, and delivered the annual Phi Beta Kappa lecture. Off campus, he spoke at banquets and graduation exercises in Denver, Lindsborg, Kansas City, Stillwater, and Newton. His speeches tended to be much longer than Murphy's and substantially more scholarly—he used the framework of many speeches as articles for professional journals, to which he contributed several times each year. *College and Research Libraries,* for example, published his 2,200 word "Acquisition Policy—Fact or Fancy?" in its October 1953, issue.[191]

When the two men took their message on the road together, their different styles blended well. After all, they gave the same message: excellence at the University of Kansas. Vosper described it as Murphy's love of "taking the university out into the counties," a public-relations practice he had begun as dean of medicine.[192] The University of Kansas, Vosper said, "had always been isolated and impersonal. Murphy began setting up special projects in central Kansas and western Kansas, and so ... we began going off together with some members of the faculty on barnstorming trips."[193] The group traveled in a small bus and put on programs for alumni all over the state. The programs in the counties covered a lot of topics, Vosper said: "I took a suitcase full of rare books that we had been buying and talked to the people about that."[194]

On one memorable trip, they met other Kansans who would build close ties to the university as a result of that suitcase. In Wichita, Vosper was surprised to meet a group of book collectors after his own heart— the Wichita Bibliophiles. This longstanding association of 25 men loved the contents of Vosper's suitcase—they were men who loved the feel of the handmade paper and the smell of old leather, who relished the adventure of the rare-book search, and who presented scholarly papers at their monthly meetings.[195] As some of them were owners of public and private presses, they often printed the announcement of the meetings. Robert Vosper was surprised to find in Wichita a group of serious bibliophiles to match any of the groups he had loved in Los Angeles. "I don't know of anything comparable in the country," he said years later. "There are bibliophilic organizations in Chicago, in New York City, in San Francisco and Los Angeles, but they're formal organizations." The Wichita Bibliophiles were different—it was an informal and casual group: "very personal, very bookish."

Both Vosper and Murphy attended their Wichita meetings once or twice each year thereafter. "The only problem," Vosper said, "was that they had such big meals that Franklin and I always fell asleep. We invited them to Lawrence a few times," he said, "and we'd have a big party over at my house or the chancellor's house. It was a lot of fun and Franklin enjoyed it too."[196] The Wichita Bibliophiles also enjoyed those dinners, as member Harry Kurdian recalled 28 years later on the 50th anniversary of the club. "On April 24th, 1954," he wrote, "the members ... were the guests, at Lawrence, of Franklin D. Murphy, Chancellor, Bob Vosper, Director of Libraries, and Dick Howey, Professor, of Kansas University. On arriving in Lawrence, we first went to the Library to view many choice and rare volumes which had been laid out for our attention; thereafter to the home of Bob Vosper for cocktails[197] and snacks, and thereafter to a private dining room in the Student Union Building for an elegant dinner of prime ribs of beef, with all the trimmings."[198]

In his 1955-56 annual report on the libraries, Vosper noted the formation of a new Special Development Committee, set up to help the KU Endowment Association acquire funds for library acquisitions. Comprising "discriminating book collectors or friends of libraries, as well as successful men of affairs," the committee included R.T. Aitchison and Harold Null, both members of the Wichita Bibliophiles.[199] "Several of those men's private collections have come to KU in their wills," Vosper said in 1989, "because we established a feeling that we understood what they were doing and how important it was to have their friendship."[200]

From the beginning, the chancellor solicited gifts in the form of money and Vosper solicited books from bibliophilic friends of the university and in the form of catalogues from rare-book dealers who might know of collections to purchase. "We're eager to buy books here and able to pay for them," he wrote to dealers all over the country. "Catalogues will be appreciated and read."[201] They arrived in droves. Vosper needed trained personnel to evaluate their promises and to access the books they produced. As early as 1953, Vosper's first year, he had added 11 professionals to the library staff,[202] including the new associate director, Robert Talmadge; Robert Mengel, bibliographer; Robert Quinsey, chief of reader services: and Joe Rubinstein.[203] A librarian from London, L. E. James Helyar, arrived in 1955 on a visiting-professional arrangement and stayed two years. Helyar returned in 1961 and remained at the library as Curator in Graphics and the Ellis Collection for his entire career.[204]

By 1957, so many books were arriving from the call for catalogs and from Rubinstein's international adventures in book-sleuthing that Vosper described Watson Library's holding as "a stack 22 miles high, give or take a mile or two."[205] As the library was adding about 3,000 volumes a month, he said, the stack would grow at the rate of about a mile a year. While he pressed for thorough structural expansion and renovation, Vosper knew that the libraries needed even more staff members.

In 1956, the University of Kansas had gained some international attention when the London *Times Literary Supplement* praised its book collections, generated by an "enterprising librarian backed by an enlightened Chancellor who knows how to make his advice persuasive to the authorities of a state as rich as Kansas."[206] The article gave Vosper an idea, he said, for finding talented employees in an age with absolutely no regional library schools. "I was stuck with the problem of trying to tell people about Kansas and our new programs," he said.[207] He had seen many advertisements in the *Times Literary Supplement* for British librarians seeking work, he said, and decided to run an ad of his own. On July 18, 1957, *TLS* carried a long advertisement in its "Appointments Vacant" section. Murphy heartily approved of the copy, being convinced that it would generate candidates of high quality.[208] "The vigorous and expanding Library is interested in applicants for visiting or permanent appointments to the professional staff," the notice stated, specifying salaries in the $3,900 - $4,260 minimum—"with no maximum salary." Vosper said he played it up a little to catch their attention.[209] The ad described the community of Lawrence as friendly, with 24,000 population, and "situated in rolling, tree-covered country (not the desolate High Plains)."[210]

The notice generated a lot of attention. "I was swamped with replies from all over the world," Vosper said, noting letters from Australia, the Gold Coast, Scandinavia, France, Belgium, Scotland, England, and Ireland. "One was the historian of the Seventh Fleet in Great Britain," John Glinka said, who read many.[211] On going through the applications, Glinka said that Vosper's eyes twinkled: "Let's fire me and hire the best in the world," Vosper told him.[212]

Eleanor Symons, who had attended Oxford University and had trained at the University of London School of Librarianship, was one of those "best in the world." She left Cornwall, England, in 1957 to join the KU staff. "Vosper made the University of Kansas and the job sound very, very attractive," she said, in 1994, upon retiring after 37 years as a Watson Library reference librarian and bibliographer.[213]

Only one of the applications originated in the United States. Alexandra Mason was one of the thousands of Americans who regularly read the London *Times Literary Supplement*. The Mount Holyoke College classics graduate said that she answered "the most marvelous ad that made Kansas sound like heaven."[214] Mason told Vosper that she would love to work with any librarian who would advertise in *TLS*. "Thank goodness she read it," he said.[215] "I'll never forget finding her," Vosper said. He explained that Mason was working in Chicago for *World Book Encyclopedia* when she applied for the Kansas position. "I hired her right away, quick."[216] Mason was hired sight-unseen to catalog rare books, Vosper said, and became one the best rare books librarians in the country. "I lived off that ad for several years," he said, describing the Kansas-England librarian exchanges that resulted. "I think we may have been one of the first."[217]

Bookmen and bookwomen not only responded to the 1957 advertisement, but also they came to the university because it "was all the talk" in library circles.[218] The London *Times Literary Supplement* continued to feature Kansas. In 1958, it published a full-page article about outstanding university libraries in the midwestern United States, notably the University of Kansas - with "the University of California at Los Angeles providing very active competition from the West Coast."[219]

Vosper's leadership in the American Library Association, his regular contributions to scholarly journals, and his insistence that his staff become involved in professional associations had given Kansas the reputation of an action-filled institution—a reputation that drew librarians, but also drew bookish faculty members.[220] Charlton Hinman, the renowned Shakespearean scholar, joined the faculty after Vosper convinced Murphy to fund a Hinman Collator, a bibliographic tool used to compare Shakespearean folios, and which would help graduate students learn bibliography. Harold Orel came as a result of the P. S. O'Hegarty Collections of William Butler Yeats and Sean O'Casey, which Vosper found and Murphy found money to purchase.

A Year of Books and Money: 1953

Passion for books lasts one's lifetime and often leads to memorable personal accomplishments. If he or she is fortunate, each scholar adventurer has one big story—of the collection almost captured, of the $1,400 first-edition purchased at a flea market for two bucks, or of the chance meeting with a little old lady who has a trunk of old letters in her attic.

Few could match the Murphy and Vosper story of the Fitzpatrick Collection. It was a book-lover's dream come true and certainly constituted the most unusual book-collection adventure of the decade for the University of Kansas. "Being in on the find is ... a high point in my life," Vosper said.[221]

The collection came to Murphy's attention not from a far-away catalogue but from his old friend, Frank Glenn, still an active dealer of rare books in Kansas City's Muehlebach Hotel, just as he had been 25 years earlier when teen-aged Murphy purchased his first original art—the Dürer. In February 1953, Frank Glenn called Murphy with some books to sell. In "one of the more sensational American book sales of the century,"[222] Glenn had purchased the entire collection of the late Thomas Jefferson Fitzpatrick[223]—"the whole fabulous tonnage of rare books and unique scientific manuscripts amassed by the late Nebraska University professor in a lifetime of feverish collection"[224] Glenn paid $53,000 for all of it. He later estimated that it would sell, broken into lots, for at least $150,000.[225]

Newspaper articles explained that three years earlier the University of Nebraska had been offered and had rejected 300 books of Linnaeus, the Swedish naturalist who founded plant classification and who is known as "the father of botany." The 300 books constituted Linnaeus' complete works—unavailable anywhere in the world. Before his death, Professor Fitzpatrick had hoped to sell the Linnaeus to Nebraska for $3,000. However, Nebraska had been unable to find money to buy the books, its director of libraries said.[226]

"It was a steal," the director said of Frank Glenn's coup. Nebraska officials explained that the university should not be criticized for failing to acquire any part of the collection: after all, the legislature and the Nebraska Board of Regents allocated money carefully and with great difficulty. "When a problem of this sort comes up—such as the possible purchase of the Fitzpatrick collection—it can only be met with money contributed by friends of the University. If this cannot be done," the official said, "we must forget it."[227]

Professor Fitzpatrick apparently hoped to live long enough to see his collections purchased and installed in the University of Nebraska's new Love Memorial Library, "a magnificent million dollar building ..., its formal landscaping featuring pink roses."[228] But NU had no money for rare-book acquisitions—neither $51,000 for half of the entire lot, all of which was now owned by Frank Glenn, nor even $3,000 for the incomparable Linnaeus.[229] Its new library, with floodlighting and pink roses, would not house the Fitzpatrick Collection.

When 84-year-old Fitzpatrick died, he left $11.84 in his bank account and at least 40 (or up to 250) tons of books and periodicals: rare histories of the Mormon church, 15,000 volumes of poetry, collections of Abraham Lincoln and Thomas Jefferson, the Linneaus collection, and the most complete works anywhere of the naturalist, Constantin F. Rafinesque. The professor had kept precise records of each volume, adding to its provenance with the skill of a scholarly lifetime.

Frank Glenn bought it all. Then he called his young friend, Franklin Murphy, and offered the entire collection. "I told him we might not want to buy everything," Murphy said, "especially the Mormon stuff.[230] First I referred him to Bob Vosper because I wasn't going to do things independently. Bob and I always did these things together."[231] As it turned out, the Kansas City Public Library wanted the Mormon materials, but most of the scientific works—including the Linneaus and the Rafinesque—were available to the University of Kansas. The price was $51,000.

Franklin Murphy didn't hesitate or worry about where the money would come from—he simply bought it. The collection was quickly out of the reach of the University of Nebraska officials, who still were trying to raise some money, and the director of libraries at the University of Oklahoma, who wanted it badly, had the money in hand, and had expected to make a proposal to Glenn.[232]

"Have not as yet told them it was purchased by the University of Kansas," Glenn wrote to Murphy. "It will be an eye-opener when it is seen in its entirety."[233] Eyes bulging, Frank Glenn and Bob Vosper had seen the "bookman's jungle" together in early February, long before either the sale had been struck or the newspapers had been alerted.[234] A man of galloping bibliomania[235] in his later years, Fitzpatrick had spent his 84 years and his tiny $1,800[236] annual professorial income on books—exceptional, rare books.

Vosper described the scene to his California colleagues: "They lived in squalor, even to gunnysack clothing," he wrote, "while their 16 room house filled with books, driving the children and the bathroom fixtures out. They even bought the house next door for the overflow and then stored the cream of the collection in metal cabinets on the Lincoln campus and the whey in a barn in Iowa."[237]

Even though the NU botany faculty had known since 1927 of Fitzpatrick's initial collections, only the professor and his wife knew its true extent in later years. He allowed no visitors into the house, but could not stop the Lincoln fire, health, police and building inspectors who investigated the structure in 1950. The city's building inspector reported that *each* of the ten larger rooms in the house held approximately 25 tons of books. City codes provided for a maximum of 40 pounds per square foot in residential dwellings; somehow, the Fitzpatrick's book house was "bearing up under a 348 pounds per square foot loading."[238] The three stories of the main house "groaned under its little-known treasure of books."[239] It bore up simply because it was solid. "It was almost impossible to work around the rooms or up the stairs," Vosper said. "The shelves were loaded three and four deep and stacked ceiling high and books were stored under the eaves. Fitzpatrick's printing press on the third floor was deluged with books and the closets were packed tight."[240] Like a rabbit warren, the structure comprised solid books, with passageways so narrow that Vosper and Glenn could move only sideways along them. Vosper was not wearing a three-piece suit in the freezing weekends at the Nebraska farmhouse, whose 16 rooms were heated by one pot-bellied stove. "Soot was everywhere," he said.[241]

KU's acquisition totaled at least 30,000 separate items—ten tons in 270 large boxes and 150 file cabinets, according to Vosper's accounting, written for Murphy's use with the Board of Regents.[242] For, while Vosper was digging through the collection, Murphy was pulling together the money to buy it. But the chancellor didn't bother his director of libraries with financial details. "Franklin just said 'let's buy it' and then he got the money,"[243] Vosper explained later. "He got it from a couple of Regents, but it was all on kind of an *ad hoc* basis," Vosper said. "There wasn't any budget for that sort of thing."[244]

When Franklin Murphy had written to Robert Vosper only nine months earlier, urging him to accept the position at Kansas, the chancellor carefully made no guarantees for acquisitions above the promised annual budget of $150,000—only a portion of which would be available for rare books, in any case. However, he described his relationship with the Board of Regents and Governor Fred Hall as "cordial" and expressed confidence that the budget might go higher in the future and that money might be obtained for special purchases.[245] Now, in February, 1953, Murphy tested the extent of that cordiality. With nothing more than his word, the Regents approved the purchase of $51,000 of rare scientific books—none of which anyone concerned had seen. In an age when Vosper was able to attract a talented librarian from the University of Illinois for an annual salary of $6,500,[246] when the director of the libraries himself earned $8,800, and when a round-trip train ticket between Los Angeles and Lawrence cost $87, the Regents' approval illustrated Franklin Murphy's persuasive power and their confidence in him.[247] Two points were obvious: $51,000 constituted a lot of money and Nebraska had no Franklin Murphy.

At the Regents' next meeting, Murphy delivered a purchase request and a logic-laden justification of the Board's speedy decision the previous month, written to provide answers to anyone who might question the expenditure. He wrote a model of persuasion to Hubert Brighton, Secretary of the Kansas Board of Regents:

> We are forwarding herewith the Purchase Request for the Fitzpatrick Collection, the purchase of which was approved by the Board at the last meeting. This purchase is in the amount of $51,000, as the Board was informed. The collection consists of more than 30,000 items—books, journals, etc.—representing the largest collection still in private hands in the country in the field of Botany, early American Natural History, and Natural History in Western Europe. Many of these books and journals are unobtainable today and are of most exceeding rarity, and yet you will note that, item for item, we are paying only a little more than $1.00 per item.
>
> As I told the Board, this is probably one of the greatest opportunities that has come the way of the University for many, many years, and it is one of the two great library collections I have had my eye on for many months now. I actually thought we would have to pay more for it than the $51,000.
>
> As you know, the Ralph Ellis collection in Natural History, which came to us as a gift, is conservatively estimated to be

worth somewhere between $500,000 and $750,000. However, the crucial gaps in the Ellis collection will be almost completely filled by the unique material in the Fitzpatrick collection. To put it another way, the Ellis collection separately may be worth three-quarters of a million dollars, but to add to it the Fitzpatrick collection would increase the value of the combined collections to well over $1,500,000. As I told the Board, it is a little like having a fine automobile with three wheels. The addition of the fourth wheel makes the automobile of a disproportionately greater value than the cost of the new wheel. —

We are not only fortunate to get this collection for the price of $51,000, but we are even more fortunate in that the University of Nebraska, Harvard, and two or three other institutions around the country had desired to buy it at this price.

The dealer who bought the collection from the estate happens to live in Kansas City, has a deep interest in the affairs of K.U. and gave us the first chance.

Frankly, although I had had my eye on this collection for many months, I had never hoped that it would go for as little as $51,000, and I never hoped that we would be able to snatch it away from the other institutions who were interested in it.

This addition will make K.U. the leading center in the country for research and graduate study in these basic fields in natural history, including ornithology, botany, mammals, etc. It is the kind of thing that really brings distinction not only to the University but to the state, and I am sure the Board will not soon again make an investment that will mean so much to the prestige of the University of Kansas.[248]

The book value of the collection made it important enough to the university, but its research value was even greater. "It extends and enriches both our Ellis and Clendening collections," Vosper said, "giving us in total a deep research collection in the history of science."[249]

The acquisition couldn't have come at a better time. In early 1953, Vosper had been on the job fewer than six months; Murphy one year and a half. With the Fitzpatrick coup, everyone could see instantaneous energy as the rocket took off. To Vosper, who had written to Murphy on accepting the position that "anything less than a renaissance will be a disappointment," the experience proved that he would not be disappointed at Kansas.[250] He was not disappointed at all. The energy continued unabated. On April 13, 1953, just two weeks after Murphy's Fitzpatrick meeting with the Regents, Vosper received a letter from Dick Howey, the library's most productive professorial sleuth.[251] He had just learned of the availability of the John Crerar Library of Economics: "I wish to urge most strongly the purchase of the approximately 30,000 volumes," he wrote. "At a price of $40,000 the collection is an outstanding bargain."[252]

Howey explained that, unlike the unorganized Fitzpatrick collection, the Crerar books would come to the university ready to use—they would come bound and complete with a card catalog. "If the books were available ... from bookdealers (which they are not) at today's prices, and if they had to be individually ordered, catalogued, and prepared for the shelves," he continued, "the cost would be ... five times the price.[253]

"Thanks to the perception and initiative of Professor Howey," the university was in a prime position to take over the bulk of the Crerar collection, Vosper wrote to Murphy, hoping "very much indeed that you can find means to take advantage of this uncommon opportunity."[254] Murphy responded with pleasure, noting by hand and with typical attention to detail to "tell about asst. editor, London *Times*."[255] The Crerar economics collection arrived just before the end of that eventful year.[256]

Where did Murphy find the money for this $40,000 purchase, just two weeks after the $51,000 Fitzpatrick? As was his habit, he played with funds—some came from private gifts and some came from Murphy's skill at moving money around. Evidence of the Crerar purchase shows up, for example, in an unusually skewed allocation to Howey's economics department in the 1953-54 budget. For that year, the department of economics received a $10,000 annual book-buying allocation, when the next largest budgets (English and law) stood at $5,000. The departments of Western Civilization, pharmacy, journalism and education were budgeted at $500 each, and thirty of the sixty-five departments received that amount or less.[257]

Certainly, the collections were not funded from the $150,000 promised to Vosper for acquisitions. That money went to departments ($90,225 for 1953-54), to subscriptions ($35,000), and to a reserve fund to be used by the director ($24,775).[258] In 1952-53, Vosper reported, a number of items had been purchased from the reserve fund, including a sixty-volume collected works of Handel, 320 pamphlets of the 17th century, 151 volumes of *Frasers* Magazine, and 33 volumes of *the Historical Records of Australia*[259] In the midst of it all, the State of Kansas purchased a James Joyce collection, of 632 items, for the University of Kansas.[260]

To succeed in building an exceptional library, Murphy and Vosper took many risks—they gambled often, never knowing whether the opportunity at hand was more important than the unseen next possibility. When an exciting collection emerged, they quickly considered faculty advice[261] as to its value for teaching and research, such important details as available shelf space,[262] and the likelihood of finding money. In spite of Murphy's confidence and success in funding the Fitzpatrick and Crerar collections within a few month's time, he could not fund everything that he and Vosper might have wished to obtain. In November of that expensive year of 1953, for example, Murphy was forced to reject a George Catlin collection, telling Frank Glenn that "we are not financially in a position to take this calculated risk, and our Board of Regents would agree."[263] In fact, Vosper's exceptional staff— notably Joe Rubinstein—had decided already that the Catlin work was neither worth the money, nor valuable for the university.

The first year as a team, with its visible energy, set the tone for Murphy's and Vosper's eight years together at Kansas. Although few acquisitions later in the decade matched the pure excitement of the Fitzpatrick, the years were extremely productive. The team made a name for Kansas in library circles around the world and they had added as many books to the library in fewer than ten years as had been gathered in all of the previous ninety-five.[26]

* * *

On March 17th, 1960, Murphy announced that he would leave the University of Kansas to become chancellor of UCLA, the University of California Los Angeles. On April 14th, Frank Glenn ended his career as a rare-book dealer by closing his shop in the Muehlebach Hotel.[265] On June 15th, Murphy moved to Los Angeles. Two days earlier, Frank Glenn had died.[266] An exceptional era was over.

"I was lucky at Kansas," Vosper said later. "I went in with a new chancellor and he was ambitious to build the university and he would do anything to find money to support the library program, so we were able to buy collections in a fashion like drunken sailors."[267]

"It was an awful lot of fun," Murphy agreed, speaking of his work with Robert Vosper. "He and I were in it together. He was the library man and I was the money man, but we both were bookmen. It was just marvelous to raise those funds privately as well as publicly, divert budgets and build a library budget. During those nine or 10 years, even if I say so myself, we put together a hell of a library."[268]

One year later, Robert Vosper left Lawrence to join Murphy at UCLA, where he became Director of Libraries.

CHAPTER 5

Civil Rights
1951-1960

In 1951, black movie-theater patrons were required to sit only in the theater balconies, not on the main floor. Shortly after becoming chancellor, Murphy met with the theater owners and "gave them a lesson in manners," he said. When they responded that it was impossible to tell the African foreign students from the African-American students, Murphy suggested that it would be much simpler to allow all patrons, whether black or white, to sit wherever they chose. And then, he began to *persuade*.

WHY WOULD A SMALL TOWN in 1855 Kansas Territory need so many Bibles? Yet, here they were in the year-old settlement of Lawrence, with its few hundred inhabitants: dozens of long, rectangular wooden crates with their contents spelled out clearly for all to see—BIBLES. The crates did contain Bibles. But with every one of the 600 books, the Lawrence settlers also found a more practical gift, a Sharps rifle—the "Bibles" of the Abolitionist cause.[2] They had been sent to this settlement on the western edge of the United States by New York preacher, Henry Ward Beecher, who raised the money for their purchase in special Sunday-morning collections.[3] The rifles, known then and afterward as "Beecher's Bibles," would help the 369 Lawrence settlers defend Kansas Territory against their pro-slavery neighbors, who used violent tactics to protect their own interests.[4] The crates and their contents lie at the core of the Lawrence mythology— the two words, "Beecher's Bibles," encapsulate the community's deserved or undeserved perception of itself as fundamentally tolerant and as the pre-Civil War birthplace of abolitionist action in America's West.

When told that he should have sent only Bibles, Beecher declared: "You might as well send the Bible to buffaloes as to those who follow (the pro-slavery cause), but they have a supreme respect for the logic that is embodied in Sharps rifles."[5] The settlers who accepted Beecher's gift had come to Kansas Territory during the previous year as part of the New England Emigrant Aid Company, composed of determined bands of men and women with such vehement opposition to slavery that they left their homes and moved West, to raise a town on the banks of the Kansas River to be the front line of the national abolitionist movement. The bands of men and women included a band of musicians. Their anthem—played and sung at their departure in Boston, on the road, and in the new settlement—was John Greenleaf Whittier's "Song of the Kansas Emigrant," which begins as follows:

> We cross the prairie as of old
> Our fathers crossed the sea,
> To make the West as they the East
> The homestead of the free.
> We go to rear a wall of men
> On Freedom's southern line,
> And plant beside the cotton tree
> The rugged northern pine.[6]

The founders of Lawrence came not only to raise a town, but also to raise a "wall of men" against slavery. They named their town in honor of one of the men who had funded their Company, Boston's Amos Lawrence. True to their New England roots, within five months they had opened two churches and a school. Within one year, the colonists had obtained land and initial funding for a college, which would become the University of Kansas. It opened in 1865.

In 1855, within one year of their community's founding, the Lawrence settlers knew that the new Sharps rifles gave their cause a distinct advantage over their enemies' old-fashioned muzzle-loaders.[7] They had many opportunities to use the rifles, but one wonders where they were during the raid by the several hundred pro-slavery raiders of William Quantrill in which 132 Lawrence citizens died.[8] Later, Kansan John Brown would carry the almost-spiritual fervor of the abolitionists to Harpers Ferry, Virginia, in his and his mixed race band of followers' doomed attempt to draw attention to the anti-slavery cause.

Lawrence was founded, in large part, to stop the advance of slavery. In its earliest days, the people of Lawrence put their Sharps rifles to good use.[9] In doing so, they fired the first shots that would end in the Civil War and in freedom for slaves. During the War, Missourians believed that Lawrence was one of the stations on the underground railroad. Richard Cordley, who lived in the town at the time, wrote in 1895 that the city probably deserved its reputation: "There is no doubt that a good many slaves," he wrote, "fleeing from bondage, made their way to Lawrence, and there were aided on their journey towards Canada. Not many of the people knew anything about this, but there were a few to whom such fugitives always went and were never betrayed. But the sympathy of the people was with every one who was struggling for freedom. The town was founded in opposition to slavery," Cordley wrote, and he continued:[10]

> The people of Lawrence were not lovers of strife. Her people were lovers of order and peace. They only stood in the gap for conscience sake and not from preference. Now peace had come after all these years of strife. And it was peace that would stay. The roots of the conflict were gone. Not only was Kansas a free state, but slavery itself was abolished. Kansas had won her case, not for herself alone but for the nation. She had not stood in the focus of the fight for naught. When Lawrence realized that peace was really assured, it seemed as if a new sun had arisen in the heavens, and a new atmosphere had given vigor to life.[11]

Civil Rights Activism in Lawrence and at KU

In spite of Lawrence founders' opposition to slavery, the sad fact was that most of the white people who came to Kansas in the 1860s were "diehard racists who believed that blacks were inherently inferior," according to historian William M. Tuttle, Jr. in his excellent 2001 essay, *Separate but Not Equal*.[12] Even abolitionists who bitterly opposed slavery also expressed their opposition to racial equality. The worst of the Jim Crow era (from the end of Reconstruction until the 1920) is seen by historian C. Vann Woodward as the period of "America's capitulation to racism" in the South and in the North. In fact, in Lawrence, Kansas, once at the heart of the abolitionist movement, a mob of 300 white men lynched three black men in 1882.

Nevertheless, the Jim Crow years were years also of black community building in Kansas and in Lawrence, including the establishment of churches, mutual aid and benevolent societies, masonic lodges, women's clubs, and schools. In Lawrence, African Americans were establishing businesses and entering professions, including several black physicians, assistant chief of police Sam Jeans, and two black lawyers, Robert B. McWilliams and John W. Clark, who earned a bachelor of law degree from KU in 1896.[13]

With the adoption of the Fifteenth Amendment in 1870 giving black men the right to vote, Lawrence's black community extended its involvement in the quest for civil rights. In 1866, for example, the Kansas State Colored Convention met in Lawrence to urge the adoption of the Amendment. In addition, it published a resolution as follows: "RESOLVED, That it is anti-democratic, inhuman and unjust of the proprietors of stages, railroad cars, barber shops, hotels and saloons, to exclude us on account of color from an equal enjoyment of the conveniences of these public institutions."[14] The University of Kansas had been founded one year earlier, in 1865, with a racially open admissions policy. The first black KU student, Lizzie Ann Smith, enrolled in 1876, and the first black KU graduate was B. K. Bruce in 1885. In the 1890s, three African-American lettermen sons of the Douglas County Harvey family had studied at KU, as had many from surrounding states that did not allow black students to enroll in their public universities. In just a few years, however, as racism swept the nation and the KU campus, the University's chancellors began to exclude African American students from extracurricular activities, including intercollegiate sports. The Harvey brothers and many others would not have been permitted to participate.[15]

Racism intensified in America during the 1920s with race riots and lynchings, and with the rise of the Ku Klux Klan. In 1924, the KKK held a statewide conference in downtown Lawrence. A few blocks away at KU, black students were barred not only from intercollegiate athletics, but also from the glee club, the band, the orchestra, the debating team, ROTC, and the student council. The student union was segregated and the student swimming pool was available to blacks only on the last day of the month, just before the pool was drained. Because black students were not allowed to live in campus dormitories, most boarded with black families in East and North Lawrence. Some white students on campus formed the Ku Ku Klan (later the Ku Ku Klub) whose members wore sheets and performed during the halftime at KU football games.[16]

"In 1927, *The Crisis* magazine of the National Association for the Advancement of Colored People (NAACP) published an article about African American student life at KU. The author was Loren Miller, a black KU student who had left the University, and who later became a historian and a judge in California. Some 150 black students attended KU, Miller explained, but "It is the official policy of Kansas to ignore their presence as far as possible," and "When colored students become too obtrusive, they are put in their place quickly." As for intercollegiate sports, Miller claimed, "Dr. F. C. Allen, head of athletics, said recently that no colored man will ever have a chance as long as he is there." Loren Miller had special contempt for the chancellor, Ernest H. Lindley (KU chancellor 1920–1939), whom he labeled, correctly, a paternalistic racist. "He is a first class Christian gentleman," Miller wrote, and he "boasts that he comes from abolitionist stock." Lindley, however, supported University of Kansas basketball coach Dr. Forrest 'Phog' Allen's stance. But more than that, he allowed the social, political, and extracurricular life of the University of Kansas to become rigidly segregated. Miller explained that Lindley had lobbied the Kansas legislature for "a new dormitory for women. It is of the most modern type. [But] Colored girls *cannot* stay there." The Chancellor said that there were so many Southern students at the institution that to permit colored girls to stay there would be unwise. One gathers," Miller said, "that citizens of Kansas owe the South something." In another interview, Allen denied Miller's charges, but did say: "I do not believe that colored and white boys should play together in any games of physical contact or combat." Obviously, he would change his mind during the '50s when he welcomed LaVannes Squires, Maurice King, and Wilt Chamberlain to his teams.

Dr. W.E.B. Du Bois, editor of *The Crisis* magazine, wrote to Chancellor Lindley to inquire about KU's racial policies. Lindley replied that black students are "given full privileges in classroom and library," but that the cafeteria and the concert series, both of which were "dependent on financial support," were different. He said that several years earlier, black students had insisted on sitting at the same cafeteria table as white students. The latter then chose to eat elsewhere, causing some loss of income for the cafeteria. KU's racial problems were largely imaginary, Lindley said, the product of troublemakers – "a small minority" of black students "who insist on the rapid and complete obliteration of any race distinction."[17]

Chancellor Lindley resigned in 1939 after 19 years of KU leadership and just as WWII began. The new chancellor was Deane W. Malott. The University became part of the war effort, and many students addressed the contradictions between the ideals for which America was fighting and the racial segregation on campus. For example, in 1942, an interracial group of Christian pacifists on campus formed a branch of the Fellowship of Reconciliation. The group attempted to change the segregated seating policy at the Memorial Union. Malott rejected their efforts, telling the Board of Regents that the group consisted of "well-meaning, but misguided students: who were "zealous," but "ineffective in the community." During the same year, a KU student organized an NAACP chapter that called upon the governor to end segregation on campus, and a group of white track athletes attempted to desegregate intramural and varsity track teams, but with little success. Thus, when the war ended in 1945, there was already a civil rights movement in place at KU.[18]

"Fortuitously for the Lawrence civil rights movement, when Deane Malott left KU in 1950, he was succeeded by a civil rights activist, Franklin D. Murphy, who accomplished as much for the betterment of race relations in Lawrence and at KU as any local citizen in the twentieth century," according to historian Tuttle, who wrote in *Separate but Not Equal.* "I see Chancellor Murphy as the twentieth-century embodiment of James Lane or John Brown. The difference was that Murphy operated largely behind the scenes." Furthermore, upon his inauguration as chancellor, Murphy led an institution almost as segregated as it had been in the past.[19]

In 1951, ninety-six years after the Beecher's Bibles arrived in Lawrence, African Americans in that same city were far from free— for them, the "new sun" was hiding behind a cloud. In 1951, African Americans in Lawrence, Kansas, were not allowed to eat in local restaurants, sit on the main floor of public movie theaters, join a non-Black fraternity or sorority, teach as a tenure-track faculty member at the University,[20] drink a beer at the Jayhawk or any other student tavern, sit any place you wished in the Kansas Union's popular fountain area, student teach in a white school, rent a room in a hotel, ice-skate at the local rink, live in a scholarship hall or dormitory, study medicine or nursing at the University of Kansas Medical Center, swim in a swimming pool, bowl in the public bowling alley, or gave birth to a baby at the KU Medical Center.[21]

1951 was the first year that coach, 'Phog' Allen had allowed a black basketball player to join the team. The league's ban on mixed-race teams in contact sports had been lifted only a few years earlier. It would be three years more before the *Brown v. Board of Education* decision desegregated schools, four years before the Montgomery bus boycott launched Martin Luther King, Jr. to national prominence, and another twenty-two years before blacks or Jews could purchase property in Lawrence's next-to-campus West Hills development.[22]

In 1951, ninety-six years after the Beecher's Bibles arrived and eighty-six years after the Civil War had ended, Franklin Murphy became chancellor of the University of Kansas—a segregated institution in a segregated community. More than any other leader in KU's history, Chancellor Murphy is credited with having erased this racial division. In the decade to come, he would not march personally in front of the students who attempted to cut down the racial barriers. Instead, he sought to raise the ethical standard for the entire community, holding it high so that everyone might see it more clearly and move toward the goal that it promised. The leader, he said later, must be the one to identify the vision and to motivate the people.[23] In his inaugural speech, Murphy shared his vision for the university. In this most-important speech of his life to that date, he urged the students and the state to a standard higher than the knowledge one expects to gain in college. He spoke of one's duty to humanity, saying that the only human effort of lasting value is the thinking of men concerned with the problems of mankind. But we must all go beyond mere thinking about problems, he said: "We insist that man must be measured by performance, not prejudice," he said. "At KU, we will not merely *discuss* human freedom and the dignity of all men—we will put them into practice."[24]

From the first speech to his last month as chancellor, Murphy not only climbed upon his bully pulpit to speak with passion, but also he worked steadily behind it, outside of public view, to put his ethical standards into practice and to try to bring Lawrence and KU back to their roots of tolerance.

Ethics. *Ethos.* Character. The source of a leader's ability to persuade. As a university leader whose articulate voice carried great weight among the pliant young and their tolerant or prejudiced elders, Murphy urged his followers to set higher standards. Often, he spoke out on controversial issues, attempting to persuade people to think for themselves. In the early 1950s, he denounced the demagoguery of Joseph McCarthy, calling upon his audiences to recognize the intolerant venom being spread by the senator. He spoke of the evil of Orval Faubus and constantly reminded his students and faculty of their role in America's future—a role that must include racial tolerance. And, he personally acted on the reminder, using the power of his institution's purse and his persona to attempt to convince the owners of Lawrence's movie theaters and restaurants to change their segregationist policies, voluntarily.

Without question, many of the people around Chancellor Murphy understood his commitment to breaking down racial barriers. As leader, Murphy urged his team to break new ground, giving them the freedom and the public encouragement to help turn the vision into reality. For example, Robert Vosper (the thoroughly trusted Murphy team member and university library director) very early brought to the university the first fully professional African-Americans—all well-trained librarians and all receiving full Academic Senate membership.[25]

In addition to altering the racial proportions among professionals, Murphy worked hard to draw students who would represent varying racial and religious groups. For a variety of reasons, he intended to increase the foreign-student presence, for example, and to help the nearly all-white student body see more color among their colleagues. "Murphy hoped," for another example, "that outstanding black athletes might be brought to the University of Kansas to promote racial tolerance."[26]

At no time did he waver in his feelings of disgust for racism, recalling that in his parents' home, for example, "discrimination was just no good."[27] He explained that he chose words carefully in an attempt to force the students to seek the highest human goals for themselves, just as he sought excellence for himself and for the university. "One should never fear belonging to a group that does not always agree with the thoughts of the majority," he said to an audience of students within two weeks of his inauguration, reinforcing the vision articulated earlier.[28]

To the 1954 governor-elect, Fred Hall, Murphy wrote privately, but no less passionately: "Particularly do I think segregation inexcusable in the state of Kansas, which was founded as a free state."[29] And, later, he firmly responded to a racist letter: "...I believe that segregation is immoral—quite as immoral as communism, facism, or any other 'ism' that denies fundamental human rights and human dignity."[30]

Regardless of his many public and private words about the evils of segregation, Murphy did not intend to lead a civil rights movement—he acknowledged many times that integration of KU was not his *overriding* goal.[31] For Murphy, the need to end segregation was part of what he called "ethical citizenship in a democracy." Simply, an ethical citizen accepted people who differ from themselves and ideas that differ from their own. A man who always sought universals, Murphy joined the values of tolerance, human dignity, free expression, and responsibility into one category—ethical citizenship. The purpose of "university" for Murphy was to help the young understand and practice citizenship. For them and for all the others, he believed that the university should stand as an unassailable beacon—as the example of a democracy's highest ethical standards.

His overriding goal was not to integrate the University of Kansas, although he intended to do that, without question. Instead, his goal was to teach about and protect the citizenship rights of all, whether African-American or Caucasian, liberal or conservative, Jewish or Christian or agnostic. Nothing could improve for any of them, he said, unless the university remained a "market place of free ideas," where all could test dogma and theories that were new to them. The chancellor's primary task, Murphy believed, was to protect that market place from the "clammy hands" of those who would suppress the full rights of citizenship.[32] Not only must he protect from outside suppression, but also, Murphy said, the chancellor must give students the confidence to think for themselves. "Future citizens should argue the political issues with which they do not agree," he told a combined meeting of science clubs in 1954. "Do not let them pass unchallenged!"[33]

The prime purpose of a university, he said in 1954, is not only to train young persons vocationally, but culturally as well, to make them aware of current economic and social upheavals which influence their times, and to help them learn that citizenship involves both rights and responsibilities. Saying that he intended to give students as much responsibility as possible, he used the analogy of a coin with two sides:[34] "The individual is master of his fate," he said, "but he must also accept the fact that self-discipline and even pain are part of the privilege of being given and accepting responsibility."[35] Moreover, the early 1950s proved that the goals of tolerance, free expression, human dignity, and responsibility could not be separated. It was the time of Joseph McCarthy, loyalty oaths, Red-baiting, conformity, and incipient integration of the races in American society.

Murphy was a Platonist in his belief in immutable *standards* that exist outside the realm of experience.[36] A scientist, he was an Aristotelian realist in his trust of the truths that can be seen and tested. But he also had learned to be pragmatic in his quest for excellence. He worked hard to keep the overriding "Purpose of University" visible but he learned, by every-day experience, that separate issues demand their own time—often, issues are given attention in proportion to many other items on the leadership plate of the moment.

Murphy's plate was very full in the early 1950s. He had made a national name for himself: the national Jaycees named Murphy as one of the 10 most outstanding young men of 1949, for example.[37] He spent more than a little time denying that he would leave KU to take on federal appointments. Just one week before the 1952 election, *Time* Magazine suggested, after Presidential-candidate Dwight Eisenhower praised Murphy, that he should be chosen as the first Secretary of Health and Welfare in Ike's cabinet. The full-page article, entitled "Ike Sat At His Feet," quoted Eisenhower: "The best plan I ever heard about came right from this state, from (Dr. Murphy). I sat at his feet for several hours. This is a man who, it seems to me, has real sense.[38] Just after the election, Murphy denied having been offered the top Federal Security Administration job.[39] In fact, he would soon be asked by President Eisenhower to become Secretary of the Army—which, like all the other offers, he would reject.[40]

He was busy enough at the university, having raised all-time high totals in private contributions and research grants.[41] Furthermore, he knew that he could not *lead* a civil rights movement and keep the money rolling in at the same time. He worked in more subtle ways; perhaps the results were less immediate, but the repercussions were fewer. Certainly the squeaky-wheel theory played a part in Murphy's choice of activities, especially in student-initiated controversies that he might have preferred to avoid. However, he did not spend his nine years at the University of Kansas reacting to the agendas set by others: he was in control—he set the tone. "Identify the vision, and motivate the people," he would say later—and don't worry about using different techniques for different audiences.[42]

In choosing differing methods of persuasion for different audiences, Murphy was not duplicitous—he was merely acting on the lessons of his past. A leader, Aristotle had written, possesses the wisdom to understand the causes of action and uses that wisdom to persuade others to join him. Murphy had learned that to be successful, he must know his audiences well enough to be able to speak and act persuasively to each. To be persuaded results in an attitudinal change, regardless of how one is persuaded. As a leader, Murphy combined *ethos, logos,* and *pathos*—ethics, logic, and passion—in varying ways.

He learned, for example, that the great jazz singer and university's guest Ella Fitzgerald had no place to stay because the local hotels did not rent rooms to African-Americans.[43] After the sold-out concert, in which students honored her with many standing ovations, Fitzgerald spent the night in a university guest house—one of Murphy's first capital improvements as chancellor.[44] Perhaps he could not change the policies of others too quickly, but he could circumvent them. That method would do for the short term.

One cannot say that the beginning of Murphy's tenure marked a clean break with the past—as if no movement toward racial integration had begun before he arrived. In fact, many changes had occurred as a result of World War II's end and the G.I. Bill students' demands for change. In 1909, the National Association for the Advancement of Colored People (NAACP) formed to gain civil rights for African Americans, and the Congress of Racial Equality (CORE) was founded in 1942 at the University of Chicago. Similarly, one cannot say that Murphy's work for civil rights stands as a national beacon, as if to say: "Here's where the change began." Certainly, the times were right to end segregation. From 1954 until 1964, the nation dealt with no issue of greater importance or of more vociferous emotion. Rules and policies changed in every community and on every campus. The University of Kansas did not make a name for itself as a national leader in this effort.

In the North and in the South, public awareness of the effects of segregation began on college campuses. Clearly, civil rights organizations in the decades prior to 1954 laid the groundwork for the Supreme Court's decision *in Brown vs. Board of Education.* According to a pre-eminent history of African-Americans,[45] the "Black Revolution" was a national movement on February 1, 1960, when four black college students in Greensboro, North Carolina, demanded service in a public lunch counter.[46] Even the multi-volume history, *Eyes on the Prize,* begins its chronological account of "America's Civil Rights Years" as late as 1954, and reminds us that events that drew national attention occurred in 1955 (the Emmett Till lynching) and 1955-1956 (the Montgomery, Alabama, bus boycott).

Before the mid-1950s, efforts for civil rights reform at universities often centered on the work of a few students and church groups, largely isolated in college communities and on campuses. That so much activity occurred at the University of Kansas during the early 1950s is remarkable indeed. When one reads the student newspaper from World War II to 1954, one is struck by the continuing interest in ending discrimination.

The extent of the interest must be viewed in light of the times. After all, the early 1950s was an age of conformity, when very few students marched to the beat of a different drummer. Author John Osborne's "last angry man"[47] would not set the stage for the Beat Generation until 1956, and Jack Kerouac would not bring that non-conformist philosophy to full voice until 1957.[48] In spite of J.D. Salinger's out-of-the-ordinary hero, Holden Caulfield, most of America's young people in 1951 were normal in the extreme.[49] In fact, *Time* Magazine published a special issue on youth, asking the overriding question: "Why haven't we heard from them?"[50] In retrospect, it was termed the "Silent Generation." Quite understandably, college men did not wish to draw attention to themselves as being different. After all, the Korean conflict needed men—students were being drafted at the rate of 25,000 each month.[51] Draft deferments for college students relied entirely on one's grades and one's college record.

To speak out in favor of African-American rights might draw undesired political attention. During the early 1950s, Senator Joseph McCarthy led the nation in an unprecedented exercise in paranoia. His successful "Joe McCarthy vs. Joe Stalin" campaign in 1952 assured the powerful anti-communist senator another term of freedom to attack subversives.[52] For Franklin Murphy, the witch hunts by McCarthy and his supporters (some of whom were alumni of KU and infatiguable letter writers) constituted dangerous attacks on free expression, the fundamental American right which he defended so often. Even though Murphy did not deny the apparent motives of the international Communist Party, he vociferously rejected the methods of those who would root out its supposed members. When called upon by a legislator to remove subversive literature from the university library, for example, Murphy directed Robert Vosper to set up an immediate display on "The Evils of Censorship," which could be used by other institutions.[53]

In a widely disseminated news release, the University of Kansas explained that the 'Burned Books' exhibit, included 200 books over which censorship has attempted to exercise its guardianship of the mind of man, and it explained:

The written or printed word has played a central and crucial role, Dr. Franklin D. Murphy, chancellor of the university, pointed out, "In the dramatic story of man's effort to scale those hard cliffs of prejudice, ignorance and tyranny. The University of Kansas dedicated now as always to the 'free market place of ideas,' is proud to present this exhibit as an expression of our belief in the right of man to proceed through reason—as well as faith—and as a reminder that this right must be guarded jealously by thoughtful men at all times."

Murphy later wrote, for publication, a strong defense of academic freedom. Near its end, he explained his opinion about Communism:

In 1952, when the Communist party stands unveiled beyond question as an instrument of international conspiracy, dedicated to the subversion of personal freedom and human dignity, one who still espouses its principles must indeed be utterly naive, profoundly stupid, or convinced of the importance of these principles.[54]

In his 1953 KU commencement address, Murphy stated his beliefs clearly. "Bigots and enemies of freedom are abroad in all generations, often well-camouflaged and occasionally well-meaning," he said. "In times of high tension, they may become the spokesmen for millions of insecure and confused people. Their effort is made far more influential by those well-meaning but naive and socially immature ones among us who either cannot or will not recognize evil whatever its manifestation."[55]

The clammy hands of those who would suppress free expression had not left the University of Kansas untouched. Since 1949, all employees had been required to sign a loyalty oath or be subjected to immediate dismissal.[56] In spite of his continuing pleas to the contrary, Murphy's hands were not entirely dry in this matter. Even though he considered himself the guardian of free expression, he was a Republican—a moderate Republican—and it was 1953. With four other university presidents, for example, he wrote a 1953 report on loyalty oaths for the American Association of Universities.[57] Published in its entirety in *Time,* it began well, but ended by upholding such oaths:

Even in the face of popular disapproval, timidity should not lead a scholar or a teacher to stand silent when he must speak in matters of truth and conscience, particularly in his own special field of study.

Appointment to a university position and retention after appointment require not only professional competence but involve the affirmative obligation of being diligent and loyal in citizenship.

Above all, a scholar must have integrity and independence. This renders impossible adherence to such a regime as that of Russia and its satellites. No person who accepts or advocates such principles and methods has any place in a university. Since present membership in the Communist party requires the acceptance of these principles and methods, such membership extinguishes the right to a university position.[58]

The report generated volumes of letters to the editors, surveys of faculties, and news releases.[59] One in the latter category, from the Teachers Union of New York City, attacked the AAU report: in Murphy's unmistakably bold handwriting, in red, one sees his reaction—"Comm. Front organization."[60] Franklin Murphy was not immune to the paranoia.

The chancellor's mail contained many warnings about subversives. The most vociferous warning has to have come from Ray Garvey, a wealthy Wichitan and a stalwart of the ultra-right John Birch Society. He wrote often. "It seems as though every now and then the University gets some crackpot to make a speech from the leftwing reactionaries," he wrote in February of 1953.[61] He objected to a speech by Palmer Hoyt, who had recently attacked Senator McCarthy. Murphy responded: "I expect that the problem of letting the students hear the expression of many points of view in these times when tensions are so high is indeed a difficult one, and yet we are determined to try to maintain a university climate where the students may, if they wish, hear all sides of every question. Whether or not we achieve this millennium is questionable, but we shall keep on trying."[62]

Another alumnus chastised Murphy for allowing a Summerfield grant to be given to an "individual who has professed a belief in socialism to at least two persons." The writer suggested that the university might investigate such young scholars' beliefs about theories of government "(not necessarily his political associations though) as a matter of routine."[63] Murphy explained in response that he had investigated the matter:

I cannot adduce any evidence that this young man is a Socialist, as such, and indeed it is rather difficult for me to believe that a high school senior of substantially less than twenty years of age could have very fixed and firm political or social views.

There can be no question as to how the administration here stands on this issue. We have publicly stated, and repeated, that we believe in freedom, American democracy and the free enterprise system. If we can bring under our influence young men who may, in their youth and naiveté, question it, and can encourage them to understand the validity of this system, we will be doing a greater service than in denying educational opportunity to a brilliant young man only because he dares to ask some frank questions.[64]

Anti-subversive emotions ran high all across the nation. Many of the fifteen million citizens who owned a television watched "I Led Three Lives" and accepted the overwhelming visual and political evidence that spies could be any place.[65] After all, Julius and Ethel Rosenberg had been sentenced to death as spies in 1951 and would be executed in 1953. In the "Freedom of Expression" file among Murphy's papers of 1952 and 1953, one finds an illustration of his efforts to learn the truth about the "tension" of the times. In that file he inserted a "Special Report on Book Censorship" reprinted from *The New Republic*, (which he would have occasion to use); an editorial from *The Milwaukee Journal* listing the illegal and unethical acts of its newly nominated senator-to-be, Joseph McCarthy, and a number of speeches.[66] Among the latter, Murphy had marked a particular passage for possible use by himself—he wrote "MB" (maybe) beside the following quotation from Ben Franklin:

Without freedom of thought there can be no such thing as wisdom; and no such thing as public liberty without freedom of speech; which is the right of every man as far as by it he does not hurt or control the right of another; and this is the only check it ought to suffer and the only bounds it ought to know. Whoever would overthrow the liberty of the nation must begin by subduing the freeness of speech; a thing terrible to public traitors.[67]

Certainly, many in Kansas and in the nation were convinced that college campuses were breeding grounds for communism and its fellow-traveler, socialism. In addition, more than a few equated all efforts for racial equality as Communist plots. The 1951 public trial of W.E.B. Du Bois and other African-American colleagues for alleged communist activities gave conservatives the justification to paint all reformers with the same brush.[68] The student who became involved in civil rights activities on campus might have been branded easily. One correspondent made his sentiments clear in a 1953 letter to Chancellor Murphy: "I noted in the Kansas City Star of last Saturday," the alumnus wrote at the end of a scathing letter about the university's lousy football performance, "that the university is now enjoying social activities among its students which are comparable to those of the Harlem Night Club. I will not pass comment on this activity, as I do not want to scorch the paper."[69] Murphy did not mention the addendum in his response.

Many white college students avoided the early efforts for racial equality for fear of the draft, and others avoided it for fear of being branded subversive. Many simply didn't think about it—it did not occur to them to become involved. In fact, few European Americans had any personal experience at all with individual African Americans. The races were segregated—isolated from one another—by law and by custom. After all, most white and black children did not attend school together, did not live in the same neighborhoods, did not eat in the same restaurants, swim in the same pools, or sit beside one another in movie theaters. Most Americans lived in small towns or rural areas with all-white neighbors. African-Americans did not appear on television or in magazine advertisements. In movies, they were cast as domestics, and in newsreels, as Mau Mau terrorists. Unless one's family employed a black servant, as was the case for many middle-class families, one simply did not see the other race. What you do not see, you typically do not think about.

Some white Americans simply were afraid of all black-skinned people at that time. In Kenya, black Mau Mau tribesmen slaughtered white colonists in 1952, the frightening details of which Americans viewed with horror in newsreels, movies, and read about, shortly thereafter, in Robert Ruark's best selling book, *Something of Value*.

Perhaps yet another isolating element entered the early 1950s social picture—polio. At the height of its deadly march during those years, infantile paralysis caused more fear and isolation than the ubiquitous Communist, in fear of whom Americans guarded their tongues among strangers and would later build elaborate fallout shelters.[70] Few knew the cause of polio, the crippling and killing disease that could strike with a simple headache or sore throat. The fear of polio changed

American's habits, especially during the summers when it seemed to strike most often. One learned to avoid crowds and exertion. Families swam in lakes with those they knew, instead of in public pools filled with unknown germs, whether white or black. Children attended fewer crowded movie theaters and took more soothing, therapeutic naps.[71] The University of Kansas did not escape the plague of polio. Its four new cases in the week of October 1, 1952, brought the *Kansas* total to 1,482 new cases for the year[72]—more than twice the number for 1951 at the same time. Even the strongest were not immune, as KU football player Morris Kay was stricken at the height of the season.[73]

So, in light of the real and imagined dangers of involvement in any out-of-the-ordinary cause, the public efforts for civil rights among students at the University of Kansas in the early 1950s constituted some degree of bravery on their parts—not at all behind the times, but instead, perhaps signs of early leadership. And, it wasn't as if the problem of discrimination in Lawrence was especially visible. In 1952, foreign students outnumbered African-American students by 122 to 113 in a total student body of 5,851.[74]

For Chancellor Franklin Murphy to have become publicly involved in the desegregation movement at the early dates of 1951 to 1953 would have been unusual in the extreme. And yet, he did just that. In February 1952, for example, Murphy spoke to 250 guests of the annual Brotherhood Dinner of the Lawrence League for the Practice of Democracy, which had been established by liberal whites and blacks in 1946. In a speech that centered on the global need to understand human differences, he reminded the group to "prove that we are not being hypocritical. To do that," he said, "we must follow our ideals, continue to minimize our prejudices and critically determine if we are to continue to support certain imperialistic practices of Western nations."[75]

Often, evidence shows Murphy attempting to set a tone of tolerance for the university. He personally arranged the visits of numerous renowned speakers, including Thurgood Marshall, for example, to broaden the moral and intellectual horizons of the campus community. Few speakers could have been more appropriate during 1950s than poet and playwright Langston Hughes, one of the most renowned of those African-American sons of Lawrence. To have invited Hughes was courageous in itself: beginning in 1950, he had been labeled as subversive by the political right wing.[76] In 1953, he appeared under subpoena before Senator Joseph McCarthy's subcommittee on subsersive activities and "conceded past mistakes as a radical."[77]

Although he was exonerated by the committee, conservative attacks would continue for many years.

In his October, 1958, visit at Murphy's invitation, Hughes recalled his segregated living with his grandmother in early 20th-century Lawrence, about 50 years after the Beecher's Bibles had arrived in the community.[78] During that time, 2,032 blacks lived in the community of 10,862 population.[79] In 1890, of 1.5 million residents of the state, about 50,000 were African-American.[80]

"Grandmother was not like the other colored women of Lawrence," Hughes said, describing her many attempts to survive financially while maintaining her dignity. A proud woman, she had been honored by President Teddy Roosevelt as the last surviving widow of John Brown's raid at Osawatomie.[81] In his autobiography, her grandson wrote that "she tried to make a living by renting rooms to college students from Kansas University"—thereby providing one of the few sources of housing for such African American students.

Hughes recalled his own money-making projects (a very real family necessity), which included collecting maple seeds in the spring and selling them to the seed store.[82] In addition, he recalled his origins in journalism:

> I delivered (the local) papers and sold the *Saturday Evening Post.* For a few weeks I also sold the *Appeal to Reason* for an old gentleman with a white beard, who said his paper was trying to make a better world. But the editor of the local daily told me to stop selling the *Appeal to Reason,* because it was a radical sheet and would get colored folks in trouble. Besides, he said I couldn't carry his papers and that one too. So I gave up the *Appeal to Reason.*"[83]

> When I was in the seventh grade, I got my first regular job, cleaning up the lobby and toilets of an old hotel near the school I attended. I kept the mirrors and spitoons shined and the halls scrubbed. I was paid fifty cents a week, with which I went to see Mary Pickford and Charlie Chaplin and Theda Bara on the screen. Also Pearl White in "The Clutching Claw," until the theater put up a sign: "NO COLORED ALLOWED."[84]

Clearly, Langston Hughes loved the movies, the music, the poetry and the stage shows in Lawrence. He wrote of his mother pointing out Lawrence poet Harry Kemp and of his family's connection with the "great Negro actor, Nash Walker, of "Bon Bon Buddy, the Chocolate

Drop"[85] fame," who lived in Lawrence, too. Young Langston Hughes loved the glamour, he said.

When Hughes left Lawrence in 1915, at age 13, he moved to large Midwestern cities and ultimately to Harlem, the black Mecca of America. There lived the wealthy and the intelligentsia of African American arts and culture. Hughes definitely found a place in the glamour of the arts. On the other hand, for those African Americans who lacked Hughes' talent or luck and who remained in Lawrence, Kansas, there was little glamour in the segregated town. For them, life changed little.[86]

The changes began with the University of Kansas students. In April 1943, the university's student leadership organization approved a new constitution that included the following non-discrimination policy: "No regularly enrolled students shall, in a discriminatory manner, be denied the privileges of membership."[87] Shortly thereafter, student (and later professor) Paul W. Gilles pointed out that the non-discrimination clause had been ignored, notably in the area of school dances, which black students were not allowed to attend. The next day, the Men's Student Council and the Women's Student Government Association clarified the matter by "guaranteeing the right of the Negro to attend the Junior Prom."[88]

Perhaps the students' governing bodies could guarantee the right of all to attend a campus prom, but that was the extent of the students' power during the 1940s in the arena of desegregation. Those who led the university feared change. The chancellor, Deane Malott, attributed aggressiveness among African-Americans to fifth-column activities led by the wartime Axis powers. He told Governor Andrew Schoeppel, in 1943, that these aggressive troublemakers at the university had been sent in from other states specifically to raise trouble. The majority of black students, Malott told Schoeppel, were happy the way things were.[89]

One of those students, Kermit Phelps, the 1987 leader of the American Association of Retired Persons and a 1952 KU graduate, earned the first Ph.D. in clinical psychology in the U.S. As a graduate student during Chancellor Deane Malott's administration, Phelps was not allowed to teach because he was African-American. While unspoken and never articulated in writing, the policy remained until Murphy took over as chancellor. There would be no teaching appointments for blacks at KU while Malott was chancellor.[90]

Malott was not alone in his attempts to maintain the status quo. The leaders of intercollegiate athletics agreed and provide a case in point. In 1925, the University of Kansas played in the Missouri Valley

Conference, which barred black players from its games. Basketball, football, and other contact sports were especially segregated because "it was believed that Negroes had sores on their bodies" that might be "catching."[91] By 1943, the university competed in the Big Six Conference: Kansas State, Iowa State, and the universities of Kansas, Nebraska, Oklahoma, and Missouri. The latter two, representing traditionally southern states, refused to compete with teams that included black players and the old white-only rule held.

In 1943, KU attempted to change the rule in order to allow Roger Whitworth, a talented African-American sprinter to compete in a Big Six track meet. In spite of editorial and student support for a rules change, representatives of the institutions refused to budge[92] The decision makers suggested that black athletes be allowed to compete in the KU-K State meet—which did not happen. The meet did not occur.

While Kansans in general do not see themselves as "southern," as do Missouri and Oklahoma, KU and Kansas State college were members of the Big Seven athletic league, which was the Big Six before Colorado joined. The league included Kansas State College, Nebraska, Iowa State, Oklahoma, Colorado, and Missouri. Faculty representatives set policy for all aspects of the league, which by "gentlemen's agreement" informally sidelined black athletes from any contest involving southern teams, notably Missouri and Oklahoma. The six founding institutions were parties to the so-called agreement since 1926. Kansas State college president Milton Eisenhower led the war against segregation on campus with notable success. His goal, according to historian S. Zebulon Baker, was to make it possible for Harold Robinson, a black football player, and for others to participate fully.

And play he did, Baker wrote. The first four games of the 1949 schedule tallied just the second and third victories for Kansas State since the end of WWII. The minutes of the league's meeting in 1950 reveal that they never formally repealed the rule—segregation as policy was voided by integration in practice—and when the 1950 edition of the rule book was sent to the printers, they discreetly deleted the segregationist bylaw.[93]

In basketball, the primary decision maker was the University of Kansas coach, powerful 'Phog' Allen, a man with decided antipathy for African Americans.[94] In 1947, the race issue arose in the Letters to the Editor column of the *University Daily Kansan*. "The apparent attitude of our genial coach, Dr. Allen, is that he would rather lose every game on the schedule than allow a Negro to play on his team.

And in fact, he has not allowed Negro students to do so, no matter how great their ability might be."[95] Allen replied that there was not much interest in athletics among black students, saying that "three Negro boys had come out for practice and had been discouraged from coming back, along with 50 white contenders."[96] He noted that it would not be fair to leave black players in Lawrence when the team travelled to play Missouri and Oklahoma, schools that barred blacks from their courts. The student newspaper, in an editorial, wrote that "it would be silly to ask schools favoring racial equality to work out two separate plans of play in order to offer Missouri and Oklahoma all-white opposition. No team is going to try to be less efficient than possible."[97]

Indeed, the issue rested on a team's desire to win. Even though he lacked the idealism of Branch Rickey, who in 1947 would bring Jackie Robinson to his Brooklyn Dodgers as the first African American to play major-league baseball, KU's 'Phog' Allen eventually integrated his teams. But it did not happen until 1951, Franklin Murphy's first year as chancellor, when LaVannes Squires joined the basketball squad as the first black player. Rather quickly, Coach Allen would be pleased that the barriers had dropped: in 1952, he learned about a black basketball player who would have an enormous impact on his future. In that year, KU Sports Information Director Don Pierce clipped a photo from a Philadelphia newspaper about an outstanding high-school player from that city.[98] His name was Wilton Chamberlain.

Not only were African-American students barred from sports until the late 1940s, but also they were not allowed to join musical groups. In 1943, for example, the director of the KU Women's Glee Club responded to charges of barring black singers: "Some have tried out," she said, "but their voices weren't good enough to make it and didn't fit in."[99] African-American instrumental musicians were not allowed to join the KU band because "it worked together as a unit, going on trips and such, and there is close bodily contact."[100]

Chancellor Deane Malott reflected the times and his own prejudices when he explained KU's policy against renting residence-hall rooms to black students. "Parents and students of Kansas are not yet ready," he said in a letter to the governor, "to live in intimate contact with the Negro."[101] Just as had been the case when Langston Hughes' grandmother rented rooms to African American students at KU 40 years earlier, their descendants were forced to find their own housing. Even the university's Home Management House, a KU Home Economics Department experiment in living, barred black women students. Chancellor Malott justified the decision by noting that it was impossible to ask white girls to share bedrooms and bathrooms with a black student.[102] As a partial solution to the housing problem, several male students formed an African-American fraternity, Alpha Phi Alpha—known as the first black fraternity west of the Mississippi. Lavannes Squires was a member in 1951.[103] Kappa Alpha Psi, another black fraternity, formed during the 1950s. In 1958, four black student athletes shared the top-floor and attic living spaces of Kappa Alpha Psi. Those students were Wilt Chamberlain, Charlie Tidwell, David Harris, and Ernie Shelby.[104]

With the crush of new G.I. Bill students after the war, housing constituted a problem for every student—they were living in closets, miles away at the Sunflower Ordnance Factory, and in tents on campus. The only inter-racial housing, the Jayhawk Coop at 1614 Kentucky, was described by a familiar campus slogan: "Some people are rich and some live in coops."[105] The issue of housing, in fact, kept Murphy very busy during the entire decade as he worked to fund and construct dormitories at a time when students were very angry at their absence.[106]

African American aggressiveness could no longer be blamed on Axis powers: the war had been won, in part by black soldiers who now demanded an equal place in American society. One organization in the late 1940s was particularly aggressive and successful: the Congress on Racial Equality (CORE). Founded to break down segregation by non-violent direct action, CORE members objected in 1947 to the university's practice of stamping *"colored"* on student-registration cards. They charged that the label allowed campus organizations to continue discriminatory practices.[107]

A few months later, CORE would begin an effort to desegregate four popular close-to-campus taverns and eateries, the Rock Chalk, the Cottage, the Jayhawk, and Brick's Cafe.[108] Three years later, Murphy became Chancellor: when he left in 1960, at least one restaurant still refused service to blacks. But many public restaurants in Lawrence had changed their white-only rule and Franklin Murphy deserves much of the credit. It involved a long, difficult fight and it relied to some degree on techniques of persuasion that the chancellor learned very soon after assuming his office—techniques that he used to desegregate Lawrence's movie theaters.

That project began with Murphy's intense efforts to attract foreign students to the university, part of his campaign of excellence. He believed that the presence of varying cultures was vital at an exceptional institution. Furthermore, he said that America's foreign policy should rest not on guns and dollars, but on "an expanded program of exchanging students, teachers and experts in many technical fields."[109] In the autumn of 1951, Murphy's first semester as chancellor, 122 foreign students attended KU. In working closely with this small but soon-to-increase number—many of whom were black students from Africa—Murphy learned that they did not enjoy the same campus and community amenities as other students.

He had been raised to be a gracious host; in this situation, he was furious to discover that his guests were ill-treated and immediately began to alter the situation. He responded first to the treatment of guests. Very soon, he would extend his ire and his action to the treatment of the 113 African American students who attended KU.[110] While "no colored" had been the policy that excluded blacks from entering Lawrence's movie theaters during Langston Hughes' childhood, in 1951 it generally had been altered to require blacks to sit only in the balcony, not on the main floor with white patrons. LaVannes Squires recalled an instance when, while a movie was in progress, he and his white team-mates were offered full refunds if he, the only African American in the group, would move to the balcony, or behind the white line.[111]

Shortly after becoming chancellor, Murphy met with the theater owners and "gave them a lesson in manners," he said.[112] When they responded that it was impossible to tell the African foreign students from the African American students, Murphy suggested that it would be much simpler to allow all patrons, whether black or white, to sit wherever they chose.[113] And then, he began to *persuade*. Very clearly, he explained an idea that he had been investigating at the university. He intended to begin a new on-campus film series, he told the group, that would feature first-run movies. Of course, Chancellor Murphy said, the KU films would compete directly with those playing in their downtown theaters, and of course, the KU films would allow unrestricted seating to anyone who wished to show student identification, and the KU movies would be free.[114] Murphy explained the proposition in terms that the theater owners could understand. As "The African Queen," and "Streetcar Named Desire" were current box-office and pocketbook hits for the theater owners, they understood the potential of free movies on campus. The chancellor's message was clear—unless you desegregate your seating, KU will compete and win. "I'm going to establish movies on campus," he had told them. They said that he had no right to do that and besides, he couldn't make it happen. "I can," he replied, "and I will."[115]

Murphy said later that he didn't want to go into competition with the theaters, but merely wanted to change their policies. Theater-manager J.D. King went to Murphy privately: "I want to change," he said, "but I can't do it alone." Murphy told him that he would make sure the Granada got "so much coverage—I'll be interviewed and I'll tell them to attend your theater."[116] King agreed to try a policy change at his Granada Theatre, and Murphy set in motion a plan that would convince King and his peers of the financial wisdom of his decision.[117] The chancellor contacted several student leaders and asked them to inundate the Granada Theater with business during the weekend to come—show the manager that he can make money with desegregated seating. "Nobody noticed the difference," Murphy said later, "because people didn't go . . . to dance; they went to see the movie. They didn't care who sat next to them."[118] Murphy had used the power of his institution's purse and its students' purchasing power to change racist policy. "In less than a month," he said, "all were integrated."[119]

In 1954, Murphy was forced to remind King of their agreement: "Enclosed you will find a brief memo," Murphy wrote, "which is the kind of thing that suggests we must continually be on the alert to move the segregation problem forward as fast as we can. As I indicated to you when I last talked with you, I think this kind of concern will be constant and increasing."[120] In spite of this later reminder, Murphy's persuasion worked, quickly and painlessly.

Convincing restaurant owners to serve African-Americans was neither quick, nor painless. He knew that it would not be easy and said that he "saved the hardest 'til last" [121] Ubiquitous, early-1960s signs warnings that "we reserve the right to refuse service to anyone" came later. In the early 1950s, many knew better than to ask and thereby invite the humiliation of a refusal. "The attitude of the waitress and the rejection of my patronage humiliated me beyond explanation," said a black KU student who was refused service at a privately owned cafe near the campus in 1954.[122]

Apparently the often-noted fear of bodily contact was thought to be most possible in restaurants, in which African American dishwashers, for example, might leave their germs on plates and forks. Restaurant segregation, which was the first to inflame emotions nationwide, was one of the last barriers to fall in Lawrence. Recognizing the emotions involved, a group of African American students in Greensboro, N.C. purposely chose to focus public attention over their inability to eat food at the same lunch counter as whites. Staging their first sit-in confrontation, in 1960, at a lunch counter was a decision guaranteed to draw local and national attention.[123]

At the University of Kansas, campus agitation for change became heated in 1952 as a result of the work begun years before by members of CORE and KU-Y, and continued by the Methodist students' Wesley foundation, a group with inter-racial membership. In April of 1952, the Methodist students attempted to find a place to go for coffee after their meetings, but were refused service by four restaurants near campus. The proprietors all justified their actions, in general, by saying that "our customers don't want it."[124] Just before graduation in May 1952, the movement to change the proprietors' minds was a month old and had resulted in a petition signed by 1,269 students—nearly one-fourth of the student body.[125] It urged the owners of the Call, Gemmell's, the Jayhawk, and the Rock Chalk to "serve all University students regardless of race or creed."[126]

While the student newspaper ran a series of articles about this "situation of long existence in Lawrence," the four cafe owners decided publicly to ignore the petition and to continue to refuse service to blacks. "I talked to the other restaurant owners," said Gleason Gregory, proprietor of the Rock Chalk cafe, "and we decided it was 'no dice'." Each of the owners explained that they would lose more business than they would gain by bending to the petition of "a certain campus group that tries to stir up trouble of this sort every year." Besides, "they have a place to eat," Gregory said, "the student union."[127]

In the few days that remained before final exams began, (when campus debates, however heated, die), the newspaper was filled with letters to the editor in support of the Wesley students' petition. One white waitress quit her job at the Rock Chalk cafe "over this discrimination thing." She said that "one of the Negroes who works in the back room as a dishwasher" was thinking about quitting, as well.[128]

The All-Student Council president acknowledged that his group could take no action on the controversy as too little time remained before the semester ended. On the last day before finals, 97 of 100 students interviewed in a *University Daily Kansan* spot poll said that they had no objection to blacks being served in Lawrence restaurants;[129] the president of a black fraternity, Alpha Phi Alpha, urged a boycott, supported by "many of our white friends."[130] As the KU students spent the weekend studying, Chancellor Murphy was scheduled to attend a public forum on campus. The speaker was to be the Kansas City head of the NAACP and his topic: "Should minority groups become more militant?"[131]

Knowing that the semester would end soon and that student-led causes rarely embroil a campus during the summer, Murphy did not become involved openly in this one. However, during the same week, he revealed some of his beliefs about discrimination in response to a letter. The writer, a woman of Overbrook, Kansas, wrote to Murphy to inquire about the credentials of a young doctor who was considering opening a practice in that community. "We do understand," she wrote, "that he is a Catholic and wonder if he might fit into the community and if he would be satisfied."[132] Murphy noted that the physician's KU Medical School class ranking and continued: "So far as his religion is concerned ... you people would know your own situation best. I must say that ... the shortage of physicians due to the military is such that one cannot be too particular about such relatively minor matters (as a man's religion)."[133]

Certainly change would have occurred more quickly had not summer breaks intervened, but change was coming. In this 1952 year of Ralph Ellison's *The Invisible Man* and of black heroes of the Korean War, more and more individuals looked at their world more critically.[134] Many of them apparently did not like what they saw. "I was really disheartened during the big week-end of the Kansas Relays," wrote one student. "Some of the teams stayed in Kansas City where the Negro participants could stay with the team instead of bringing them on to Lawrence where they would have been divided. My biggest disappointment was in the case of the Drake University track team. Two Negro members, Arnold Betton and Ray Eiland, were not permitted to stay with the team at the Eldridge in downtown Lawrence. Betton was one of the athletes who made up the U.S. entry in the Olympics of 1952."[135]

In the autumn of 1952, a student-government pronouncement supported "continued and emphasized efforts against racial and religious discrimination,"[136] at the same time that the Supreme Court of the United States began to hear arguments in *Brown vs. Topeka Board of Education*,[137] the defining issue of America's 20th century civil rights campaign. However, another semester passed before the University of Kansas students took up the campaign again in force.

The next autumn, the student newspaper asked editorially what had happened to all the fervor of the previous years.[138] The editorial elicited a number of calls for student boycotts of four restaurants that refused to serve blacks. Apparently the newspaper's efforts for reform were not appreciated by all on campus. A large, bold, unsigned advertisement asked that "ANYONE interested in starting up a newspaper for the University of Kansas, Call 2569W. [139] One of the students who sought reform, James L. Blair, planned a meeting at his apartment and invited "those persons interested in cautiously searching for a solution."[140] Thirty showed up and promptly formed themselves into The Jayhawk Brotherhood. Not so promptly, however, did they settle on the words to use to define their purpose. Spurring on the group, the editor of the *University Daily Kansan* wrote that "time was wasted discussing the purpose of ending discrimination, when the time could have been used in planning some positive action. The group could do a great deal through church organizations, who are solidly back of the drive to get equal rights for Negroes. The group could work through the All Student Council in bringing about some positive action. One positive step has been taken by the group in finding out the opinion of the faculty and administration."[141] The group chose to conduct a scientific study of segregated eating facilities in Lawrence.

It was a busy semester for the Jayhawk Brotherhood. The group found, for example, that only five of 40 eating places (exclusive of those owned by African-Americans) were non-discriminatory.[142] In addition to its survey, they spent time investigating Kansas law and learned that the 1874 civil rights statute did not cover restaurants or movie theaters.[143] The members then conducted a massive poll on campus, this time involving 3,479 returned ballots. It concluded that 75.6 percent opposed racial discrimination in Lawrence's restaurants.[144] And one week later, it published a series of articles ("compiled not by members of the *Kansan* staff, but by members of the Jayhawk Brotherhood") entitled "How Does It Feel to Be a Negro?"[145]

Chancellor Murphy said later that he had hoped that the massive expansion of the eating facilities at the Kansas Memorial Union would convince the recalcitrant restaurant owners to end their discriminatory practices, a ploy that had worked with the theaters.[146] No written evidence exists of attempts on his part to convince them of the financial wisdom of such a move, however. Murphy later said that several of the merchants went to the Kansas legislature in an effort to stop the university from competing against them in food service. Those efforts were in vain.[147] In fact, the union's expansion may have taken the heat off the private restaurants by providing the community with several integrated dining areas. Kansas legislators no longer heard complaints about black students lacking a place to eat and few made any policy changes until 1956.[148]

The Chancellor clarified the policy of the Kansas Union in a letter to a representative of the National Student Council of the YMCA and YWCA. It hoped to hold a meeting of 2,000 delegates at the university and enquired specifically about the "university attitudes toward an interracial meeting" and whether "all... university facilities ... would be open to interracial groups."[149] On the matter of the university attitude toward an interracial meeting, Murphy replied, "we have no feeling on that score. We have long had a tradition of racial freedom on our campus and each year entertain many conferences with mixed groups. Normally at Christmas time we hold a large conference, regional or national in scope, with students of all races from all parts of the country."[150]

Apparently, "how it feels to be a Negro" did not concern many students or administrators at the University of Kansas for some years thereafter, even though campus civil rights organizations, such as the Lawrence League for the Practice of Democracy (LLPD) was active. Between 1954 and 1958, KU students learned about the Supreme Court's monumental desegregation decision, with the plaintiff's team led by Thurgood Marshall of the NAACP, the Montgomery bus boycott, the attempts by black students to attend the University of Alabama, and the school-desegregation crisis in Little Rock. They staged none of the promised boycotts of Lawrence restaurants, nearly all of which continued to refuse service to African Americans. Certainly the problem still had not been resolved in 1956, when Dr. E.D.B. Charles, a visitor to the campus from England and a black-skinned man, was not allowed to eat in several Lawrence restaurants.[151] The Jayhawk Brotherhood was subsumed by the Group for the Improvement of Human Relations, the student newspaper printed twice-annual calls to action in the form of editorials and student polls, and the only evidence of Chancellor Murphy's involvement in racial issues involved the Kansas Technical Institute, in 1955.[152] Lloyd Kerford, a member of the board of directors of KTI, the only state-owned trade school in Kansas, urged Murphy to reconsider his recommendation that the school be closed because it was a segregated institution. Kerford, an African-American, (who would soon play an important role in University of Kansas affairs), praised Murphy's reason as "reflecting a highly democratic ... concept of the importance of the individual man, regardless of race, creed or color." He explained that Murphy was mistaken, that the institution had accepted students of all races since 1949, at his own insistence. "However," he continued, "KTI, along with other state schools, does not yet have an integrated faculty although such has been the desire and ultimate intent for several years."[153] Murphy replied that until he could see more persuasive data than that in the hands of the Board of Regents, he would have to maintain his present views. He explained that "although KTI may not officially be a segregated institution, it certainly operates as such, in the main, de facto."[154]

Wilt Chamberlain Comes to Kansas

The early 1950s were over. The Korean War had ended, and students no longer feared the draft. Senator McCarthy's reign of terror had died with his censure. The new polio vaccine was available and fear of that disease was eliminated.[155] President Eisenhower played golf and made the nation feel more relaxed. He had halted the steel strikes and had put big construction projects back on schedule. At the University of Kansas during the 1954-1958 years, the biggest construction project of all had been completed. At its 1954 dedication, Allen Field House became the most important building on campus. To obtain the steel necessary for the building during a national steelworkers' strike, Murphy designated the structure as a National Guard armory. Apparently, most of the people connected to the University of Kansas between 1954 and 1958 had decided to put aside civil rights in favor of basketball—and Wilt Chamberlain.[156]

In no small part, the decision to recruit the seven-foot-tall Philadelphia high-school star arose out of Franklin Murphy's idealism. 'Phog' Allen's "desire to put the greatest basketball player in the world in Allen Field House meshed with an even more important dream held by Chancellor Franklin Murphy," according to Mike Fisher, in his history of Dean Nesmith, the university's long-time trainer and coach. "That dream centered on breaking down the racial barriers that still blighted the nation in 1955. Murphy hoped outstanding black athletes might be brought to the University of Kansas to promote racial tolerance through their athletic contributions to the university."[157]

Murphy organized the effort, Fisher said. Years later, Murphy agreed and told about his efforts to recruit Chamberlain, beginning with a call to his old friend and fellow-KU-alumnus Ben Hibbs, the editor of the *Saturday Evening Post*—a Philadelphia enterprise owned by Curtis Publishing Company. Wilt's father worked on the loading docks for Curtis, Murphy said. Ben Hibbs and another KU alumnus from Philadelphia "went to work on the father," Murphy said, noting "there's nothing illegal in that." They also contacted Wilt's mother and told her about the good education her son would receive at the University of Kansas. "I never wanted to know how they did it," Murphy said in 1992, "but I guess that they got Wilt's dad promoted or something. Anyway, they convinced him to come."[158]

While Hibbs was working the Philadelphia angle, several African-American KU alumni organized to recruit Chamberlain as well. That effort was spearheaded by Dowdell Davis (a KU classmate of Murphy and publisher of Kansas City's newspaper for African-Americans, *The Call*) and Lloyd Kerford, the wealthy quarry owner with whom Murphy had corresponded earlier in the year about the Kansas Technical Institute. Coach Allen and Skipper Williams provided the overall coordination of the intense campaign to convince the most-heavily recruited high-school senior to attend the University of Kansas. Fisher described athletic trainer Dean 'Deaner' Nesmith's version of the campaign: Williams, who had been one of two Americans picked for the United States' 1952 Olympic skeet shooting team, took Chamberlain into his home during his two visits—supplying good food, good music, and gracious living, Lawrence, Kansas, style.

"We wanted another Jackie Robinson," Allen said later, referring to the baseball player who broke the color barrier with the Brooklyn Dodgers.[159] "We needed one good push," Dowdell Davis emphasized, indicating the hope that Chamberlain's presence might increase racial tolerance in the lagging southern and Border States. Maurice King, who preceded Wilt by a year on the Jayhawk basketball team, agreed with the theory that Wilt may have chosen Kansas to further the cause of his race. "Wilt is a young man who thinks he might do a lot to improve racial relations," King told reporters.

Later, Jerry Waugh, who had been an assistant basketball coach during Chamberlain's playing days at Kansas, and who remains active in KU sports, disagreed that Wilt would have been a willing vehicle to break down racial intolerance. "I'm not sure Wilt wanted people using him," Waugh said. "He resented that. I'm sure he had a good relationship with the Chancellor, but I think he would have resented the thought that that was the reason he was here."[160]

'Phog' Allen, called the best coach in the country by his former player, Kentucky's Adolph Rupp, and many others, had learned how to recruit "super" players in the late 1940s. Although never proved, allegations of alumni pot-sweetening continued through 1952, when Jayhawk super-player Clyde Lovellette led his team to the national basketball championship.[161] Lovellette's prominence reflected well on his coach: Allen was pleased indeed when congratulatory letters flooded the Lawrence post office, some simply addressed to, "The Nation's Greatest Basketball Player, Lawrence, Kansas."[162] A man of no small ego, Allen knew that Wilton Chamberlain would draw even more attention. But mostly, Allen wanted Chamberlain because he was an astounding athlete.[163] Racial equality did not enter the picture for the coach, whom Murphy described as "not at all liberal."[164] Allen saw no reason to change his winning streak or his successful recruiting strategy, and went after Chamberlain with a vengeance. And Allen got his man. All kinds of stories embellish the real or imagined enticements that may have convinced Chamberlain to choose Kansas. Whatever the truth of the stories, Wilt Chamberlain indicated that KU's earlier decision to desegregate its team had been *at least part* of the deciding factor in his decision.

When Wilt was a KU student in 1956, the *Saturday Evening Post* published an article by Jimmy Breslin that used an interview with the young KU basketball star as evidence. In this article, Breslin had quoted Chamberlain: "The first time I went to Kansas, the Missouri Coach (Wilbur Stalcup) met me at the airport—he was kind of cutting in—and asked me if I wanted to be the first Negro to play at his school. I told him no. Same as I told Oklahoma A & M. And I crossed off a lot of other schools because they never had gone in for colored athletes."[165] Although he said that he would not comment on the charge made in the *Post,* Chamberlain did say that Breslin had misquoted him. It wasn't Coach Stalcup who actually intercepted him, Chamberlain said, but a Missouri alumnus. He did not deny having said the other words.

However, racial discrimination almost made him leave as soon as he had arrived. In his 1973 autobiography, Chamberlain wrote (with co-author David Shaw) that after an all-night drive from Philadelphia on his way to his freshman year at KU, he stopped in Kansas City for food. He was told that he could be served only in the kitchen. Furious, he went directly to Coach Allen, in Lawrence, who tried to calm him down. Chamberlain continued:

> Well, it took me about a week to realize the whole area around Lawrence, except for one Black section in Kansas City, was infested with segregation. I called on a few of the alums who had recruited me, and I told them in no uncertain terms what they could do with Kansas if things didn't get straightened out in a hurry.
>
> A couple of them told me, "Look Wilt, you just go wherever you want. You sit down in those restaurants and don't leave until they serve you." That's exactly what I did. It took me about two months, but I went into every damn place within 40 miles of Lawrence, places I didn't want to go into. I'd just sit there and glower and wait. Finally, they'd serve me. I never got turned down or badmouthed or anything, and when I got through, other Blacks would follow me.[166]

Perhaps Chamberlain had not wanted to help break down racial barriers by coming to the University of Kansas, but he seems to have done just that—at least for a few African-Americans. For those who were not seven feet tall, discrimination continued as it had. Certainly, Wilt Chamberlain's primary reason for choosing Kansas rested on his desire to work with an outstanding coach. "I went to the University of Kansas just because I respected their coach so much," Chamberlain wrote in his 1992 autobiography. "He was Dr. Forrest C. Allen. He learned his basketball from a guy named Naismith—perhaps you've heard of him? Dr. Allen also taught Adolph Rupp and other great coaches."[167]

As for the other recruiting enticements, Chamberlain continued to raise questions as late as 1992. "Amateur sports have always been controlled by dollars and cents," he wrote in his autobiography. "Even in *my* time, money was given under the table to players to entice them to go to various schools. Is this wrong? Look at the revenue athletes generate for those schools. Star quarterbacks, Heisman Trophy winners, an NBA number-one draft pick can bring in millions and millions of dollars to a university. It was said that I helped to build the Kansas Turnpike—they needed it, so people could come to Lawrence to watch me perform at KU. If this is true, they didn't pay me *nearly* enough money for my three years as a Jayhawk."[168]

The most visible black student at the University of Kansas in the mid 1950s, "Wilt, the Dipper" averaged 40 points per game and took his team to first-place rankings, though not to the championship. After watching his first scrimmage, one of the Kansas State University coaches put his head into his hands. "I feel sick," he said.

Chamberlain played for Coach Allen for only two years. The end of Wilt's sophomore year coincided with Coach Allen's 70th birthday. After 39 years at the University of Kansas, 'Phog' Allen would be forced to retire, at the height of his fame and to his vocal objections. He and many loyal supporters across the state mounted a campaign to convince Chancellor Murphy to waive the mandatory-retirement policy so that Allen could continue as coach until the end of Chamberlain's career. They even introduced a bill into the legislature requiring Murphy to allow Allen to stay.[169] Murphy had recently been forced to end the teaching career of Professor John Ise for the same reason, and refused to treat the popular coach any differently. "The law's the law," Murphy said.[170] 'Phog' Allen's tenure ended officially on March 29, 1956, not at all quietly.[171] Soon, all would know that Murphy had good cause to have insisted on letting him go. On May 1, Murphy received a two-page telegram from the president of the

National Collegiate Athletic Association, placing KU on a one-year probation for recruiting infractions.[172] "'Phog' went," Murphy said.[173]

Chamberlain was not pleased to be working with Allen's successor, Coach Dick Harp.[174] Furthermore, many listeners to the radio program that Wilt hosted objected to his playing so much Elvis Presley, who had hit the nation in 1956. But, he was more than displeased—he must have been hurt and angry—when the newspaper published a photograph of three gleeful students holding two puppets that they had made in art education class. The puppet on the left in the picture was white and smiling. The puppet on the right was all black, with menacing eyes and no other facial features. The cutline read: "No offense intended, Mr. Chamberlain, but that's you on the right"[175] When Wilt complained to the Chancellor, Murphy responded— recognizing easily the blatant racism in the photo and knowing that "Dear Wilton" was not having a good year:

> I looked up the picture which you mentioned to me and must agree that it was in very poor taste. Although I am sure that the youngsters involved did not mean it in the least in the manner in which it appeared. Suffice to say, I have made it very clear to the staff of the *Kansan* that it was in extremely poor taste and that such lack of maturity, no matter how well-meaning, is simply inexcusable.
>
> This all leads me to say what I have many times wanted to say to you, namely that I think you have no idea of the real affection in which you are held by the student body here at the University. They are proud of you, not only by way of your athletic skill but even more so because of your dignity, good humor and friendliness. I hope you will not elevate out of proportion such an episode as the *Kansan* picture. As I indicate above, I am sure no harm was meant and it is but a tiny, passing breeze without any real significance as compared to the broad area of respect and affection which is yours.[176]

To Chamberlain, the offensive puppets and the *Kansan's* words cannot have illustrated "affection." If anything, they must have represented to him yet another example of white students' thorough lack of understanding of what it means to be a black-skinned student and in the minority. Perhaps his initial impressions of Kansas had hit home, again.

In October, 1957, Chamberlain joined three other African Americans in an extraordinary meeting with Chancellor Murphy, the result of which did more to end segregation in Lawrence than had any earlier attempt. Ernie Shelby, All-American track star and future captain of the 1959 KU track team, explained the meeting in a 2013 letter reproduced in the Appendix.

In spite of Murphy's efforts to desegregate Lawrence restaurants and movie theaters, such services still were not entirely available to African Americans. According to Shelby, "as late as 1957, African Americans were still being forced to sit in the balcony at the movie theaters, were not allowed to dine in any restaurant and were compelled to wait (while standing) for food orders, which were brought to us in brown paper bags. In addition," Shelby wrote, "we were not provided service in barber or beauty salons, or allowed in public swimming facilities, etc."

The puppet incident convinced Chamberlain that even his celebrity had not resulted in significant change. He lived, with three others, on the top floor of the predominately African-American Kappa Alpha Psi fraternity. The four friends scheduled an appointment with Chancellor Murphy to express their frustration with segregation.

The meeting with Murphy included Wilt Chamberlain, All-American basketball star and captain of the '57-'58 KU basketball team; Homer Floyd, All-Conference football star and future captain of the '58 football team; Charlie Tidwell, All-American track star and world record holder; and Ernie Shelby, All-American track star and future captain of the '59 KU track team.

In fact, Shelby wrote, "it was our collective agreement that we would ALL leave KU if the problem was not immediately addressed."

"During the meeting with Dr. Murphy," Shelby wrote in 2013, "we established the areas of concern that we had, informed him of our collective decision to leave and suggested to him the myriad problems that would be derived from the perception of Kansas University losing its key African-American athletes due to racial discrimination. Dr. Murphy's reaction was extremely attentive, accompanied with great understanding and empathy."

"In response, he shared his straightforward plans to declare the city 'Off Limits" to all students if all retail establishments of Lawrence did not cooperate. At that point in time his plans were incomplete and still unvarnished. There were rumors that he also threatened to open a free, on-campus interracial movie theater, showing the same movies playing at the local theaters, to expand the menu of the campus cafeteria to compete with the local restaurants, and to open an on-campus, interracial beauty salon/barber shop."

"Dr. Murphy got back to us within a few days to inform us that the businessmen of Lawrence had almost immediately capitulated and agreed to desegregate, due to their heavy dependency on KU patronage. We promptly checked it out," Shelby wrote, "and found it to be true!"

Had the four students left KU after the 1957 meeting with Murphy, two historical events would not have occurred, according to Shelby. For the first time in American sports history, he wrote, captains of three major NCAA division 1 sports programs in adjacent and contiguous years were African-American. And, in 1959, Kansas University won the National Men's Outdoor Division 1 Track and Field Championship, with Tidwell and Shelby being the high-point men. "This categorically would not have occurred without the desegregation intervention of Chancellor Dr. Franklin D. Murphy, which prevented the exodus of KU's best known African-American athletes at that time."[177]

* * *

The next year, coach Allen announced his belief that Chamberlain would leave KU, to play for the Harlem Globetrotters. "Why, Wilt made more than $100,000 for the University of Kansas last year," he said. "He thinks it is time he made a little for himself. And he will get $20,000 when he turns pro."[178] 'Phog' Allen was partially correct. Chamberlain left KU the next year, exchanging a second season under Coach Dick Harp and the probability of a college degree for a contract with the Harlem Globetrotters.[179] But he was hired for $65,000, a bit more than Allen had predicted.[180] Many observers at the time concluded that the $65,000 prompted Chamberlain's decision to leave the University of Kansas. As he returned only once in the years that followed, later observers have credited Chamberlain's disdain for KU to Coach Harp's decision in the final minutes of what might have been an NCAA championship, in March 1957.[181] "I don't know what the circumstances are," said Harvey Pollack, a long-time Chamberlain friend, "but he left [Kansas] early. He didn't graduate. He had no real glory. They didn't win the championship."[182] Chamberlain wrote later that he did not leave Kansas on bad terms: "I had a pleasant talk with the chancellor, Franklin Murphy," he wrote, "and he said he thought I was making the right decision."[183] Perhaps the racism of the puppet photograph in October, 1957, helped make the decision final.

Discrimination at KU Set Aside "for future study."

Wilt Chamberlain left at the end of the 1957-'58 season and, at almost the same time, the students at the University of Kansas resumed the fight for racial equality. Only sporadic attempts had been made between 1954 and 1958 to interest the students in that issue. In 1956, in the same week that Spring Vespers was cancelled for lack of interest, the campus sponsored Religious Emphasis Week, which featured DeWitt Baldwin as its speaker. "The great issue of today," he said, referring to the "color problem" of every nation, "is not the fact that color is one of the major issues in the world, but isn't it that you have made it one of your problems?"[184] Baldwin was speaking of the entire country, which indeed had taken up the issue. The same was not true at the University of Kansas.

Only the *University Daily Kansan* editorial staff continued the fight between 1954 and 1958. After a February, 1957, plea for comments about the state of integration, for example, it acknowledged having received pitifully few. L. C. Woodruff, KU's dean of students, spoke for the administration when he told the Group for the Improvement of Human Relations that he was "pleased and amazed beyond measure of the progress we have made in the last six months. However, I would hesitate to do anything that smacked of violence," he added, obviously referring to some students' wishes to boycott restaurants.[185]

In a portent of things to come in the arena of intolerance and civil rights, the KU Band Director, Russell Wiley, announced that "women have no place in the band." Chancellor Murphy agreed.[186] And, the lone female member of the debate team urged others to join her, saying that "women debaters can do just as well in college as they did in high school."[187]

Just before the basketball team would enter and lose the NCAA playoffs, the editorial writers noted that the Group for the Improvement of Human Relations had received absolutely no offers of help or financial aid from Lawrence institutions, including the churches. "In a university community one would expect to see the first signs of social progress, but here in Lawrence, the town newspaper does not allow the issue on its editorial page, or any other page."[188] The non-supported group decided to set aside the discrimination problem "for future study."[189]

Even through the Orval Faubus vs. President Eisenhower standoff over the Little Rock High School desegregation, in September, 1957, the university students did not rouse themselves.[190] Murphy immediately commented, however, in a speech to an overflow audience at the International Club. "Since the twelfth century," he said, "we have had a free marketplace of ideas, and always there have been tyrants trying to close the door."[191]

Just five days later, about one-third of KU's students watched television[192] to hear President Eisenhower explain how he had taken responsibility for resolving the Little Rock crisis, and to watch televised film of bayonet-toting paratroopers escorting nine black children through the mob of screaming adults.[193] As is often the case, college students' attention-spans do not linger long on issues that do not concern them directly. Just as they had during the basketball heyday, KU students moved on to more exciting, more local matters of interest, such as the October 8, 1957, visit of Senator John Fitzgerald Kennedy. The largely Republican campus was just settling down from that excitement when another event took them farther away than ever from the problems of African Americans. On October 8, 1957, the Russians launched Sputnik. Within a few months, they sent up two others. A new age had arrived.

Thurgood Marshall, chief counsel for the National Association for the Advancement of Colored People and hero of the 1954 *Brown vs. Board of Education* triumph, tried to steer the national conversation away from the "Russians' little Red balls" and back to the fight for racial equality. In his February, 1958, speech at the University of Kansas, Marshall said that Orval Faubus was causing the integration process to falter. Unless such incidents as these are prevented, he said, the U.S. is going to get a "black eye" in its dealings with the Middle East and Asia. "Three Sputniks in the air cannot bring Asia and Africa to our side," he said, "as readily as a successful integration in Little Rock."[194] Murphy agreed with Marshall's message and, as host, undoubtedly applauded his words. The guest's words were vital to Murphy's vision, but the chancellor's mind was on the little Red balls circling the earth—and probably spying on America. As chairman of Eisenhower's National Security Commission, Murphy was responsible, in no small part, for the nation's security and Sputnik was not a far-away, minor threat to him. Unless forced into it, Murphy had no intention of using his time on race relations and he did not refer to it at all for many months. For better or worse, he was forced into it shortly after the autumn 1958, semester began. The push came from student politicians. In a typical, beginning-of-term statement, the Allied Greek-Independent Party called for changes. It sought increased student wages on campus and the elimination of racial discrimination in Lawrence public places.[195] These were not new issues. The only difference lay in the source of the call for integration. This was the All Student Council speaking, not a group of liberals.

All of a sudden, the Lawrence Chamber of Commerce decided to get involved and spoke through its manager, E.R. Zook, who warned the students not to push this issue. "There is enough confusion on this subject already," he said. "If there is a lot of demanding made about it the confusion will increase. Little Rock is an example of this."[196] Zook said that two years earlier he had attended a meeting with Lawrence restaurant owners and university officials and that that meeting had resulted in some restaurants beginning to serve blacks. He said that the group agreed to work on this problem on a gradual basis. "If those people in that party on the hill would go to the chancellor," Zook said, "they would find out that rushing this thing isn't going to do any good."[197]

He was right. Obviously, Murphy did not care to enter a fracas at that moment. When those people from that party on the hill went to his office, later the same day, the chancellor replied with words decidedly conciliatory and ill-informed: "I have no comment on Mr. Zook's observation," he said to the students and in a written statement:

> I am grateful for the support which Mr. Zook, the Chamber of Commerce and other enlightened citizens of Lawrence have given us over the past years in the progressive elimination of the residual discrimination in Lawrence. I am personally distressed that any discrimination continues to exist, since it is inconsistent with the basic principles by which Americans purport to live. I hope that this remaining small amount of discrimination in Lawrence can be eradicated as soon as possible by all thoughtful but effective means.[198]

Murphy had not seen the latest survey, which was published the day after his "residual ... small amount of discrimination" words to the students. In fact, of 40 Lawrence restaurants, only ten would serve black patrons in mixed groups, at all times. Only a few would serve African Americans alone.[199] Apparently, Murphy's years-earlier attempt to prod change with the financial threat of expanded and integrated service at the Kansas Union had resulted in nothing more than an agreement to *begin* the process.

Lawrence's mayor, John Weatherwax, said that integration was not a step to be taken by the city government, although he personally wished that the restaurants were integrated. "If a man wants to open a business and serve only white or Negro customers, that is his privilege," he said, reflecting the point of view of many. "And to force him to serve both is to infringe upon free enterprise."[200] Apparently, Mayor Weatherwax wished that the restaurants were already integrated so that he would not have to deal with the problem.

The University of Kansas student government decided to set up a special, non-political committee to "promote the work of any organization concerned with racial discrimination,"[201] and Al Jones, a student editorial writer, blasted Zook: "In Arkansas, at least," Jones wrote, "they can claim a southern tradition of intolerance and tyranny. In Lawrence we have our own version, home-grown and free-lance, just as vicious, and just as stupid."[202]

Although the editorial's timing proves that it could not have included Murphy among the cited intolerant tyrants, he did not come out of the incident unscathed. In a letter to the editor a few days later, a student had a new idea for those who say they seek brotherhood. "Before we, of the University, cloak ourselves in this 'holier-than-thou' hypocrisy, shouldn't we ask ourselves a few critical questions?," he asked of Al Jones, the editorial writer of the previous week, and continued:

> If Chancellor Murphy and especially the ever-righteous Greek organizations that function on brotherhood hill really believe in the dignity and equality of all men, why are these organizations not integrated? Have any steps been made to rewrite the charters of these philanthropic organizations so that they may practice what they preach? If Mr. Jones and the University feel free to chastise a man for being afraid to put his livelihood in jeopardy, can we not, then, be twice as critical of these sanctimonious snobbish little cliques that breed and nurture intolerance.[203]

In the one year past, the civil rights campaign had expanded, just as would occur on a national level. Women were beginning to ask why they could not play an instrument in the KU Band and students were questioning the discriminatory policies of fraternities and sororities, nearly all of which existed under the aegis of national rules that specifically excluded African Americans and Jews. Murphy would deal with each, to a degree. For the moment, however, he spoke forcefully about racial discrimination. "Governor Orval Faubus is a venal man taking advantage of the color of innocent children for his own political purposes," he said in a keynote speech to the Kansas Tuberculosis and Health Association, one week after his less-than-strong response to students on campus. "This man from Arkansas is doing a great violence to the traditions and dignity of our country."[204] He told the group about his three-week visit to Russia the previous summer and about the 40,000 mile trip through Asia and the Middle East at the same time. He explained that, with Sputnik, the Soviet Union had drawn this country into a real contest of education and research, "for it is through these achievements the Soviet hopes to win a large percentage of the undeveloped nations of the world," he said. "This country, however, possesses a secret weapon," Murphy continued. "That weapon is its fundamental concept of human dignity, individual opportunity and freedom from tyranny." But this man from Arkansas, he concluded, "is writing black headlines around the world which tarnish our weapon and eat into the hearts and ego of our fellow men."[205]

The speech elicited a number of letters from irate Kansans, as was always the case when Chancellor Murphy raised his voice in moral indignation. One writer included in her letter so many of the sentiments of others that it deserves full reproduction: [206]

> After reading of your criticism of the Governor of Arkansas, I am writing for information.
>
> Through some research work, I thought I had learned that 25 years ago the communists in New York City were plotting and planning to use Arkansas as a place to stir up trouble. They were using young men and women through preparation of a detailed plan as is outlined in the Communist Secret Report.
>
> And I thought I learned also that the NAACP is a group organized so the communists can use the negroes as tools to win their goals, only to later enslave the ignorant negroes also.
>
> When, Dr. Murphy, did our Constitution or the Congress give the U. S. Supreme Court the ability or privilege of *making* our laws? Some of the court's recent decisions have been deplorable and—if it so continues with its communistic sympathizers, how can we as a once so privileged country expect to stay free?
>
> Haven't we, for a good many years been getting along fine with the Negroes? Isn't the *enforcement* of integration by the communists that is hurting and causing this recent feeling and

ill will, thus causing a damage the communists hope never can be corrected?

I, too, thot [sic] the Governor wrong when the trouble first broke—but, learning he's upholding his state's rights and that it is an issue *between communists* and *American freedom*—not between races—I think we should uphold him instead of criticizing him. Don't you?

Tho [sic] I no longer teach—I have—and have also been a Sunday School teacher for years—and lately have been doing *considerable* research work via the Bible, F.B.I. (Hoover), Un-American Activities Committee—the government, etc.—until I could shudder (and maybe we will!)—but—hope and pray that America will again (?) return to God before it is too late.

I would appreciate very kindly a few moments of your time if you would write in answer. I think my husband was in a meeting with you a few years ago, in Burlington, I believe.

Did Murphy need to respond to this letter? The writer was one elderly woman in a small Kansas town—one who could influence few and one who had probably been ignored by many who made public speeches. Few would see his response to her; she would not publish it. She was unlikely to give money or refuse it, or to influence any who might. Like all of the dozens of letters he dictated each week, this one responded specifically to the individual who had written and contained no "stock" paragraphs—which he did not use, except perhaps in one instance.[207] He had nothing to gain politically, in the state or on the campus, by answering her letter. And yet he did, at length:

My criticism of Governor Faubus is based upon the established fact that the School Board in Little Rock, Arkansas, had spent an entire year carefully working with organized groups in the community so that the integration of the high school would go forward smoothly. It is also an established fact that this year of preparation had been eminently successful, and no responsible person expected any difficulty. Only when Governor Faubus realized the need of a major issue for reelection and moved into the picture did difficulties develop.

> In the second place, I believe that segregation is immoral—quite as immoral as Communism, Fascism, or any other 'ism' that denies fundamental human rights and human dignity.
>
> Jesus said, 'Let the little children come unto me'—not the little *white* children, but simply the 'children'. The Preamble to the Constitution of the United States seems fairly clear, too, to me.
>
> I personally believe that Little Rock and the whole matter of segregation in the South is doing more to harm the United States in all parts of the world than any other single thing. A dozen Communist spies, working twenty-four hours a day, could not do as much damage as Governor Faubus has done as far as the very necessary friendship that we must gain and maintain with millions of people all over the world whose skins are other than white.[208]

Murphy had expected to persuade Lawrence restaurants to integrate easily, and years before. He had not wished to force the issue, but believed it to be just and may have expected others to recognize the justice of integration as well. In the end, the restaurants were integrated legally not by words from Murphy's bully pulpit, and not by the efforts of four black athletes, but by the Kansas legislature. In October of 1959, just five months before Murphy would announce his resignation as chancellor of the University of Kansas, House Bill No. 467 passed. It provided, in part, that:

> If any of the regents or trustees of any state university, college, or other school of public instruction, or the state superintendent, or the owner or owners, agents, trustees or managers in charge of any hotel... or of any place of public entertainment or public amusement, for which a license is required by any of the municipal authorities of this state, or the owner or owners or person or persons in charge of any railroad, bus, streetcar, or any other means of public carriage of persons within the state, shall make any distinction on account of race, color, religion, national origin or ancestry, the person so offending shall be deemed guilty of a misdemeanor....[209]

Even though the new legislation did not cover most taverns, which did not prepare food on the premises and which, therefore, could not be categorized as restaurants that were covered by the bill, it did open the eating establishments to any who could pay the bill. In her research, Heidi Pitts drew the conclusion well for the restaurant-integration issue: Eight months after the bill became law, a memo passed through the Dean of Men's office saying the "restaurant problem is pretty well solved."[210]

The floodgates had opened with the restaurants and students had become very interested indeed in matters of racial and religious bias. As he was embroiled with Kansas politics, Murphy did not get involved in race-based issues on campus in 1958 and 1959, but left them to other members of his team. Clarke Wescoe, Dean of the Medical School, dealt with most of the very real segregation issues at its hospital, for example, and among its professional staff.[211] A year later, in 1960, when the Greensboro, N.C. students staged the first lunch-counter sit in, the KU Medical Center still had two infant nurseries—one for white babies, and one for black babies.

Another campus issue that Murphy dealt with only at its conclusion concerned the embarrassing revelation of racial bias in university housing. Dean of Students Laurence Woodruff and Dean of Women Emily Taylor had spent months attempting to deal with student allegations that the housing office handed out different "apartments available" lists, depending on the race of the potential renter. In early 1959, the *Kansan* checked the lists carefully and discovered the differences—an embarrassing turn of events for the administrators, who had denied often that such lists existed.[212]

At the end of the 1959 legislative session, in which HB 467 had been one of very few bright spots in the midst of attacks by Governor George Docking, Chancellor Murphy met with students, in part to assure them that the very-public budget disputes with the governor had not harmed the university irreparably. On the issue of the *Kansan's* recent proof of racially biased housing lists, Murphy told the students that he approved of the *Kansan's* work to check the lists. "Students should not take the word of the administration," he said, presaging his own career at UCLA during the Black Power, anti-war, student-uprising days of the 1960s to come. "For this reason the check was justified."[213]

However, the KU leader had a few more words to say on the subject of discrimination. Recalling the student's question of the previous semester about bias in fraternities on "Brotherhood Hill," Murphy called the racial and religious clauses in national charters of Greek letter organizations "inexcusable."[214] Franklin Murphy, the loyal member of Beta Theta Pi who had known since his fraternity days that they "wouldn't consider pledging a Jew," he said later, "to say nothing of a black," did not want to tackle this one, he said.[215] "I decided to leave that to the next guy."[216] He did, however, ask the University of Kansas Senate to study the existence of such exclusionary clauses and to prepare a policy statement, although he did not announce its work to the students. Its report would not be presented until Murphy had left the University of Kansas, but it did reflect his sentiments, especially in its first clause:

> We believe that the presence, in the constitution of a national fraternity or sorority, of a discriminatory clause based upon race, color, religion, or national origin—except for a religious clause in the case of a group primarily religious in purpose— is both ethically wrong and so incompatible with the status of the local chapter as a living group enjoying recognition by the University of Kansas.[217]

At about the same time as the Spring 1959, meeting with students, Murphy had launched another of his new ideas in the arena of human rights. At that time, he had gone to the largest Jewish temple in Kansas City and asked for the members' help. "I want a Jewish presence at the University of Kansas," he said to them.[218]

In September, a Jewish freshman named Yale Dolginou moved into his dormitory at KU. He hated it, he recalled later, especially the food. "There were not many Jews," he said, "and they served pork in the dorm every day." Dolginou went first to the dietician, who said that nothing could be done about the menu, and then sent him to Donald Alderson, the dean of men. Alderson agreed with the dietician. "We can't change the menu," he said, and sent the young man to the next individual on the upward chain of command, who told Dolginou to "go see Murphy," which he promptly did. It didn't take Murphy long to settle the issue of appropriate food for the Jewish freshman (who would graduate in 1964 and who now owns a national merchandising firm, Dolgin's). Murphy called every person in the aforementioned administrative hierarchy: "We want this guy to stay," he told them firmly. "Feed him steak!"[219]

For Murphy, a democracy could not survive without citizens who acted upon the highest ethical standards. For him, activities to integrate the community and the institution appeared to stand as his part in that effort. It was not undertaken or accomplished for African-American rights or Jewish rights, but as his responsibility as an ethical citizen.

The fourth print of the series of one of Dürer's best known woodcuts. In it, the Four Horseman—representing from left to right, Death, Famine, Pestilence, and War—ride rampant over the earth. *Time Life Library of Art: The World of Dürer 1471-1528*, by Francis Russell and the Editors of *Time-Life Books*, Time Incorporated NY 1967, property of the author.

Murphy leads entourage from Strong Hall to Hoch Auditorium where he is to be installed as University of Kansas Chancellor, September, 1951. Kenneth Spencer Research Library, University of Kansas Libraries.

Murphy family portrait. Kenneth Spencer Research Library, University of Kansas Libraries.

Board of Directors for Truman's Presidential Library. Murphy is second from left. Kenneth Spencer Research Library, University of Kansas Libraries.

Celebrating KU's basketball success, 1952. Judy and Franklin Murphy with Coach 'Phog' Allen. Kenneth Spencer Research Library, University of Kansas Libraries.

Dr. Franklin Murphy was the last KU chancellor to participate in the Nightshirt Parades. He also presided over the University's first "Tradition's Rally," which replaced the annual parading on September 19, 1958. Image: University Archives.

Stork Club in New York City, 1951. Charles Boyer, Noel Coward, and Franklin Murphy. Kenneth Spencer Research Library, University of Kansas Libraries.

Informal discussion at the Lawrence Brotherhood Banquet among (left to right) Homer Floyd, Chancellor Franklin Murphy, Thurgood Marshall, Charles Tidwell, and Ernie Shelby. February 11, 1958. Kansas Memorial Union. Kenneth Spencer Research Library, University of Kansas Libraries.

Coach 'Phog' Allen and freshman basketball phenom Wilt Chamberlain, 1955. Kenneth Spencer Research Library, University of Kansas Libraries.

Governor George Docking with his wife, Virginia, and Chancellor Franklin Murphy with his wife, Judy. 1956. Kenneth Spencer Research Library, University of Kansas Libraries.

Murphy, left, opening part of Kansas Turnpike, 1954. Kenneth Spencer Research Library, University of Kansas Libraries.

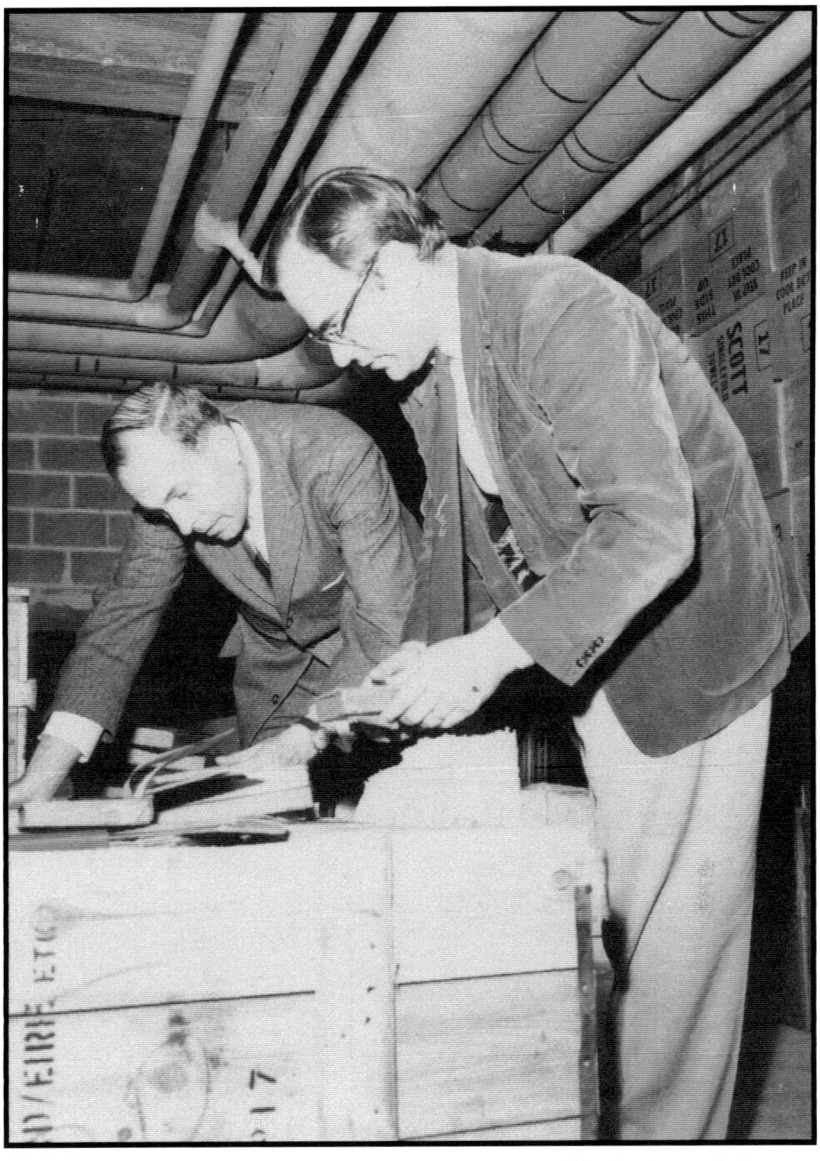

Murphy and Library Director Robert Vosper open crates of books. Kenneth Spencer Research Library, University of Kansas Libraries.

Students gather to protest Chancellor Murphy's decision to leave KU, March 18, 1960. Kenneth Spencer Research Library, University of Kansas Libraries.

Chancellor Murphy speaking to students about his resignation, 1960, near Potters Lake. Kenneth Spencer Research Library, University of Kansas Libraries.

CHAPTER 6

Kansas Political Wars
1951-1960

Apparently, President Dwight Eisenhower considered Murphy sufficiently political to suggest that he might be trusted with the highest political office in the nation. In 1955, he wrote to thirty-nine-year-old Murphy, complaining about the traditional Republican Party view that younger men are not electable, which "kind of thinking—or rather lack of thinking—infuriates me," Eisenhower wrote. "I most earnestly believe that we should constantly seek out relatively young men to occupy the high positions of government. I can name a dozen men in the forty to fifty year group—including yourself—to whom I would gladly entrust the duties of the Presidency."

KANSANS have never really warmed to labor unions. To the typical Kansan, labor unions mean bosses forcing you to join if you want a job. Labor unions mean strikes and battles with the police. In 1956, just after the McCarthy-led frenzy over Communist infiltration, the average Kansan probably was convinced that labor unions were filled with pinkos. Certainly, labor unions were filled with Democrats—and Kansas was not.

Kansas is Republican. It was settled by farmers, by men and women who avoided the big cities on purpose, who reveled in their independence, and who thought nothing of living in the isolated center of their 160 acres—miles away from neighbors and as far away as possible from anyone who might attempt to run their lives. The 19th century Kansas-led Populist movement set the tone for the Kansan's "I'll do it my way, thank you very much" brand of individualism, which was strong enough to elect two governors for its cause.

Nationally, labor unions had flexed their muscles during the early 1950s and effectively shut down the construction industry at the height of the Korean War with steel, mining, and railroad strikes. In Kansas, meat packers, railroad employees, and airplane-plant workers in Wyandotte, Shawnee, and Sedgwick counties constituted the largest enclaves of union members in the state. Kansas was not the only state whose voters fundamentally opposed unions. In the mid-1950s, many state legislatures attempted to weaken unions by passing bills that halted organized labor's power to force workers to join. Such bills were called "right-to-work" bills—they gave employees the right-to-work, whether or not one chose to join the union.

Basically, right-to-work legislation forbids any union-shop contracts ("closed shop") between management and labor that would require employees to join a union within a prescribed time in order to be hired or retained. Proponents of right-to-work favor an "open shop" and argue that such legislation has no intention of doing away with unions. The issue, proponents explain, centers on whether an American worker should be forced, under penalty of losing his job, to join and support a particular organization—whether a union, church, or civic club.

Opponents of right-to-work legislation typically include members of labor unions and others who favor the "closed shop" and "union-security agreements." They argue that right-to-work legislation would kill unions, lower wages, and hurt business in general. While countless other arguments for and against occur, these are the basic strands. Historically, Republicans favor right-to-work bills and Democrats oppose them.

In 1955, the Republican-controlled Kansas House of Representatives introduced a right-to-work bill and promptly passed it, as did the Senate. Republican Governor Fred Hall, humiliated by his Republican predecessor's lame-duck appointments to 27 plum jobs (including two appointments to the powerful Kansas Board of Regents), the Governor raised his hackles and vetoed the measure that had been passed by his own party. It proved to be his own party in name only. It isn't that Governor Hall favored unions and closed shops or even that he opposed right-to-work. More likely, he opposed the Old Guard, more-conservative Republicans who had shepherded the legislation.[1] On March 28, 1955, he vetoed the bill, saying that his office had received 23,000 messages concerning right-to-work, with about two-to-one opposed to the measure.[2] The next day, the House failed to override his veto by six votes.

The right-to-work issue was dead for awhile and Governor Hall soon was out of office, having been defeated in a bitter 1956 primary by Republican Warren Shaw, whom Franklin Murphy had supported[3] and who lost in the general election to Democrat George Docking.[4] According to Kansas historian Bliss Isely, numerous friends of Hall voted for Docking rather than support Shaw.[5] George Docking replaced Hall in the governor's office, having won the 1956 contest with the largest majority ever given by Kansans to a member of his party.[6] Clearly, many Kansas Republicans had voted for Docking, a Democrat, as governor—a major surprise. After all, Kansas had been solidly Republican throughout its history, with all except eight of its thirty-two governors being members of that party— and with two of the eight remaining being members of the Populist Party. Of the twenty-four Republican governors, seventeen were elected for two terms. None of the six Democratic governors had been re-elected after his two-year term.[7]

Governor George Docking, the first Democrat in that office in twenty years, recognized his debt to the many Republicans who had voted for him. Elected on a tight-money, fiscal-conservatism platform at the height of a Plains-states drought, he would do everything possible to avoid raising taxes. This surely would appeal to the Western Kansas farmers and other Republicans. He did not want to deal with right-to-work, a straight-party-line issue that he opposed, and that most Republicans favored.[8]

When the right-to-work effort first hit the Kansas Legislature, back in 1955, some business vs. union controversy was assured, but few expected the venom that would result in the next three years. Certainly, Franklin Murphy did not expect it to embroil the

University of Kansas as it did in 1958.[9] His response to the right-to-work controversy illustrates Murphy's dealings, successful and unsuccessful, in the Kansas political arena—with the university community, with its potential donors, with state politicians, and with his nemesis, Governor George Docking.

Furthermore, the right-to-work issue and the political climate that surrounded it illustrate Murphy's efforts to persuade with logic; *logos*—the ability to move people intellectually, using solid reasoning. In this, he succeeded and he failed. He needed to move people intellectually—they would need solid reasons if they were to support the vision that he articulated so often. Murphy's vision for the university required money—a lot of it. Without adequate funds, his vision could have no chance at all, however articulate or logical.

Murphy's task was to raise that money. As must all leaders of public universities, he struggled constantly for revenue from four sources: public funds derived from state taxes; student funds derived from tuition; research funds derived from federal or foundation grants; and endowment funds derived from private donations. Because the core of that revenue comes from the state (53 percent in FY 1960), the university leader is constantly drawn into political battles, whether they involve money or whether they involve ideological issues.[10] Although not an elected official, the leader of a public university must be political to the extent that he or she is able to protect and enlarge the institution's budget.

Murphy knew that he could win some and lose some. In March 1953, for example, Murphy expressed his "distress" at the Kansas Legislature's killing of a $450,000 appropriations bill to provide educational television at Kansas State College and the University of Kansas. He had worked hard to convince the Ford Foundation to match the state funds with $200,000 to establish TV stations at both institutions.

One month later, in April 1953, Murphy noted the "thoughtful and kind treatment" of the Legislature for its increased appropriation that "will permit us to maintain our present standard and level of activities as well as to make an honest expansion of effort."[11]

Unfortunately, in 1956 agricultural-based Kansas was in the midst of a drought and many in the state could not balance the long-term promise in Murphy's words against the shortfall in their bank books. Murphy was not an elected official who could generate the funds by raising taxes or shifting allocations himself. His task was to persuade the people of Kansas, in every manner possible, to support the elected officials who would support his vision. But he did not consider his role "political." Murphy viewed his role and his actions as standing outside politics, saying on one occasion that "educators of Kansas must be given the opportunity to proceed with their difficult tasks unencumbered by extraneous and traditionally unrelated matters. Politics and education," he said, "simply cannot be mixed."[12] Clifford Griffin, an historian of the University of Kansas, did not agree: "It was, of course, not true. Politics and education had to be mixed in public institutions."[13]

Certainly, Murphy may have *desired* that such would be the case, but he was not naive. In making such statements, he spoke of the best of all possible worlds, but appears to have knowingly shaded his eyes from the truth. After all, he was a Republican and he had promised the state party to help its cause in the 1956 election.[14] He promised to remind Kansans of their recent heritage of progress, saying "we shall do our bit to see that this story is told."[15] Although he said that he remained aloof, Murphy was no stranger to politics. In January of 1955, for example, he wrote the legislation that would exempt certain university income from control by the Board of Regents. In a letter to President James A. McCain of Kansas State College, Murphy said that he had been advised to keep the number of funds to be handled locally to a minimum, and "this I have tried to do in the language in this bill."[16] The bill proposed that all charges or receipts collected shall be remitted to the State Treasurer, except those to be "administered at the institutions as provided by this act." Such exempted monies would include gifts, bequests, student union receipts, intercollegiate athletics receipts, and other specified categories. It was an important document for the future financial stability of the Regents' institutions, and it was political.

Apparently, President Dwight Eisenhower considered Murphy sufficiently political to suggest that he might be trusted with the highest political office in the nation. In 1955, he wrote to thirty-nine-year-old Murphy, complaining about the traditional Republican Party view that younger men are not electable, which "kind of thinking—or rather lack of thinking—infuriates me," Eisenhower wrote. "I most earnestly believe that we should constantly seek out relatively young men to occupy the high positions of government. I can name a dozen men in the forty to fifty year group—including yourself— to whom I would gladly entrust the duties of the Presidency."[17]

Murphy had tested his political instincts as the leader of the KU Medical Center. His success with the Kansas Rural Health Plan taught him to trust those instincts. He had learned how to raise money and from whom. He had learned which newspaper editors to court and how to court them. He knew the legislators' interests and their wives names.[18] He had been successful as dean of the Medical Center and during the first years of his work as University of Kansas chancellor.

A new test of those political lessons began in November 1956, a month when Murphy realized unmistakably that he faced a challenge of enormous importance to the university—"a crossroads—a crisis" for the future.[19] It involved money and politics. It threatened to obliterate his vision for the University of Kansas. His vision was simple—make the university into one of the nation's finest. The man who expected excellence in everything could aspire to no less for the institution he led. Murphy especially expected excellence for the state of Kansas, which he believed deserved greater recognition than it received.

From his days as a medical student, in the late 1930s, Murphy had seen the Midwest export its youthful brainpower to the East. He said that he considered such exportation of intellect a good idea, in that "it has guaranteed that the blue has received a continuous infusion of red blood."[20] However, that brain drain must stop, he said as KU chancellor. The universities of the Midwest—led by the University of Kansas—must stand as qualitative equals to the best universities in the East. The state or the area or the institution that reaches the heights of Murphy's vision would be the one "which invests the most in the intellectual equipment to produce trained and education people...."[21] He knew about the brain drain to the East from personal experience and had come far from the University of Pennsylvania when the "little ole' Kansas boy" captured the medical-school top prize, beating out students from Harvard and Yale. To his death, that acknowledgement of Midwestern brain power pleased him as much as any in his honor-laden life.[22] Now, in 1956, the presidents of Yale and Harvard were his colleagues: Murphy and Yale's president A. Whitney Griswold had written the American Association of Universities' public response to Joseph McCarthy's threat to academic freedom, in 1953.[23]

Now, in 1956, Murphy of Kansas had friends in high places indeed. He had rejected an appointment as Secretary of the Army from President Eisenhower,[24] who invited the young KU chancellor to the White House often, the first time being to "an informal stag dinner with a very few men" to which the President noted he would be wearing black tie, "but dark suit will be entirely appropriate;"[25] who signed "as ever, D. E." to most of the 26 letters that he wrote to "dear Franklin;"[26] and who would send Murphy as his personal emissary to Winston Churchill, just a few months later, in April 1957. In his letter of introduction to Churchill, Eisenhower would describe Franklin

Murphy and Joyce Hall, who accompanied him, as "two of my very good friends."[27]

Now, in 1956, Murphy had been the focus of several articles in national magazines. Undoubtedly in part because of his relative youth at age 40, but certainly as well because of his ability to articulate a message with logic and words that needed little editing, Murphy of Kansas gained the reputation of being one of the nation's fastest-rising and most-respected spokesmen for education. When he spoke, people listened.

At no time in his life could Murphy allow himself to accept second-best—it made him angry with himself, he said.[28] Now, in 1956, he did not want his institution to accept mediocrity. As passionately as he considered the University of Kansas to be at a crossroads, he must have believed that he, himself, was very much on the line as well. An Aristotelian realist, Murphy knew that turning his vision into action—making his university "a cornucopia of all good things"— would require money in larger amounts than ever before.[29] However, he believed that he could do it: his success in the state and in the nation would have made even a modest man believe that he could pull it off. Although certainly a team player in the best public-spirited tradition of Benjamin Franklin, Murphy cannot be described as modest.

Having succeeded as a non-political politician and money raiser since his days as dean of the KU Medical School, Murphy had approached fund raising with confidence—from all of the four sources available to him. Since becoming chancellor, he had crisscrossed the state making friends among store owners and bibliophiles, and convincing even Western Kansas parents to send their children to Lawrence, instead of to Kansas State, thereby increasing tuition income. He paid attention to the students, attended their weddings and wrote notes to their parents when their grades dipped. He had courted old friends and new among the wealthy. He sent arcane monographs and small gifts that would appeal to the interests of each, and then appointed them to university boards, thereby increasing endowment funds markedly. He spent a growing proportion of his time in Chicago, New York, and Washington as an active member of a dozen national boards. Most importantly, he led the Commission on National Security at the behest of President Eisenhower—placing Murphy in the pipeline to obtain research grants for the university. And to legislators he sent a continuous stream of courtly prose and basketball tickets.

He had been successful in generating non-state income, particularly in private gifts to the Kansas University Endowment

Association. Initiated to keep gifts of land and money under the control of the university instead of the state, the Endowment Association substantially increased its reach and importance during Murphy's tenure.[30] He organized the Greater University Fund in 1953, he said, which generated $42,000 from 1,600 individuals in its first year and which, in 1960 alone, had increased to $243,000 from nearly 6,000 alumni and friends.[31] From 1951 to 1959, according to Griffin, the book value of the Endowment Association's assets rose from $3,835,000 to over $8,252,000.[32] The credit belongs to Murphy, Griffin acknowledged, and to Alumni Association Secretary Fred Ellsworth, the Endowment Association's Executive Secretary Irvin Youngberg, and to Kansas City banker and Executive Committee President Maurice Breidenthal. Murphy's many speeches, his Niagra of personal letters and his hand-on-the-elbow style of persuasion combined with Breidenthal's extensive contacts to increase private gifts substantially. Without question, Murphy needed to keep potential donors in the university's camp.

He had worked hard to generate such gifts and support, and the work had paid off. In 1953, for example, Murphy attended the International Universities Congress and met A. John T. Ford, who served as administrator to the Australian Vice-Chancellor's Committee. Ford also served on the board of the Carnegie Foundation. At their meeting, Ford asked if he might visit the University of Kansas. Murphy arranged the visit, apologizing that there would be no football games at that time (about which Ford had enquired specifically).[33] Ford stayed for three days as Murphy's guest. Two years later, on November 17, 1955, the *University Daily Kansan* announced that "Chancellor Franklin D. Murphy has been elected as a trustee of the Carnegie Foundation for the Advancement of Teaching."[34] That connection would pay important dividends to KU.

However much those private funds had grown, they could not compensate for the loss of income that had accompanied each of the GI Bill students, the flood of whom had ended early in the decade. Private funds could purchase the rare books that flowed from Murphy's cornucopia, but they could not provide retirement funds or salary increases that were so necessary to keep and recruit the finest faculty and allow the chancellor to realize his dream.

Now, in late 1956, Murphy knew that he faced a crisis. Quite suddenly, he realized that very little time remained to turn his vision into action. At recent meetings of several national boards—notably the American Council on Education, the Ford Foundation, and the Carnegie Corporation— he had become convinced that many other states were investing in higher education at rates far beyond the commitment of Kansas.[35] "This is a crossroads," Murphy wrote, "it is a crisis—and lack of vision, shortsightedness, political in-fighting at the expense of adequate investment in higher education could be devastating."[36] In the same month, November 1956, George Docking had been elected governor. Without doubt, Docking did not share Murphy's vision.

The chancellor knew that he would need to be very persuasive indeed. Franklin Murphy, who had privately but fiercely supported Docking's opponent, faced what he hoped would be the only two-year term for the new governor-elect.[37] Though timing was crucial if the University of Kansas were to remain in the excellence race, Murphy believed that he would succeed. If nothing else, he said later, he confidently believed that he could ride out the two years without too much damage.[38]

Both men had crossed paths often, as Docking campaigned unsuccessfully in 1954 and successfully in 1956, and as Murphy travelled the state as chancellor. They both lived in Lawrence. Each was fully aware of the other. Murphy had tried to set the tone for the working relationship when, in August and November of 1956, he had written congratulatory letters to Docking, the successful candidate. Citing the experience of Edmund Muskie of Maine, who, like Docking, was a Democratic governor with a Republican legislature, Murphy urged the governor-elect to view the coming term as an opportunity for creative leadership, devoid of political infighting.[39]

Docking's personal responses do not survive, but his use of newspapers gives a fairly clear indication that Murphy's idea of creative leadership did not match his own.[40] Immediately, "the fur began to fly—to the delight of the press."[41] Newspaper reporters soon learned how to ask questions that prompted front-page stories and, according to Nichols, "the governor was his own press agent. He was endowed with a quick wit in reply to questions, even though at times his replies were unduly critical of individuals, in particular persons at the University of Kansas."[42]

Docking raised more than a few hackles even before he took office by using the press to speak to the Board of Regents. In a published letter, Docking asked a series of questions about the state system of higher education. "The questions literally ran the gamut," Nichols recalled, "ranging from philosophical issues to attempted interference with higher education."[43] By releasing the letter to the press before having asked the questions (whether "pertinent or impertinent") of the Regents or of the Legislature, Docking set the tone for the administration to come.[44] In defense, university and college administrators quickly became vocal, perhaps out of proportion to the importance of the questions.[45]

In a speech to the Greater University Fund Committee, in December 1956, Murphy vowed to defend the university's budget in the face of expected reductions by the new governor. Murphy warned that such actions would "dilute university education to the point where we are giving a trade school education. The next five years," he declared, "would determine if KU is to become a truly great university or is to drop back."[46]

The crisis at the crossroads and the crisis at the ballot box were one in the same—it would be a difficult two years for Franklin Murphy. Within three weeks of the election, the governor-elect had made his agenda clear. He had "inherited a state with no money," Docking said, and began a campaign of financial micro-management, a portion of which was directed at the University of Kansas.[47] He recommended enormous cuts in the university's budget, notably in the art museum, the library, and the Kansas Geological Survey.

This policy is understandable for a governor who knew that he could not succeed (and certainly could not be re-elected) by raising taxes. To avoid raising taxes, he needed to squeeze the money from some existing source, hence the micromanagement and the cutbacks. The university system, a fat calf indeed, constituted an easy place to begin. Unlike visible, local school districts, universities are rarely local and few voters across the state are close enough to see the blood or hear the cries of pain. After being inaugurated, Governor Docking spent the next year and one-half attempting to slice the higher-education budget and to generate new monies for the state. In February of 1957, for example, he suggested that part of the gate receipts from KU's athletic events (especially basketball) should go into the state's general fund.[48] In spite of Murphy's continuous work to bring legislators into the KU fold, the governor nipped continually at the KU budget.[49]

In 1960, for example, Governor Docking recommended substantial cuts to Regents' institutions budgets: Pittsburg State College asked for a total operating budget of $251,009 but the governor recommended $141,315.

"Dr. Murphy asked that the University of Kansas be given $9,323,000 recommended by the Regents. The Governor asked $8,606,000. The governor also asked for $76,391 less than the $3,711,000 recommended by the Regents for the University of Kansas Medical Center at Kansas City and Dr. Murphy requested the larger amount.[50]

While the governor searched for ways to trim the state's budget, the Republican-controlled legislature raised the right-to-work issue, dormant since the previous session, when a Republican caucus from the House of Representatives voted overwhelmingly to submit it to a statewide referendum. Let the people decide whether a worker must join a union, its members concluded. Both houses of the legislature followed suit. It would appear on the ballot as a proposed amendment (Amendment 3) to the Kansas Constitution. Even though the vote would not occur for many months, right-to-work raised emotions on both sides and debates began all over the state.[51]

On the KU campus, for example, faculty members began the right-to-work debates in December 1957, when John Ise, professor emeritus of economics, and Dan Hopson, Jr., assistant dean of the school of law, faced secretary-manager of the Lawrence Chamber of Commerce, E. R. Zook. On the question "Resolved: That Kansas should adopt the right-to-work amendment," Zook spoke for the affirmative and Ise and Hopson for the negative.[52] (Ise, one of Murphy's favorite teachers as a student, had been painted as a "leftist liberal"—though never "subversive"—during the Red-baiting paranoia of the early 1950s.[53] Zook was busy during the same 1957 period attempting to keep desegregation "gradual.") The debates were public and reported in the press. No evidence exists that Murphy concerned himself with the debate or with right-to-work at all. He was busy attempting to keep his vision before the public and his budget intact.

Murphy had been successful in persuading the Board of Regents to support his vision with a recommendation for increased funds. Early in Docking's term, the Regents had recommended a ten-percent pay hike for KU faculty and staff, double the five-percent increase included in the governor's budget. Docking countered by announcing the names of those faculty members who earned more than $750 per month, fully 115 individuals. (The average factory worker's take-home pay at the same time amounted to less than $300 a month.)[54] He pointed out that Murphy earned the highest salary of all— at $1,500 per month, plus housing.[55]

In spite of Docking's efforts, the Senate Ways and Means Committee recommended the ten-percent hike, thereby prolonging an issue that would embroil Murphy and the university for years to come. Murphy ultimately would win, but only through the strength of the Republican-controlled Senate and its effective Ways and Means Committee chairman, A. W. Lauterbach, a staunch Murphy ally.[56] "Finding and keeping top notch faculty members is a grim business these days," Murphy said. "With all the raids going on on our campus and other surrounding schools, I believe this is the worst period we have faced in a long time."[57]

In rapid succession, the governor found additional ways to attack the university. He proclaimed, for example, that all faculty travel requests henceforward would be approved by his office, instead of by the Board of Regents. He had found a part of a 1949 law that required his consent for out-of-state travel by faculty and intended to enforce it.[58] He cancelled two requests from faculty in the anatomy department who wished to attend a professional meeting in Washington D.C., charging the KU administration with "lack of co-operation in reducing travel expenses."[59]

"I hate to interfere with their management," Docking said, "but it is necessary when they can't manage themselves. This department has been so inefficient that something has to be done."[60] Murphy accused the governor of ignorance of the needs of the intellect, according to Griffin: "In any field you cannot keep up very long by locking yourself in a closet."[61]

Governor Docking next described college faculty members as underworked and overpaid, and called for a careful review of all programs that did not contribute directly to on-campus education.[62] And, he announced that, in the future, no university administrator would be permitted to address the legislative budget committees directly. Those budget presentations would be made by the Board of Regents, he said. The obvious result was to gag the chancellor, an effect not lost on students and other KU supporters.[63] On the day following the effective "gag order," the *Lawrence Journal World* reported Murphy's reaction to the governor's order, calling it "the first time Dr. Murphy has been publicly critical of any Docking action or comment." According to the newspaper, Murphy had reacted by saying:

> If the state school situation should develop as some would like to have it, Kansas indeed will have the best highways in the country. But they will merely serve as highways for the state's youth to drive to better education institutions in other states. There are those who evidently think Kansas can afford only a mediocre university or an "average" or "adequate" institution. But I maintain that Kansas cannot afford not to have the best possible state institutions. Otherwise, we will lose our outstanding young men and women to other states.[64]

Furious with the local newspaper, Murphy denied having criticized the governor, or having spoken to anyone from the *Lawrence Journal World*, and added:

> We face very complex and growing problems relating to education in Kansas. The complexity of the problems naturally lead to different points of view as to solution. All interested and responsible persons must co-operate in a statesman-like fashion to solve these problems to the end that Kansas youth is always guaranteed the highest quality of educational opportunity. Certainly I and the faculty of Kansas University intend to do just that as we always have tried to do.[65]

Throughout Docking's first year as governor, Murphy attempted to conduct business in a statesman-like manner, using logic and reason to persuade the politicians that the very future of the nation, if not the state, depended upon vision, not penny-pinching and back-biting. As was so often the case, Murphy turned to friends who edited Kansas newspapers. They were his spokesmen—they carried his vision to the people of Kansas. To Whitley Austin, editor of the Salina *Journal*, a firm Murphy supporter, and soon-to-be member of the Board of Regents, he explained his frustration: "It is ironic that in the middle of the 20th Century and the greatest scientific revolution the world has ever seen, one must still devote a substantial amount of time in defending the needs for the highest quality of higher education and research."[66]

As the second legislative session of Docking's term drew closer, the attempts by Murphy and the Regents to increase faculty salaries grew more heated. The Regents, led by its chairman McDill "Huck" Boyd, refused to retreat from its recommendation of 10 percent increases and the governor continued to find fault with the University of Kansas. As the session opened, Docking announced that he would support no increases until the "clutter of courses" should be cleaned out and the "faculty members squeaking around" the state universities should be fired.[67] He listed courses he would drop and departments with too many "squeakers."

In this, Docking the politician reflected the view of many voters, then and now, who cite the ubiquitous professor who is seen mowing his lawn at two in the afternoon and giving all the others a bad name while the rest of the taxpayers are at work. Docking used this fairly common perception among voters as an easy target. He said that the problem of faculty being lost to industry was not a problem of the faculty or its salaries, but rather a fault of the institution's administration. "The school budget is getting to be pure politics and the college administrators are getting to be nothing but politicians," Docking said. "We have to change the thinking of many of our administrators. We have to get them out of politics and back to the job they are supposed to do."[68]

Two days later, Murphy explained his bewilderment to Frank Theis, a Democrat and, later, a federal judge: "As you know, I have actually leaned over backward to keep out of politics and have always said that we dare not let our institutions become so involved. I have privately and publicly stated that I would never be a candidate for public office. I simply do not know how one can stay isolated from political affairs more than I have tried to do," he wrote, and continued:

> Needless to say, at a time when we are experiencing ever greater difficulty in keeping faculty and when we stand well behind competitive institutions, government and industry in salary scales, gratuitous insults to our faculty do not ease this problem. In any event, I stand again bewildered and puzzled. It is almost to the point that if these accusations are true I should be dismissed by the Board of Regents.[69]

In a *Kansas City Times* interview the next day, Murphy noted that many failed to comprehend why faculty members were being hired away from higher education. "If the U.S. is to survive the next 50 years as a first-rate power," Murphy said, "there must be a change in attitude toward the intellectual on the part of the American public. This is a plea for the egghead," he said, in a barely veiled attack on the governor. "The egghead has been maligned by the short-sighted fatheads in all fields."[70]

As early as 1953, Murphy's correspondence pounded out the same message. He wrote to Tom Kiene, managing editor of the *Topeka State Journal*, saying that the record shows beyond question that great universities are the product of great men and women:

> The question of recruiting and keeping first class teachers in our colleges and universities has become one of the most pressing problems of higher education. Men and women are prepared to make moderate financial sacrifices in order to satisfy their great desire to teach and do research in a

university. It is, however, unreasonable to expect them to make disproportionate sacrifices.

If we are not able to keep our fair share of the brains and skill of America in the colleges and the universities and if we continue to lose them in large numbers to industry and the professions, we run the grave danger of killing "the goose that lays the golden egg."[71]

It had become very personal and very heated, indeed. The next response came from the governor who said that his reported differences with Chancellor Murphy were not personal, but instead constituted "a battle between the salesman and the auditor." Docking, the auditor, once again put himself in the voters' place and spoke as the one who had been elected to guard the state coffers from such profligate spending as the University of Kansas chancellor proposed. Docking said that those legislators who are too "shallow minded" to see the differences in the two men's roles "are not mature enough."[72]

"Dr. Murphy and I have had no personal disagreements," he said to newsmen, "but we have disagreed on issues and methods of operations. Dr. Murphy has some good qualities, but some of his ideas cost the taxpayers. Those who think it a personal matter just aren't civilized enough to realize that people can differ on issues and still not be emotionally involved," the governor said.[73]

In spite of the extensive newspaper coverage of what appeared to be a running feud between himself and Docking, Murphy abhorred such public wrangling, but preferred to use his influence in quieter ways that would take him out of the spotlight held by Docking.[74] "Chancellor Murphy was a master of getting things done by others," according to Frank Burge, whom Murphy hired to manage the Kansas Union in 1951. "This is the mark of a true leader."[75] Although the chancellor traveled around the state often, he knew that his own voice would be insufficient in convincing voters in the state to support the changes that he considered so very important to the nation's future. He needed many other voices to speak for him—voices that had earned the respect of those who listened. Most often, he turned to newspaper editors, as had been his policy since the KU Med School days.

He knew, for example, that western Kansas viewed KU as radical and snobbish and that he would need to try to change that perception. To John McCormally, powerful editor of the *Hutchinson News*, Murphy sent an idea for a series of articles and offered to provide any statistical data that would be needed. He stated his purpose clearly:

Due to the interest especially of the *Kansas City Star*, Alvin McCoy, Dick Fowler, etc., we have no problem ... in keeping the eastern part of the state informed as to programs and problems at K.U. I am sure we are not nearly as successful in central and especially in western Kansas... Of course, the *Hutchinson News* is the key paper in the west-central and western parts of Kansas. I am thinking of more than merely news releases about people and specific things, and certainly far beyond athletics. I am thinking more of feature stories about programs in science, research, gifted students, foreign language developments and related matters, suggesting that the University of Kansas is moving forward with vigor. On the other hand, I am thinking also about stories suggesting some of our deficiencies and what we are trying to do and what our needs are in correcting them.

In short, how could we best develop a relationship with the *Hutchinson News* that would be continuous and mutually beneficial? Needless to say, I do not seek to propagandize but merely deal with the facts whether they stimulate pride or concern.[76]

Another important newspaper supporter was Marcellus Murdock, publisher of the *Wichita Eagle*. In the morning's *Eagle* Murdock wrote to congratulate Murphy for "that analysis of the university's needs," which he called "a stem-winder."[77] Murphy's response expressed his appreciation for "publishing our statement."[78]

Throughout Docking's first term, Murphy worked behind the scenes to promote his KU-as-outstanding agenda by using the methods he had found so useful of letting *others* speak for the university. Often, Murphy turned to his friends, especially to his Democratic friends, to attempt to override the governor, Murphy later acknowledged that these activities had made Docking furious.[79] It is no wonder that Docking was upset. People love to carry tales, especially when the result curries favor with the powerful. In spite of Murphy's attempts to stay outside the fray and to let others speak for him, surely at least some of his letters, statements, and comments got back to Docking.

One instance that backfired, at least for the messenger, arose when Murphy was approached by his college fraternity brother, Lewis Oswald, an active member of the Democratic party, former mayor, and attorney in Hutchinson. Oswald asked Murphy to comment on an article that Oswald intended to write.[80]

Indeed, Murphy commented and modified the copy, as Oswald had asked. Murphy added a section in praise of the other four state-supported institutions and then suggested that Oswald say: "I have used the University [of Kansas] as the prototype only because at the moment I am more familiar with its activities."[81] Murphy suggested that his friend Oswald insert the following into his article:

> But the point I rise to make is that we, Kansans, should and must insist that no unreasonable or illogical interference be visited on the heads of our state institutions and their distinguished faculties—for our youth, for our state and for the nation, time is too short and the implications too terrible to permit anything but unstinting support and understanding of the importance of these institutions to our future.
>
> After all, the men and women in Lawrence, Manhattan, Pittsburg, Emporia and Hays are not playing a little personal game for their own benefit. They are the main players in a game that involves the security of this country and the future standards of living of its people. They deserve positive support, not disinterest; they must have adequate funds, not pious platitudes.[82]

Oswald proved to be a loyal friend of KU. In May of 1958, a few months following his article, Oswald spoke to the Fifth District Young Democrats in Dodge City. His keynote speech blasted Democratic Governor George Docking for having "exhibited a vicious bitterness" and for threatening to "get rid of Chancellor Franklin D. Murphy of the University of Kansas." Docking's attempt to get rid of Murphy was not an idle threat. Docking had said publicly that he was not sure that the state was getting its money's worth with Murphy, and the chancellor knew of the governor's efforts.[83] One day early in 1958, Murphy went into the office of the Dean of the university, George Baxter Smith, put his feet on the chair and pushed back his hat. "I think this guy Docking's going to get me fired," Murphy said.[84]

Oswald claimed that he had personally talked the governor out of firing Murphy at the executive mansion late one night in January 1958. "The Governor came panting into the parlor, threw down his top-coat, and exclaimed, I am going to blow hell out of that little punk tomorrow'."[85] The same evening, Docking told Oswald that he had considered appointing Oswald to the Board of Regents, but had decided against it because Oswald was a friend of Murphy.[86]

Docking did not fire Murphy, but the word spread. The governor attempted to put down the rumors of a potential firing, responding to a reporter that he would not fire the chancellor even if he could.[87] Nichols verified Oswald's claim, years later, saying that Oswald had told Murphy that George Docking was vindictive because he had never been invited to KU affairs. "They snubbed me," Docking told Oswald. "Time and time again he [Murphy] could have invited me to University affairs, and he snubbed me."[88]

In calling on Docking to desist, Oswald said: "We Kansas Democrats do not want a personal government with all of its latent possibilities of oppression, favoritism and caprice."[89] While he mentioned Murphy and the University of Kansas, Oswald's speech centered on Docking's failure to follow the advice of other party leaders with regard to state appointments. However well-intentioned, Oswald's efforts quite naturally created additional tension between Murphy and Docking. And, it did not serve Oswald particularly well, either. Oswald's attack on his party's leader was seen as the "remarks of a bitterly disappointed man who expected to be the vice-governor of Kansas," according to a national committeeman of the Democratic Party.[90]

Docking did not step aside, but instead announced his intention of running for a second term. No Democrat in the history of the state had won a second term as governor.[91] With Docking firmly in the 1958 race, Murphy doubled his behind-the-scenes efforts on behalf of another candidate. While continuing to court the pro-KU speakers and the newspaper editors, he began to work extremely closely with Clyde Reed, Jr., one of the several August-primary candidates who might oppose Docking in the upcoming November election. Murphy's own name had been mentioned often as a candidate, as had that of Attorney General John Anderson, former governor Fred Hall, and El Dorado publisher Rolla Clymer.[92] Murphy's choice, however, was Clyde Reed.

Reed was one of those newspapermen with whom Murphy had kept in close touch. In late March of 1958, Murphy wrote to Reed in response to the candidate's query about an upcoming campaign speech in Troy, Kansas. Murphy urged his friend to "start talking about 'The roaring '60s'"—a reference to the "fact that industrial leaders throughout the country are predicting an era of unprecedented industrial prosperity and expansion during the '60s," he wrote, and continued:

The point here is that in order to be prepared to share in this development, we must get ready now. This then leads into all of the matters of education, research, vocational education ....

On the other hand, when you speak out in the wheat country in the west, rather than emphasizing [the] food processing industry, I would talk most about agriculture and industrial research leading to industrial uses of agricultural products. In every case, however, I would keep emphasizing "The roaring '60s" concept.[93]

Clearly supportive of Murphy and KU, Reed spoke early and often against the governor's treatment of Murphy, in particular, and education, in general. He charged, for example, that the Docking administration's attitude toward schools is "full of tragic libels against the dedicated men and women devoting their lives to your education and to the education of all young people."[94] Pledging his "full and untiring support" to the educational system of Kansas, Reed lambasted Docking for referring to teachers and professors as "underworked and overpaid." The people of Kansas cannot afford, he said, "a 1910 government in the atomic age."[95]

Reed and Murphy worked hard to focus the 1958 campaign on higher education and the need for funds to support it. The majority of Kansans, however, were interested in another topic—right-to-work. Both gubernatorial candidates, incumbent George Docking and *Parsons Sun* publisher Clyde Reed, Jr., opposed it.[96] Reed would not state an opinion, leaving the issue of right-to-work "to the will of the people," but his newspaper, *The Parsons Sun*, had attacked the proposed amendment. His no-stand stand is not particularly surprising in that his home area, southeastern Kansas, traditionally voted Democratic and comprised a vocal proportion of union members. However, those voters were few in number. It is rather surprising that Republican Reed was accepted by so many as a strong candidate in light of his silence on an issue that most Republicans favored.

Regardless of the lukewarm commitment of both candidates to such an emotional issue, the party lines were clear: the Democratic Party opposed right-to-work and the Republicans favored it. Moreover, although it was not a presidential-election year, the turnout was expected to be heavy. The right-to-work issue *could* determine the outcome, if it generated enough interest. Right-to-work was the hottest issue in the campaign. Predicting a close vote, Kansas editors concluded two weeks before the election that it probably would pass.[97]

Votes in favor would come from the less-populous, more-conservative rural districts, while those opposing right-to-work would come from the populous industrial areas. "Many voters," the editors said, "are keeping silent while the tempest by vocal opponents is raging around their heads."[98] Neither gubernatorial candidate directly tied his campaign to the right-to-work issue, calling it "one of those emotional things" that could be the deciding factor in a close election.[99] Murphy believed that the paramount question in the 1958 campaign should have centered on the candidates' level of support for higher education, and he concentrated his efforts on it. To him "the crossroads—a crisis" had grown much worse than it had been in November 1956, when he first used the words. He certainly believed that the 1958 election would spell either success or utter mediocrity for KU. He could not accept the latter option.

To Murphy, in fact, the future of the nation depended on its commitment to higher education. He had spent three weeks in Russia during the summer of 1957 and had been impressed and frightened by that nation's commitment to education. Shortly thereafter, in October 1957, the Russians orbited Sputnik, and Murphy's speeches dealt overwhelmingly with the need for increased efforts in American education. He laid out the argument over and over. "The Russian Sputnik is a Pearl Harbor for American Education," he warned. "We are in a position of world leadership and must deal with people who do not look like us or think like us. We must gain the knowledge for this."[100] That knowledge costs money, Murphy told his audiences. Now is not the time to retreat from the investment in higher education—now is the time to double it. "If we continue to measure things in the amount of alcohol, tobacco or motor cars that can be purchased, we will be working in the next 50 years for someone who has out-thought us," he said, in one of many pleas for a change in public attitude toward the American intellectual. "It will be impossible for American universities and colleges to compete with Russia without it," he said.[101]

Although never in public print, he definitely preferred the moderate Republican, thoroughly supportive publisher Clyde Reed, Jr. to the "enormously abusive" standing governor, George Docking, with whom he had tried to work, with little success, for nearly two years.[102] 1958 was a vital campaign. Reed supported the University of Kansas and Murphy's vision of its leadership role. Docking did not.

In Murphy's view, Docking's policies concentrated at best on "alcohol, tobacco and motor cars," instead of on the desperate need to strengthen America's ability to compete with mind power. He did not relish the prospect of another Docking term—the first had been difficult enough. The two previous years had taught the chancellor that Docking would use every avenue to undercut the University of Kansas, in general, and Franklin Murphy, in particular.

Although the true reasons for Docking's vehement opposition to Murphy and to KU are unclear, many potential explanations exist.[103] It could rest, for example, on the realities of Kansas politics. In order for a Democrat to win statewide office, that individual must garner all the Democrats' and a healthy share of Republicans' votes. This fact is especially true in the solidly Republican western half of the state. Furthermore, western Kansas historically has favored Kansas State University over the University of Kansas. Perhaps Docking's anti-KU message was a concerted effort to draw to his campaign those western Kansas Republicans who distrusted KU and viewed it as an enclave of liberal professors and snobbish Kansas City coeds.

Perhaps Docking, a Lawrence native, considered it necessary to show no favoritism to his hometown university. More likely, Docking felt no favoritism at all toward Lawrence, a community that had never supported him—neither in his unsuccessful race against Fred Hall in 1954, nor in his 1956 race against Warren Shaw. Without question, he did not like the leadership of either the *Lawrence Journal World*, which he referred to as "that self-styled newspaper," or the Lawrence Chamber of Commerce.[104]

Perhaps Docking distrusted Murphy because he considered the young and articulate chancellor a formidable political rival. After all, Murphy had been asked to run for the governorship since 1952 and his name had been included among those who might challenge Docking in the 1958 campaign.[105] In public and in private, Murphy consistently denied interest in such political races:[106]

> The most important reason [for refusing to consider elective office] is that I have a great dedication to the conviction that we can here build at the University of Kansas one of the truly significant institutions of higher learning in the United States. With every passing year I am more convinced that this is possible, and indeed I believe we are making consistent strides in this direction. In the long run—that is to say over a twenty-year span—I am firmly convinced that my few talents, whatever they are, can most effectively be brought to bear on behalf of the state of Kansas and this entire mid-western area by way of my present responsibility rather than any other.[107]

Years later he explained that he felt lucky to have realized very early that he could be much more effective by standing outside politics.[108]

Franklin Murphy and the men around him attributed Docking's actions and personal attacks on Murphy to fundamental differences between the two men. "Franklin was urbane and wealthy," Raymond Nichols said. "He was well-connected and thoroughly respected across the state, and in many circles, across the country. President Eisenhower and Winston Churchill were his personal friends. George Docking— even as governor— lacked everything that came to Franklin Murphy quite naturally."[109]

Perhaps the two men clashed because Murphy had supported Shaw, Docking's opponent in the 1956 election. Maybe it was due to a combination of reasons: after all, Lawrence in the 1950s was a small town and Docking was a small-town Kansas banker. Into Lawrence strode Franklin Murphy, son of a concert pianist and a famed physician, top in his class at Penn, and the dynamo cover-boy of national magazines and savior of the KU Medical Center before he was thirty-five. His friends were powerful men in Kansas City, he actually loved opera, and he read dictionaries for fun.[110] Nearly everyone described him as charming. Perhaps Franklin Murphy intimidated George Docking. Certainly there was a personality clash between the two men.

"The Docking story," Murphy said, later, "is interesting and sad." He described Docking as "a very difficult man: a real loner, who was not a team player. The result was that Docking was not involved in town; he was not invited to join athletic and other events. From the day he took office," Murphy said, "Docking went after KU. Because I was the symbol of KU, he went after me—over and over."[111]

Chancellor Murphy had to cover all the bases. While feting legislators and commenting on candidate's speeches, he appealed to groups of natural supporters, just as he had done with the Kansas Farm Bureau in the rural-physician effort of the late-1940s. To C.O. Wright, the executive secretary of the Kansas State Teachers' Association, Murphy wrote a typical plea for support in thanks for the publication of a series of Murphy-supplied articles. He urged Wright to consider using the last two paragraphs on page forty-one of the October 14th issue of *Look Magazine*, and concluded:

> Off the record, you will be interested in an impression that continually grows on me. I have just returned from a full day's visit to southwest Kansas [Garden City] where I found among

our representatives, farmers and businessmen a new, serious interest in our problems in education in Kansas and a determination to solve them. I get the same general word from a member of our Board of Regents who lives in northwest Kansas. *[McDill "Huck" Boyd].* The thing that really frustrates me is that apparently our leadership is way behind the people, and we somehow must do something about it. Again I emphasize that the above comment is strictly between you and me.[112]

Murphy worked closely not only with Clyde Reed, the Republican candidate, but also with legislators who wished to promote the Murphy vision. In his correspondence one finds letters to and from legislators. A typical sampling appears in the account of the 1959-60 efforts to generate construction funds on campus.

With the 1958 election one month away, Murphy was attempting to keep himself and those directly connected to the university out of the conflict. He had managed to do that fairly well until KU students created new headlines and generated renewed anger from Governor Docking.[113] On September 30th, a busload of KU Young Republicans picketed a Democratic fundraiser in Leavenworth, carrying signs and handing out Reed-for-Governor folders in front of the hotel and in its lobby. One of the students handed a folder to Governor Docking and asked: "Why don't you vote for the next governor of Kansas?"[114] Angered by the picketers, Docking heard one of the students being addressed as "Joe Reed," of Topeka.[115] "Oh," the governor shouted, "you must be the illegitimate son of the Republican candidate."[116] Newspaper accounts noted that the governor was grabbed quickly by his people and led inside. On the students' return to Lawrence, the bus was stopped by Leavenworth Sheriff's deputies, who described their search of the bus as "a routine check for ICC and KCC registration."[117] A full year later, in the heat of the most virulent attacks on Murphy, Docking's temper had not cooled over the Leavenworth affair.

The incident cast KU students in a bad light. Murphy hadn't counted on belligerent students (in an age of docile, conforming youth) to create additional anti-KU headlines.[118] Try as he might to keep himself and the University of Kansas out of direct conflict in the gubernatorial race, Murphy was finding the going tense indeed.

It was a tight race—it could go either way. During the final days of the campaign, Murphy wanted the university to be seen by the voters as beneficial, as an island of reason, as the best hope for the future, as deserving of a governor who would support it. He needed no more student rallies to grab headlines, if Reed were to win. Murphy needed to control any references to KU. Having spent an increasingly greater proportion of his professional time on public relations, attempting to extract money from the state legislature, Murphy knew that he should have done more— because of a "frankly hostile and profoundly reactionary governor who believes that most educational effort is unnecessary."[119] But there was no time. With only one week before the election, polls conducted by *The Salina Journal* and *The Hutchinson News* (covering more than half the state's counties) indicated a neck-and-neck race for the governor's seat.[120]

Throughout the campaign, Murphy had centered his efforts on the role of and support of higher education. Without question, Murphy did not expect that such labor debates as right-to-work would embroil the University of Kansas. He considered that issue peripheral to the larger, education-based political issues that had filled his time for nearly two years.[121] But right-to-work embroiled the campus indeed. With it came a memorable test of Murphy's philosophy— of the university as the free marketplace of ideas—and illustrated the often-conflicting roles that a university chancellor must balance. As that free marketplace, the university community had debated the issue of right-to-work during 1957. In September of 1958, the Governmental Research Center of the University of Kansas published an issue of its regular newsletter, *Your Government*, "issued as a public service." This particular edition laid out the "unbiased facts without emotionalism" on the question of the right-to-work amendment—No. 3 on the ballot. Attributed to Chester Newland, research assistant, and carrying the union label (as did everything published by the State printer), the two-page, September 15th bulletin was sponsored, it said, by the Voluntary Committee of Kansas Clergy and Educators Opposed to Amendment No. 3. "READ IT BEFORE YOU DECIDE," it urged boldly, just before offering reprints from the University of Kansas Governmental Research Center.[122]

During the pre-election month of October, more faculty members joined the campus fray, solidly and vocally in opposition: Clifford Ketzel, assistant professor of political science, announced a straw poll of his classes;[123] John Grumm, another assistant professor of political science, was interviewed by the campus newspaper and spoke in opposition;[124] and Charles Oldfather, Jr., professor of law, blasted Amendment 3 as "false, misleading, and deceptive."[125] Groups and individuals all over the state were organizing to support or defeat the amendment, using full-page ads to tell their stories.[126]

Evidence of one such effort arrived in Chancellor Murphy's hands on October 28, (just eight days before the election) when he received copies of two letters relating to the right-to-work issue from his friend Kenneth Spencer, President of Spencer Chemical Company and member of the very loyal KU-benefactor Spencer family.

The first, written on October 6th and addressed to J. Earl Schaefer, vice chairman of the Boeing Company in Wichita, comprised an attack not only on Schaefer, but also on the business community in general. It was written by George D. Bell, County Superintendent of Public Instruction for Wyandotte County, the strongest labor-union area in the state. "You and your side," Superintendent Bell wrote in closing, "have fought every movement that tended to give more of that dollar to the masses of people. You cover up your motives with high-sounding talk that is a lie to your real interest, and I hope you are whipped on November 4th. By the way, I shall be voting NO!"[127]

The second letter that Spencer sent to Murphy was a copy of Schaefer's three-page response to Superintendent Bell. After stating his case in favor of the right-to-work amendment and for the need of educators, like Bell, to help their students understand the role of business in a democracy, Schaefer continued with a litany of his individual and company attempts to discharge their responsibilities to the state's educational system:

> A check of the records will show that I was partially responsible for the acquisition of the Science Building by the University of Kansas, and that I was active not only in the University of Kansas Endowment Association, but also in many other organizations dedicated to improving our educational systems and programmes.[128]

Schaefer noted the scholarships his company had given to Kansas colleges and universities, including the University of Kansas, and told of his assistance "just this week, to the Dean of the School of Architecture at the University of Kansas. It seems to me that those responsible for educating our youth must have a clear and concise understanding of the needs, functions, and motives of business," he concluded. "That you apparently do not have this understanding is the reason for my concern."[129]

Schaefer had copied and mailed both letters to some of the most powerful men in the state, most of whom were conservative Republicans, friends of one another and friends of Franklin Murphy.[130]

More importantly, all were exceedingly important to the University of Kansas.[131] Few could have been more important, in fact, than Schaefer or than Kansas Citians Kenneth Spencer (who had sent the package to him), Harry Darby, and Willard Breidenthal, all of whom had received the exchange of correspondence two weeks earlier.

Years before in late 1951, Schaefer introduced Murphy's ideas to Schaefer's first-name-basis friend, General Dwight Eisenhower.[132] On January 24, 1952, Eisenhower wrote to Schaefer about Murphy. "I read the memorandum written by Chancellor Murphy," Eisenhower wrote, "and found that he was stating authoritatively what had been, for a long time, hazy impressions of mine .... The first time I get back to Kansas, I shall hope to have a real discussion with him."[133] The relationship that followed had a profound impact on Murphy and his career, in particular, and on the University of Kansas, in general.

Schaefer had been correct in his litany of services to KU (in spite of a near break with Murphy over the latter's objections to allowing Wichita University to enter the Regents' system).[134] He served as chairman of the board of the KU Research Foundation and, in November 1954, he gave the keynote speech at the opening of the Physical Sciences building. The newspaper account noted that "Mr. Schaefer played an important role in the construction of the building by telling the legislature of the need for first-class science teaching and research facilities."[135] In March 1955, he instructed Lynn Whiteside, Boeing's Training Director, to take "initial steps toward a more intensified coordination between Boeing Airplane Company and mid-western colleges."[136] Julius Earl Schaefer was a man to whom Franklin Murphy listened.

Another was Harry Darby, a close friend of President Eisenhower, a U.S. Senator, a Republican National Committeeman, and one of the most influential Kansas City citizens. The Darby family stood as one of the University's most loyal supporters: family members would contribute immensely, especially to athletic programs. The Darby family, for example, later would commission the athletic mural room in the "Boots" Adams Alumni Center.[137]

Kansas City, Kansas, banker Breidenthal was the brother of Maurice Breidenthal, who had served as chairman of the Kansas University Endowment Association since 1952 and as a trustee for 30 years. Maurice Breidenthal stood as the man most responsible for the initiation and growth of the Greater University Fund, Murphy's primary source of private monies—the kitty that bought the books and art and distinguished faculty upon which he insisted.

Kenneth Spencer, founder of the Spencer Chemical Company, had been a member of the Endowment Association's Executive Committee since 1950.[138] Later, both the University of Kansas' Spencer Research Library and Spencer Museum of Art would be built from bequests of the family.

Murphy could not afford to alienate this important group—this core of donors that represented one of the four sources of university funds. In fact, he acknowledged that private contributions rather than increased state support should provide the financial base for support of university excellence.[139] He spoke to those who served on the Greater University Fund in March 1957: "If the University is to continue to grow, the present program of channeling private funds for various school purposes into areas not covered by state funds must be increased. Unless we can continue to expand our tradition of private support, we can be accused of being naive in expecting KU to grow."[140]

At this moment in late 1958, just before an election that might result in substantial losses of state revenue for KU, the sources of private funds were particularly vital. In a cover letter, Spencer wrote Murphy that he considered the Bell letter alarming. "I was distressed that this situation could exist in my own native State of Kansas." "Is there any remedy from the standpoint of public opinion? What can be done to bring this situation to light?"[141]

Franklin Murphy, a man who gave serious consideration to public opinion, generally, and to that of KU's staunch supporters, in particular, was in no position to give his exclusive attention to Spencer's inquiry. A challenge of much greater magnitude had surfaced—the day before, Murphy had received correspondence from Wichita that would hit the Kansas City papers at any moment. The correspondence included copies of a large anti-right-to-work advertisement, published in the *Wichita Eagle* and soon to appear in newspapers all over the state.[142] Most disturbingly, it was signed by 25 University of Kansas faculty members who had identified themselves as such.[143] The signers were C.H. Oldfather, Harold Baumgartel, Elliot C. Dick, J. Elden Field, Edward Grier, John G. Grumm, Marvin Harder, Dan Hopson, Jr., Paul E. Wilson, George G. Worth, Clifford Ketzel, Roy D. Laird, Earl Nehring, Edward G. Nelson, James E. Titus, E. J. Baur, W. J. Argersinger, Jr., Robert Vosper, Ambrose Saricks, James E. Seaver, Charles E. Staley, Jacob Kleinberg, F. J. Moreau, James K. Logan, and William A. Kelly.

"It was a slap in the face," Murphy said.[144] Focused on the intricacies of a very public confrontation with Governor George

Docking, just days before an election that would spell success or failure for his vision for the University of Kansas, Murphy was shaken. The problem was the impact of this advertisement on his carefully constructed network of supporters, many of them potential donors, wealthy and conservative Republicans, most of whom supported the right-to-work amendment and who had been brought, with such hard work, into the University of Kansas fold.

Why would the right-to-work issue, only one of several topics discussed in the election, be so critically important to Franklin Murphy? As the leader of the university, he understood his constituencies. He understood the men on whom he relied to donate the money that must be raised in increased amounts if he were to balance the funds sure to be lost from the state. He knew they were conservative. Murphy must have understood the importance of athletics to some individuals of this sort—it gave them a close tie that had nothing to do with the ideologies they disliked, but which were always lurking beneath the surface, in any university. Athletics might take their minds off the distasteful things that the left-leaning liberals were doing on campus. The wealthy, conservative potential donors could tolerate a few crazies, if they were not reminded too often of the liberal connection to *their* university.

However, every once in awhile an issue comes along that they just can't abide. Right-to-work was such an issue. It was a litmus test: a knock-down-drag-out fight between business and labor unions. These men were the leaders of business. They might pass off a few belligerent students as a necessary evil in a large university, but they would not overlook the university's involvement in right-to-work. It was not difficult to imagine the impact of 39 column inches strongly opposing Amendment No. Three, and filled with names and titles, nearly half of whom were identified as professors at the University of Kansas.

Murphy received the first copy from John Boyer, a Wichita attorney. Beginning with his "considerable embarrassment" and ending with his "disgust," Boyer's letter centered on his "regret that the feature portion of the endorsement is always the "University of Kansas.""[145]

The advertisement, signed by 54 clergymen and educators across the state, urged voters to "say no to Amendment 3." Extremely visible, the huge, black-bordered ad drew the reader's eye with "SAY NO" in inch-high bold type. The group had devised the ad after forming a committee earlier in the year. This was the same group that had sponsored the September 15th edition of *Your Government*, a University of Kansas publication, just one month earlier. Now, in October, the committee sent a policy paper and a copy of the ad to groups and individuals across the state, mailed to arrive at the same time the advertisement appeared.[146] The cover letter urged readers to examine the attached explanation for its opposition to the amendment, which statement "appeals, as it should, to reason rather than to emotion. We think it of the utmost importance that as many of us as possible, who have no axe to grind in this controversy, make our position known to the people of Kansas, and particularly to those people in Kansas who are looked to for informed opinions on matters of legal and political controversy." The printed letterhead included the names, titles, and institutional affiliation of 28 individuals, most of whom were KU professors.[147]

The statement explained six areas of opposition, concerns that encompassed the varying arguments against right-to-work as a constitutional amendment. According to the ad, it had been "paid for by the The Voluntary Committee of Kansas Clergy and Educators Opposed to Amendment No. 3," but it seemed to have been funded largely by a Wichita-based union.[148]

Murphy said that he did not mind at all that the 25 KU faculty members opposed the measure, or even, he said, that they had signed the ad.[149] But he was very angry indeed that the University of Kansas faculty members had identified themselves as such.[150] Murphy knew that a great university must have a great endowment, must attract students, and must keep itself outside the public political arena. The chancellor also knew that this advertisement carried the message to many readers that *the university* opposed the legislation—that it had taken sides in a divisive election issue. He spent several days trying to control the damage. Immediately on learning of the ad, Murphy responded to John Boyer:

> Thank you for your letter of October 23, with the clipping from the Wichita Eagle enclosed. I had not known of the existence of this right-to-work advertisement until you sent it along. It is signed, as you note, by a group of clergy and educators, 25 of whom are members of the faculty of the University of Kansas. I would comment as follows.
>
> In the first place, I regret that members of our faculty have permitted themselves to get *publicly* involved in this controversy. If any one of them had talked with me about the matter prior to their agreeing to participate, I would have

advised strongly against it. Furthermore, although I am not privy to any of the facts, I cannot believe that this advertising effort has been "paid for by the voluntary committee of Kansas clergy and educators opposed to Amendment No. 3."

I am glad that you observe that members of a faculty of a university are entitled to express their opinions on matters such as this quite as freely as any other citizen. I have always felt that no faculty member should be penalized in the matter of free expression merely because he is a member of a university faculty. He should have the same rights as any other citizen, regardless of employment.

University administrators, however, have been struggling for years on a question which is still moot and I suspect will be so forever—namely, whether a faculty member has a right to use his title and his association with the university in such matters. One point of view, of course, has always held that he has the same right to identify his occupation and basis of experience (or lack of it) as a man who is president of a corporation, a minister, or independently employed as a professional man. The other side of this argument, of course, is related to whether or not one can do this without implying approval by the organization itself. There can, however, be no question, in my judgment at least, about the right of any citizen to state his views on a matter of this sort either publicly or privately, no matter how foolish it may be.

Another point that must be considered is that, regardless of how each of us feels in the matter of the right-to-work amendment, it must be admitted to all that this is a controversial matter and one in which quite properly substantial differences of opinion exist. Indeed, across the country one can identify a variety of sound, decent and objective persons who have diametrically opposite opinions in this matter. I know a number of people on this faculty who propose to vote for the right-to-work amendment, but in that group I can identify at least three basic but different reasons on which they will base their vote for the amendment. By the same token, those whom I know who are opposed to the amendment also have differing reasons. For example, some of our Law School faculty feel very keenly that a bad precedent will be established if issues of this sort must be made the subject of a constitutional amendment rather than legislative statute. It is, I think quite a mistake to reduce this ultimately and exclusively to simple a vote for or against labor.

But the main point I would wish to make is that 25 members of the faculty of the University of Kansas at Lawrence signed the advertisement. This is 25 out of 440 full-time members of the faculty at Lawrence, or approximately 6%. In other words, 94% of the full-time faculty of the University are not listed in this advertisement. Although it would be quite as wrong to state that 94% of the faculty are for the amendment as to state that the advertisement represents the position of the University, it is still a fact, in my judgment, that the vote here at the University on this matter will roughly approximate the final total vote in the state of Kansas.

Let me re-state that which I have said many times before. A university, to be worthy of bearing that name, must be a "free market-place of ideas". If freedom of expression (of course within the broad ground rules of good taste and the Constitution of the United States) is not to be found in the great universities of this country, history suggests then that it would not be long until freedom of expression would be denied to everyone, except of course those in the ultimate position of political power.

On nearly every subject from alcohol to foreign policy and from the role of the labor union to the role of the business organizations you can find broad diversity of opinion among this faculty. This is of course predictable as long as we maintain ourselves in the position of a university and do not fall into the stultifying tradition of trade school.

Let me be very clear that I am not in any sense trying to justify the position on right-to-work which these 25 members of the faculty have taken. Indeed, I have spent a good many hours arguing the matter with some of them. I am simply saying that members of the faculty, like all other loyal Americans, have a right to an opinion and a free expression thereof. I am, however, vigorously noting the fact that only 6% of the full-time faculty of the University of Kansas at Lawrence are so identified publicly and that this can by no stretch of the imagination be construed as University endorsement. In fact, it can only be said that a small minority of the faculty are against right-to-work as far as the public record is concerned.

Although I would not wish my letter to be used in the public press, I am taking the liberty of sending copies of it to others who have queried me concerning this matter.[151]

Murphy called first on his publisher friends. "I could pick up the phone and talk to my many schoolmates who owned Kansas papers, " he said.[152] "And that was the end of that."[153] He fired off a news release setting out the university's policy, dated October 30, 1958, but sent to many publishers earlier:

It has been brought to my attention that 25 of the 440 full-time faculty members of the University of Kansas have associated themselves with others in the sponsorship of an advertisement running in Kansas newspapers in opposition to the right-to-work amendment.

It has been suggested that this sponsorship implies a position of the University of Kansas itself. I have been asked to clarify this matter. "It is the traditional policy of the University that a member of this faculty has the same rights and privileges as any other free American to express his personal point of view on matters of public policy. To deny a faculty member this right would impose an unreasonable and unfair restriction of this rights as a citizen.

On the other hand, the University of Kansas as an institution never takes a position, pro or con, on such matters and it is not doing so now. I am quite sure that the 25 members of our faculty who have signed this advertisement never intended that it be thought they were speaking for anyone except themselves as individuals.

(Signed) Franklin D. Murphy
Chancellor, University of Kansas[154]

As angry letters poured in, he sought to make the best use of the little time remaining before the election. First, firmly dispel the fears of the influential and then attempt to *guide* the controversy among the general public, many of whom might be brought back to a consideration of the nation's need to invest heavily in higher education, which translated into strong-gubernatorial support for KU. Those whose minds he obviously could not change would be answered last—whether they opposed KU fundamentally, whether they had supported KU and were angry about its faculty's involvement in the right-to-work issue, or whether they were die-hard Democrats who would support Docking in any case.

Murphy set into motion a campaign of personal letters, accompanied by the formal statement, that went out within just a few days to the congressional delegation, the legislators, the Regents, the leaders of the alumni and endowment associations, and to Kenneth Spencer, Earl Schaefer, and all the others who had sent clippings and angry letters.[155]

On Thursday, October 30, Chancellor Murphy moderated a Kansas Union Ballroom debate that he considered vital to the university. It featured two state senators (Democrat Joseph McDowell and Republican Donald S. Hults) and the topic was Governor George Docking's attitude toward aid to education. This was the most important issue for Murphy—he had spent a full year dealing with little else. Originally planned as a Political Emphasis Week debate between Docking and Reed, the event changed when both candidates cancelled on October 18th.[156] By the 30th, interest wasn't high and only 50 individuals attended the debate in the 700-capacity hall.[157]

Although he was disappointed with the turnout, Murphy moderated the meeting, and was angry during the entire event. He could think of little else than his meeting the next day with the 25 men who had signed the ad, and with the Board of Regents shortly thereafter.[158] On Friday, the 31st, Murphy had Dean George Baxter Smith convene the faculty signers in his conference room, where he let them have it.[159] "We went in there at high noon and got a verbal spanking," according to Paul Wilson, then associate professor of law and one of the signers. Only Murphy and those he would chastise were in the room. "This is a family gathering," Murphy said, "and you've let us down![160] Any faculty member has a right to say whatever he wants," Murphy remembered saying to the group, "but you damned well can't wrap yourself in the flag of the university!" He said that he really spanked their faces ("verbally, at least") for using this strategy.[161]

To the newspapers, later, Murphy said that he had called the 25 men together to get the facts, not to censure them.[162] "There was no fist-shaking, shouting scene of the sort popularly imagined when a university head calls a meeting. The chancellor neither censured nor censored, but simply got the facts and explained the University's position," according to an editorial later.[163] Ambrose Saricks remembered it differently. "He didn't conduct himself in a calm manner at all," he said, "or in a manner that showed much leadership. He lost his head."[164]

The two men who worked most closely with Murphy on a day-to-day basis, Ray Nichols and George Baxter Smith, would have been surprised at Saricks' impression of Murphy's anger. Even though he often described himself as a "wild Irishman" and as "going up through the ceiling like an Irish skyrocket,"[165] Murphy seemed rarely to have let his anger get the better of him. "I never saw him lose his temper,"[166] Smith said, and Nichols agreed.[167] However, neither man was in the conference room that day. Regardless of the tone, the message was clear to all who *were* in the room: the chancellor said clearly that he agreed that each person has every right to speak for themselves in public, but *not as the university*. "Irv Youngberg will have to close up shop!" Murphy said, referring to the executive secretary of the KU Endowment Association.[168]

Balancing the dual roles as leader of his faculty and leader of his donors posed an incredible challenge. For these 25 professors to put their chancellor in such a box made Murphy very angry, he said. "You had no right to sign any such ad, especially under union auspices,"[169] he said, grilling the group on their knowledge of the ad's alleged sponsor. The labor unions, Murphy was convinced, had paid for the ads. He referred to a late-October article in *New York Times* outlining the intensive work by AFL-CIO to defeat right-to-work legislation. According to the *Time*,

> "The National Council (of labor) has really hurled itself into this bitter fight. Its liaison with the AFL-CIO is Andy Biemiller, the labor organization's Congressional contact. He and Redding are constantly on the road. They've hit most of the six states— California, Kansas, Colorado, Idaho, Ohio and Washington. In each of these states there is a central committee of citizens—under various names."[170]

Charles Oldfather, associate professor of law and chairman of the steering committee that sponsored the ad, told the *University Daily Kansan* later that "the Kansas Federation of Labor gave the organization $10,000 with no strings attached. Most of the money was used for political advertising."[171]

As the university had not been faced with a similar situation before, neither it nor the Kansas Board of Regents had formulated a policy to guide faculty members' public identification with the institution. The faculty had broken no rules, but merely had used exceedingly poor judgment, in Murphy's opinion, especially in light of the tense situation between KU and the governor. He had formulated a policy that he intended to present to the Regents immediately after this meeting and he now presented it to the faculty gathered in the conference room—speak your mind in public on any issue but do not use the name of the university. Many of those who signed the ad agreed that Murphy's suggested policy was correct. "Certainly any controversial political matter whereby the individual's use of the University's name might be read or misused to indicate that this is University policy is unwise" Roy Laird, for example, said. "I do not think that the advertisement... should have been so construed, but apparently many people who wrote Chancellor Murphy thought it was." Like others, Laird agreed that the use of one's title alone, without the institutional name, carries sufficient authority to make a personal impact on political matters.[172] E. Jackson Baur, associate professor of sociology, said that "as long as a person is identified as a professor living in Lawrence, there would not be much doubt that he is affiliated with the University."[173] And from John G. Grumm, who had been vocal on the issue for several months, came agreement with Murphy: "In the future I will not involve the University," he said. "It is important that the professors be identified by title in an advertisement of that type, but the chancellor's requirement is reasonable."[174]

On the same afternoon, in Topeka, the Board of Regents agreed as well. Later its president, McDill "Huck" Boyd, would explain it carefully. "Faculty members can publicly ascribe to any campaign issue or cause as long as they do so without involving the use of the name of the University," he said. "The Board of Regents has always encouraged faculty members to be active in public affairs because it is a sign of good citizenship," he said, describing the Regents' new policy on political involvement. "We think when a faculty member becomes a precinct committeeman, library board member, or has any other non-paying political job it is good. But the board draws the line when it comes to paid political jobs and where the institution is involved."

By November 3, the day before the election, Murphy and his staff appeared to have covered all of the bases. With so many angry letters to answer, they had resorted to the 1958 state-of-the-art response. In

1958, Murphy's three secretaries sent out mimeographed form letters, each of which opened with a name typed into a blank space and which was signed by Murphy's stamp.

The difference between the letter to Boyer, on October 25th, and this November 3rd form letter is the difference between an instant response and one that had been considered carefully for its audience, its timing, and its impact. He wrote on November 3rd:

Dear

I have your letter in which you register your strong protest at the action of twenty-five members of the faculty of the University of Kansas in associating themselves as members of the faculty with others in an advertisement in opposition to the right-to-work amendment. In reply let me say the following:

(1) No administrative officer of the University was aware that this project was contemplated or under way until I was sent a copy of the first advertisement from one of the Wichita newspapers.

(2) I personally deplore the fact that members of this faculty became involved in an advertising campaign in which their relationship to the University of Kansas was featured. I further deplore the fact that the advertisement was misleading, at least to the extent that it obviously was not funded by the signers of the advertisement but by funds which I assume have come from organized labor.

(3) This is apparently the first time the question of the propriety of a man's using his rank and position at the University to such a degree and in such a manner has come up. As a result, the Board of Regents has had no policy in this regard. These faculty members then have violated no ruling of the Board of Regents. On the other hand, I am sure that this incident will encourage the Board to examine the matter in order that such problems may be avoided in the future.

(4) I must say that I strongly support the right of these gentlemen as *individuals* to take a position on this matter of public policy, whatever that position might be.

(5) Completely obscured in this controversy is the simple fact that this advertisement was signed by only 25 of the 440 full-time members of the faculty. This is to say, less than 6% of our full-time faculty members agreed to do this. Furthermore, the substantial majority of these 25 had no notion that they were being involved in a massive state-wide advertising campaign. They are now quite as distressed as you or I.

Our faculty as a whole is too busy to take part in campaigns of this sort. If you were on this campus today you would see hundreds of dedicated scientists, historians, mathematicians, humanists, etc., working in diligent and dedicated fashion in the classrooms, libraries and laboratories of this institution. You would also find thousands of eager young Americans working equally diligently— most of them concerned with the major objective of extracting new knowledge, testing it and communicating it. The testing of scientific, social and political matters has always been and will always be one of the major functions of any institution that is worthy of being called a University. Because putting the status quo to test always causes ferment there will always be controversy or at least differences of opinion in, about and related to any great university. But, examined over the long period, you will find these same institutions, year after year, producing our physicians, our lawyers, our engineers, our chemists, our mathematicians, our business executives, and in addition to that producing new knowledge of the type that is absolutely indispensable for our ultimate national defense as well as the continuing expansion of business, industry and agriculture.

I want you to understand that I hold no brief for this kind of thing and if our positions were reversed I am sure that I would be registering my dissent, just as you have done. I only seek to keep this matter in its proper perspective. For our part, we shall try to create policies that will prevent this kind of thing from ever happening again. On the other hand, I hope that this episode will not obscure the fundamental fact that today more than ever before in our history we need strong, vital institutions of higher learning where the highest quality of teaching and research go forward.

For this transitory incident to impair the growth and development of the State University would be tragic, not primarily for the members of the faculty who in large numbers would be more than welcome in institutions of higher learning elsewhere, but for the people of this state, for their children, and for its economic development. Two wrongs never make a right.

Very sincerely,
Franklin D. Murphy, Chancellor.[175]

If the advertisement hadn't hit so soon before the election, Murphy might have been able to respond to all of the angry voters in time to turn the controversy back to the issue of support for higher education, as he attempted to do in news stories and in the form letter, reproduced above.[176] With one week more, he might have been able to aim this statewide spotlight on the University of Kansas in the direction he chose. However, in spite of all the frenetic effort, there simply wasn't enough time.

In the election on November 4, Democrat George Docking carried the state of Kansas, again—this time, by 23,000 votes.[177] Even though his margin of victory amounted to many fewer votes than his 115,000 plurality of 1956, it certainly reflected the shift of substantial numbers of Republicans to his side. Many of those who supported Docking, however, split their tickets on the issue of right-to-work. The Republican-supported right-to-work amendment won the voters' approval by an 18,000 vote margin, thereby prohibiting closed shops in the state.[178] It is ironic that the Democratic candidate won, the Republican candidate lost, and the Republican right-to-work proposal passed.

One cannot know precisely why Docking, the Democrat, won an unprecedented second term. Perhaps the ticket-splitting voters supported the governor in his role as fiscal watchdog.[179] Perhaps Clyde Reed, Jr. (whose name recognition in no way matched Docking's) did not excite the voters' enthusiasm or trust as a gubernatorial candidate. Perhaps Murphy's appeals for higher-education support appealed to, and reached, too few. Perhaps too many of the voters who heard Murphy's message believed that university professors *were* underworked and overpaid, as Docking charged—or that eggheads *were* different. Perhaps many voted 'yes' for right-to-work and skipped the governor's race altogether. Perhaps western Kansas voters' traditional antipathy for the University of Kansas was tested in the ballot box and proved to be more than a cliché. Perhaps Murphy ran out of time, tied up as he was during the final two weeks before the election. Perhaps the anti-right-to-work ad angered a sufficient number of pro-KU/pro-Reed voters enough to shift their allegiance, just as the bitter Hall vs. Shaw race of 1956 had tipped the balance to Docking.

Murphy certainly was correct in trying to persuade the voters of the state to take a long-range view. However, his efforts to focus a statewide election (in which he was not a candidate) on such nebulous idealism smacks of hubris. Perhaps he was so wrapped up in it that he could not recognize the truth—the average voter really did not care whether the University of Kansas was one of the nation's best. Perhaps Murphy was too optimistic.

Or, perhaps the moment was not right. In the first century of the Common Era, Seneca explained a Stoic's rules for living. A man could control part of his destiny, Seneca wrote, but not all of it. That which one cannot control is in the hands of fickle gods and fate. Seneca believed that this approach to life and leadership would help men weather difficulties. One should not expect to win in every race, Seneca said; that a leader conducts himself well in defeat should be some consolation.[180] One doubts that Murphy felt consoled.

For whatever reason, it was a fateful election for Murphy. He would have been much happier with Clyde Reed, Jr. as governor. On Election Day and after, Murphy responded to the many letters from those whose minds he knew could not be changed earlier. The following letter to Kansas Senator Merl L. Lemert of Sedan (one of the originators of the 1955 right-to-work legislation that Governor Hall vetoed) illustrates his honest ire at intolerance and his vocal advocacy of freedom of expression.[181]

> I am distressed by your reference to "left wing" activities and thoughts at the University. If one looks across this country, one can find not only in Kansas but in every other state of the nation a very sharp difference of opinion about right-to-work amendments. On both sides of this question, one can find honorable, loyal, decent Americans. For example, I have some very conservative lawyer friends in Kansas City— good Republicans and conservative by every conceivable measurement—who are strongly opposed to the right-to-work *amendment*. They believe that it is quite wrong to use the amending power of the constitution to deal with matters of

this sort. By the same token, they would vote for any *statute* which would do the same thing.

This, I happen to know, is the conviction of a great many of the twenty-five members of our staff who signed this advertisement. There are others who believe that right-to-work laws or amendments will not come to grips with the real cause of the sickness that exists within labor today. They are fearful that the mere passage of a right-to-work act will obscure the fact that the real necessity is such things as the guarantee of the secret ballot by union members both in the selection of their officers as well as in decisions on strike votes.

These are men who are violently concerned with the excesses of labor bosses as exposed by the McClellan Committee, but who honestly do not believe that this is the way to get the needed job done.

I must insist, at least from my point of view, that to interpret a position on this right-to-work matter as being "for or against labor" is much too over-simplified, and surely has nothing to do with "left wing" activities.

When I was a student in this University, the Kansas Legislature was about to investigate the University because, among other things, of the activity of one Professor John Ise, who was being labeled a radical, Socialist, Communist, etc. What were the three things on which he was attacked as Socialistic at that time? They were as follows:

(1) He preached the need for some governmental control over the stock markets and stock exchanges to drive out evil and dishonest speculators. Today we have the Securities and Exchange Commission and I know of no banker, broker or anyone else in the field of investments who would vote to get rid of the Securities and Exchange Commission. On the contrary, it is recommended and supported by the entire investment industry, and we must admit that these are very conservative people indeed.

(2) He espoused some kind of governmental control in the matter of oil production, declaring that the only way to stabilize

the oil market was to have such. (You will recall these were the days of "hot oil" with prices for petroleum measured in cents rathers than dollars.) Today we have pro-rationing and the oil industry itself would be the first to fight the removal of pro-rationing.

(3) He insisted that the federal government had a heavy responsibility in the management of public lands available for grazing so that these lands would not become so overgrazed as to become utterly eroded and destroyed. For this he was attacked by certain groups of cattle men. Today, the concept of scientific management of pastures, be they public or private, is a fully accepted concept in our culture.

In any event, as I have indicated in the copy of the letter which I am enclosing [*he sent a copy of the Boyer letter*], this is a most unfortunate matter but I hope that none of us lose perspective in the important business of research and education in which, for better or for worse, the University of Kansas plays a significant role not only in Kansas but in the middle west generally.

With kindest personal regards,

Sincerely, Franklin D. Murphy
Chancellor.[182]

"There was a turning-point in the 1950s," wrote Clifford Griffin in his history of the University of Kansas, "although there is no way to fix the date—when realistic observers knew once and for all that the University would never catch up with the institutions ahead of it in the race for quality, wealth, and renown, that the best it could do was continue to improve itself."[183] The fixed date of the turning point seems clear. Murphy must have known on the evening of November 4, 1958, when the results of the second Docking election came in that his vision would not become reality. He had convinced himself that the university and his dream for it could hold out for two Docking years, but he must have known that four years would kill it. No evidence exists that he acknowledged this realization to himself or to others, but he must have also known that his future in Kansas would be limited.

However, in November 1958, Franklin Murphy was not quite ready to give up either the fight or his message. The day after the election, he participated in a panel discussion in Hutchinson and the following day, he received a thank-you letter from an audience member, B. L. Humphreys, President of the Barton Salt Company. In the letter and in Murphy's response to it, one sees the very real disappointment that the chancellor's face, words, or actions must have revealed. Humphreys wrote:

> The panel discussion and meeting you conducted last night was another confirmation of the fact that the State of Kansas possesses one of the greatest universities of the country—if not in the world. I relearned this fact last summer while a student of the University in the Executive Development Program. The highly trained and capable professors and lecturers that were scheduled for that Program ... impressed me deeply, as I wrote you upon my return home.
>
> All of the students in the Program last summer and all of those in attendance at the dinner last night, caught the spirit of the ferment that you have so richly ingrained in the hearts and minds of the faculty and administrative staff of the University. You have indoctrinated a dedicated will to teach, which in my humble opinion, is at least equal to the educational training and degrees held by professors.
>
> The man re-elected governor of Kansas has demonstrated in his present term that he is no friend of the University or of Education in general. I challenge you not to lose heart, or faith in your destiny as the outstanding exponent of Education in our state. Kansas and its young generation of men and women need you infinitely more than the present governor.
>
> In Biblical times, when the Jews were being persecuted, Mordecai sent Esther to intercede for her people in the presence of the King, saying to Esther, "Who knows but that you have come to the Kingdom for just such a time as this." Who knows but that you were chosen to lead Education in such times as these— as was Queen Esther in her time.[184]

Four days later, an obviously refreshed Murphy responded, thanking Humphreys for a "wonderful letter" that had been "read and re-read by me."

The problem of communicating and understanding the needs for the highest type of education and research today sometimes seems insoluble, and yet the sun shines again, and very brightly indeed, when I receive a letter such as the one you wrote: May I simply say that I am deeply grateful.

Let me assure you that the matter of the highest quality of education for our state is of such personal and total concern to me that I certainly have no intention of giving up the fight but actually would propose to intensify it.

Very sincerely,
Franklin D. Murphy,
Chancellor.[185]

Murphy returned to the lobbying work that would be necessary when the legislature convened, just one month later.[186] Immediately after the election, for example, he wrote to John Conard, newspaper owner of Greensburg, to congratulate him for having won a seat in the Kansas Legislature. In addition to "taking the liberty of sending some materials ... which may give you a broad picture of our problems and requirements,"[187] Murphy added: "I hope very much you may see fit to make a request to serve on the Ways and Means Committee of the House. Again I say, in confidence, but frankly, that there is no more important committee for the welfare of our state."[188] He closed the letter by inviting Conard to visit the campus more often and by mentioning the name of a Conard friend at KU, "who shares this same hope."[189]

Quiet lobbying efforts did not predominate in 1959, however. The governor's attacks intensified and the newspapers carried his charges against Murphy almost daily. In fact, the fracas escalated far beyond the comparatively tame attacks of the previous years. The depth of the governor's animosity for the University of Kansas may be seen in an exclusive interview with the student editors of the *University Daily Kansan*, on February 20, 1959.[190]

"KU is a trouble spot," Docking shouted at the students, "that has run wild for 20 years and that needs cleaning up." He cited financial troubles at the University of Michigan and said that "that's what comes from letting institutions, or whatever they call themselves, run wild. We don't intend to allow that to happen here."[191] Docking had not forgotten the public humiliation of his own anger at the months-earlier picketing incident at Leavenworth: "If proper management was in effect at KU that incident would never have happened," he shouted, visibly stirred. "This is about as low as you can get. They should have been put in jail or a psychopathic ward."[192] He accused the university administration of being out to get him, citing the case of Fred Ellsworth, executive secretary of the KU alumni association, whose son, Robert, was chairman of the Douglas County Republicans. "They're tied up together," he said. And, referring to an article in the *University Daily Kansan* comparing faculty salaries in Kansas with those of other states, Docking rejected the figures that had come to him from Murphy. "I'm getting awfully tired of phony statistics," he said, not at all calmly. "Your schools are supposed to teach ethical conduct." As the students stood to leave, the governor warned them sternly to quote him correctly. "I've been misquoted more in Lawrence than any other place," he said. "One of the newspapers in your town has consistently misquoted me for the past four years."[193] The response to Docking's attack was speedy and statewide. The next day, the United Press International's Topeka bureau chief asked the governor whether he had been misquoted in his 'clean up the trouble spot" remarks to the *University Daily Kansan* story. He admitted that he had not been misquoted, but vowed "not to talk to unfriendly amateurs at press conferences."[194]

On the day following the *University Daily Kansan* interview, the governor added flammable fuel to the fire by telling a Democratic rally that "the Republican legislators can be bought very cheaply, sometimes by money or even social distinction."[195] An editorial in the *Topeka Capital Journal* called the governor's attack on KU "one of the most intemperate comments ever made by a Kansas chief executive." The *Wichita Beacon* attempted to center on the issues, instead of on personalities, by publishing a series of articles about the role KU played in the life and future of Kansas. The writer, Mark Clutter, concluded that "if the politicians will let him run a school, it is unlikely that Chancellor Franklin D. Murphy will leave the University for a higher paying job in education."[196]

State Senator Verne Hoisington, a Republican of Paradise, Kansas, and vice-chairman of the Senate Education Committee, responded in a prepared statement:

> Governor Docking's 'rule or ruin' attitude toward the five state institutions of higher education is a result of a combination of ignorance of the facts, personal prejudice and political demagoguery.

It is very apparent that Governor Docking, having failed to impose his prejudiced will on the Board of Regents and the administration, has now set out in irresponsible fashion to destroy the confidence of the people in these institutions. In short, having failed to rule, he has now determined to ruin.

We cannot now sit idly by and let this great tradition be destroyed by a man who apparently learned his political techniques from the life of Huey Long.[197]

In the middle of Docking's second term, in 1959, Murphy acknowledged that the governor's apparent hatred of him was seriously hurting KU—that no efforts on his part, as chancellor, could overcome the damage.[198] Furthermore, he acknowledged that he could do little to change the facts. In a letter to Alvin McCoy of the Kansas City *Star* (and a member of the Board of Regents), Murphy wrote that "I have made one very fundamental error. I had just taken for granted the fact that the leadership in this state wanted a high quality of educational opportunity and performance. All of our plans, of course, have been built upon this indispensable foundation. It would seem that I erred and that they are much more interested in highways, dams, state parks, and the non-productive mentally ill. To me," he concluded, "this is no longer a temporary personal or political controversy—it is just a state tragedy."[199]

During one of the most virulent attacks, Murphy was approached by representatives of the University of California at Los Angeles. Even though he had been offered, and had rejected, the top post at Brown, Johns Hopkins, Minnesota, Wisconsin, and others during his KU tenure, Murphy had still held hope to effect change at Kansas. In the midst of the daily 1959 attacks by the governor, that hope had faded. As the new year of 1960 opened, Murphy gave it one more try. Writing to KU libraries director Bob Vosper (on sabbatical in Europe), Murphy said that Docking "thinks the way to political power is posing as a great economizer, and if... education ... goes to the dogs, that is of no interest to him."[200] In words that seem less enthusiastic than ever, Murphy promised that "we will ... beat him again, as we have done in past years."[201]

Vosper had reason to wonder about the governor's hostility as the costly renovation of the Watson Library, along with a new engineering building, comprised the bulk of a "crash program" of construction that would be debated in the 1960 legislative session. Murphy had attempted to accelerate construction for years, but in 1959, State Senator Verne Hoisington devised a plan that would allow the request to originate from a sub-committee of the Senate Ways and Means Committee, which he chaired. He believed that he, Murphy, and Kansas State's McCain could build a quiet coalition to assure passage in the 1960 budget session of the legislature.[202]

In July 1959, Murphy offered public relations advice. "The issue must not primarily [be] 'the need of K.U. or K.State, etc' but rather the emphasis must be placed upon the 'opportunities and facilities for the education of Kansas boys and girls'," he wrote. "This makes it personal and takes the message potentially into a very large number of Kansas homes."[203] He was not pleased that the state's newspapers failed to cover the universities' need for new structures and noted, in October, that the student reporters of the *University Daily Kansan* had "cut to the core of the issue far more precisely than their elders active in the profession of journalism."[204] Assuring Senator A.W. Lauterbach, Ways and Means chairman and a member of the "quiet coalition," that the administration had had nothing to do with the students' articles, he admitted that he found himself in an "untenable" position over the entire "crash program" matter and that, very soon, he would have to decide where his primary loyalties should lie.[205]

The building proposal did not originate with Murphy, the chancellor emphasized, certainly realizing that such identification would kill it with the governor. A month before the legislature convened its short budget session in January 1960, Murphy sent a personal and confidential letter to Hoisington, with the enclosed "accelerated Building Program *created by the Educational Subcommittee of the Senate Ways and Means Committee.*" (emphasis in original).[206] He explained that McCain endorsed the plan, and while they had not yet seen it, presidents of the other Regents institutions (John E. King, president of Kansas State Teachers College in Emporia and Leonard Axe, president of Pittsburg State) would be apprised. He said that he was confident they would approve "since they get fair treatment."

After notifying Hoisington of the other supportive legislators and Regents who approved as well, Murphy wrote, in the same letter, that he would meet in two weeks with Whitley Austin and Claude Bradney (members of the Board of Regents) "at which time I shall unveil *your* program to them as per our agreement."[207] The goal was for Bradney to "speak vigorously" for the program in Senate Ways and Means Committee hearings. "The above is all I dare do," Murphy concluded, "under the delicate circumstances and I guess it is now up to the Subcommittee to carry the ball."[208]

Unfortunately, one president of a Regents institution did not agree that he was getting "fair treatment" in the building program recommended by the sub-committee. John E. King apparently wanted a larger piece of the pie. In the middle of the session, he effectively killed the plan. On January 5, 1960, Murphy put his anger into words in a letter to King:

> Yesterday I spoke to you by phone, three times I think, about matters relating to buildings for the institutions of higher education. I made it clear at the outset that I was speaking to you in confidence. Today I learn that in the last twenty-four hours you have discussed this matter by phone with at least one, and apparently several persons. Furthermore, I understand that your discussions had little to do with provable need but basically the application of power to get a larger piece of the pie.
>
> On first learning this, I was angry. I am now merely saddened to realize that I cannot rely on confidences with you. In any event, as far as I am concerned and as a result of the above, any informal agreements we may have made yesterday are now completely null and void.
>
> Furthermore, if an honest attempt to get adequate physical facilities for our institutions ... is defeated in the coming Legislature (as was our attempt to get a decent retirement program for our faculty in the last Legislature), the implications of this defeat for higher education in Kansas will have to be borne by those who helped make it possible.[209]

During the session, the first round went to the Murphy-McCain-Hoisington team. It was helped by a massive campaign of articles and petitions from thousands of students at KU. The legislature approved the building funds. The governor promptly exercised his veto, but the legislature overrode, at least in part. The University of Kansas would maintain its operating budget—"minimum but adequate," Murphy said—but it would construct no Engineering Building that year.[210]

"I shall never forget what you did and what you tried to do," Murphy wrote to Lauterbach "with sincere gratitude for the wonderful fight you led." The session was over, he had the flu, and he had just received more bad news.[211] Murphy's good friend Harry Darby had announced his decision not to run against Docking in the campaign that would begin a few months later.[212] Murphy and his wife, Judy, went to New York to visit a potential KU faculty member and then left for 18 days in South America.[213] As chairman of the Council on Higher Education of the American Republics, Murphy would attend meetings under the auspices of the Carnegie Commission and the U.S. Department of State.[214] The Murphy couple would spend part of their time discussing the tempting offer from UCLA.[215]

During his absence, the governor met with a group of Democrats in Great Bend and told them what he thought of certain university administrators. His remarks appeared on the front page of the *Great Bend Tribune* on February 28th. "Without naming Murphy," the article reported, "he referred to one administrator who is paid $22,000 a year, plus a free house and a car, and 'free junkets around the country.'... 'He is in South America now,' Docking said. 'I think that he's getting enough. We can get others as good for less.'"[216]

The next day, Whitley Austin defended Murphy in a Salina *Journal* editorial entitled "His Jealousy is Showing." Austin wrote that the "chancellor's job is a far higher and bigger one than the Governor's. And the qualifications are higher. So Docking, because of a personal feud, to cover his own grievous faults as an administrator in the hopes of getting a few votes from the envious, makes the chancellor a target."[217]

On his return, Murphy objected very strongly to Docking's assertion that he had misused state funds. He wrote to Ray Evans as Chairman of the State Board of Regents, and sent copies to all Regents. "I bitterly resent his deliberate misuse of the truth," Murphy wrote in this official letter, "and his repeated use of the technique of innuendo to imply that the State of Kansas and its taxpayers are somehow paying for 'free junkets around the country' and my recent trip to South America." In three pages, he explained precisely how much of the state's money had funded his travels outside the state: $96.00 in FY 1959, of which $56.40 had been used at the request of Governor Docking, when he had attended a meeting of the National Committee on the Eisenhower Library.[218] He listed the trips he had undertaken on behalf of the Carnegie Foundation, the Kress Foundation, and at President Eisenhower's request. "*In no instance*." he wrote, with emphasis, "*has the State of Kansas paid one nickle of the expenses of these trips.*"

> For four years I have patiently and deliberately refused to respond to this type of attack. I have felt that the dignity and the prestige of the University were at stake and as its chief

executive officer I was obligated to keep the University out of this kind of vicious and unprincipled controversy. However, I am only human. My patience has come to an end.

The time has come when I must express my resentment at this shameful performance on the part of a man who has the responsibility of giving not only administrative and political but moral leadership as well to the people who have elected him to high office.[219]

While Murphy was away, the Board of Regents (which in three Docking years better reflected his philosophy than Murphy's) had refused to rise to his defense over the governor's Great Bend attack, and George Docking had announced his intention of running for a third term. Meanwhile, Murphy was considering the UCLA offer very seriously.[220] He accepted an invitation from Clark Kerr, the head of the University of California system, to visit Los Angeles, hoping that the trip would bring about improved support from the Regents.

Ray Nichols and others were aware of UCLA's offer to Murphy. Nichols attempted to build support to convince him to remain, writing to Senator Glee Smith that "the Chancellor has not yet decided as to whether or not he remains in Kansas or moves west. It seems to me," Nichols wrote, "that if he does decide to stay we need a statewide appreciation of his contributions. Anything that you can do in this respect will be appreciated."[221] It was really too late. There would be no outcry from the Regents. "When it became clear that such was not to be," Nichols said, "Murphy agreed to accept the offer to become head of UCLA."

Murphy said publicly that he made his decision on Monday, March 14th, but he did not announce it until Wednesday, March 16th. Even on that day, at the Faculty Forum luncheon, he did not mention his decision. When the faculty heard the news, many of them donned black armbands in mourning.[222] The resignation would become effective on July 1, Murphy said in his announcement.

"You can only cut bait so long," he told a reporter after the announcement, "and I decided to start fishing Monday."[223] He referred to the governor's veto of the proposed KU engineering building and said that the regents in California offered him the position with no financial limitations for operating the university. "They told me that they wanted me to build the University into one of the great universities of the nation," he said. "It is a great challenge that I am looking forward to."[224]

As hundreds crowded onto the Murphy lawn on the evening of the announcement, burning Docking in effigy and begging Murphy to reconsider, the governor publicly responded to the news of Murphy's decision.[225] "I like to see these young fellows getting ahead," he said, and promptly announced the names of two men who might replace Murphy as chancellor of the University of Kansas.[226] One of Docking's choices was "a good man," the governor said, John E. King, president of Kansas State Teachers College in Emporia.[227]

King, who had wanted a larger piece of the construction pie a few months earlier, did not become KU's chancellor. In spite of initial reports of a long search, the Regents moved with unprecedented speed. Albeit on a split vote, they rejected the governor's candidates and, only three days after Murphy's resignation, had appointed Clarke Wescoe as the new chancellor.[228] Wescoe had been recruited by Murphy to take his place as dean of the KU School of Medicine, in 1951, when he had hoped to return to his medical practice but was instead "seduced" into becoming chancellor. In 1960, Murphy's man got the KU job and Murphy became chancellor of the University of California at Los Angeles.

George Docking campaigned for a third term as governor. Just a few months earlier, in the heat of the 1960 legislative session, Murphy had received some friendly advice: "A newspaper friend said that if I should resign during a Docking attack, then it might defeat him," Murphy said. "This intrigued me." Did Murphy's resignation end Docking's chances for a third term? "Maybe," Murphy said, "and maybe not. But I did resign, and he was defeated."[229]

CONCLUSION

The Patterns of Leadership

Franklin Murphy was the man of the century for KU. They broke the mold with Franklin. There's not another leader like him.

Raymond Nichols
University of Kansas

MURPHY used a meteorological metaphor in his farewell remarks to the University Senate on May 19, 1960. "No sooner had I accepted the appointment in 1951 than Kansas suffered the most economically damaging flood in the state's history," he said. "There followed immediately a long and costly drought." Although the climate has moderated meteorologically, he said, the past four years have been marked "by a climate of demagoguery" from the executive branch of the state government.[1]

There can be little doubt that the *timing* of Murphy's decision to resign from the University of Kansas resulted directly from the political climate. Even though he resigned on March 16th without having notified the Board of Regents officially, the news cannot have surprised any of its members.[2] The emphatic letter four days earlier had not mentioned resignation, but many of those who knew Murphy also knew about the offer from UCLA. The offer was very attractive. "The State of California, with its dedication to and central involvement in the great thrust to the future, is a compelling magnet," Murphy wrote in his resignation statement. "The University of California at Los Angeles has the intense and active interest and support of Californians at all levels. The creative educational opportunities are unlimited."[3]

UCLA enrolled 17,000 full-time and 10,000 extension or night-school students when Murphy accepted the offer to lead it. With its teaching staff of 1,500 and a non-academic staff of 3,250, it stood as one of the largest educational institutions in the nation.[4] Murphy would direct a university nearly 300 percent larger than KU—in people, in land, and in financial support from the state.[5]

In his preliminary discussions with Clark Kerr, who would soon become the chancellor of the University of California system of higher education, Murphy had been assured of "unlimited support" in his drive to create one of the nation's leading universities. He would not need to spend his time convincing Californians and their legislators of the need to invest in higher education, he was assured.[6] Moreover, he had been selected from more than 100 "leading educators," according the UCLA officials when they announced his appointment.[7] Murphy knew all of the enticing details of the offer.

Those in Kansas did not know the details. Judging from the editorials and statements made when he announced his resignation, many editors certainly believed that he was leaving because of Docking—that he had been driven out. In fact, many KU students must have blamed Docking, as 4,800 signed a statement objecting to the abuse that Murphy had taken from the governor.[8] Murphy insisted that his decision was more complex than merely a fight with the governor. "I want to set the record straight," he said to 750 KU alumni in Kansas City in mid-May. "I don't think I'm being chased away from Lawrence. If I thought that, I'm sure I wouldn't leave."[9]

Perhaps he protested too much. Perhaps he would have stayed a few years more had he not effectively lost the battle with the governor. Certainly, forces *were* pushing him out—notably Governor George Docking, who, Murphy said later, "took all the fun out of the job."[10] But other forces certainly attracted him to California. As much as Docking pushed, California pulled. After all, that state measured astounding population and revenue growth in the 1950s and 1960s. It offered an appeal somewhat different from Michigan or others that he had rejected. To have been offered and to have accepted, at age 44, all that California promised would be a compelling magnet for anyone. He had been at KU for nine years—it was time for a change, especially when the realization of his vision in Kansas had looked more and more dim since late 1958, when Docking won re-election. As the second term progressed—or degenerated—the offers that came to Murphy, well-known nationally, must have begun to look more attractive to him. He said that during his last year at KU, he rejected "many fine offers."[11] When Harry Darby, a man with whom Murphy could work well, declined to enter the gubernatorial race early in March 1960, Murphy had all but finalized the decision.

After having negotiated with UCLA for several months, Murphy's real decision seems to have been one of timing. The UCLA chancellor's position would be open on July first. If he intended to accept it, he needed to act quickly in order to allow time to select a successor at KU. Whether serious or not, he said he was intrigued by the idea of resigning at a time that would help to defeat Docking in his try for a third term.

Harry Valentine, a member of the Board of Regents, said on hearing the news of Murphy's resignation that "it may hurt Governor Docking's vote very materially."[12] It is true that George Docking failed to win another term and Franklin Murphy became chancellor of UCLA.

It is also true that Murphy failed to generate sufficient change to allow his vision for the University of Kansas to be fully realized. Is he less a leader because the sacrifice from the state of Kansas that he called for was not forthcoming?[13] Is he less a leader because the University of Kansas did not become the equal of the University of Pennsylvania, his standard, or Michigan, or Stanford as he wished and worked toward? To answer affirmatively is to deny the definition of leadership as he set it out. Leadership requires two things, he said:

"the ability to identify the vision and the ability to get the people motivated."[14] Just a few years later, that definition hadn't changed appreciably. "My job," he said, reflecting on his entire career, "was to share the vision, find the talent, provide the freedom, and secure the funds."[15] From his first days at the University of Kansas, Murphy set goals and articulated them clearly. He shared his vision with all. A roster of those who joined his intimate and his wider teams proves that he persuaded people to join him in the quest he had articulated. Certainly he demonstrated skill at finding ways to pay for what he wanted.

A leader does not succeed in every attempt. Some of the attempts fail. Franklin Murphy did not integrate Lawrence restaurants singlehandedly, as the folklore suggests. In fact, his primary contribution to that effort emanated from his bully pulpit—from occasional speeches exhorting the community to ethical citizenship. Had he intended to force Lawrence restaurants to serve African Americans, he would have left evidence in the form of correspondence, as is the case with his successful effort to change the theaters' racial segregation policies. He might have delayed the expansion of the student union, using it as leverage. He did not. However, working with four black athletes, Murphy deserves credit for having forced the integration of Lawrence theaters.

Did Murphy's view of himself as protector of the marketplace of free expression survive the test of the right-to-work controversy? The situation he faced pitted all of his varied responsibilities against one another. During those weeks, Murphy was forced to balance the right of his faculty to speak freely against the perceptions of donors, voters, students' parents, and elected officials. Appropriately, he attempted to minimize the impact of the anti-right-to-work advertisement that was signed by 25 faculty members. He understood his varying constituencies, but did not hide his adherence to the role of the university as guardian of free expression. He lost his temper, but would seem less than human had he not. Franklin Murphy, the man who would put his vision into action elsewhere, did not fail as a leader in Kansas. He succeeded, and in a style all his own.

Perhaps the words on the occasion of his leaving from those who shared his time during the 1950s at the University of Kansas offer the best judgment. After three years as dean and nine years as chancellor, he left few detractors and a legion of admirers. Ray Evans, chairman of the Kansas Board of Regents, cited his "leadership, vision, and inspiration" as reasons that "we knew he would be hard to keep."[16]

In its formal resolution of "regret and appreciation," the University Senate proclaimed: "The many accomplishments which have owed much to his leadership are well enough known to this Senate and have been clearly recognized in newspaper articles and editorials throughout the State." Thanking him for his "energetic and inspired leadership," the Senate unanimous approved its statement of gratitude, and concluded that "his brilliant talents will continue to champion the cause of education in this country. His work here will long be an inspiration to all to enlist in this cause."[17]

At his last commencement ceremony at KU, Murphy received an unexpected honor from his alumni colleagues. In its Citation for Distinguished Service, the KU Alumni Association praised his leadership as well:

> Franklin David Murphy, graduate of the College of Liberal Arts and Sciences with the Class of 1936, is chosen now, on the eve of his departure from this campus, to receive the citation for distinguished service. While Dean of the School of Medicine he made a dramatic and successful effort to improve the health service of this state, including mental health. As Chancellor of all the University these past nine years, he has given the entire educational enterprise a new and expanding purpose. He has led the way to doubling the library holdings, and greatly increasing their scholarly quality. He has insisted on greater emphasis on instruction in music, in art, in art history, and in acquisition of notable art collections. He has stimulated the expansion of student living quarters and of academic halls. He has worked for vast increases in scientific research both at Lawrence and Kansas City. His realization of the necessity for understanding peoples and cultures of others lands has resulted in the maintenance of a distinguished program of student exchange. His unwavering devotion to excellence is reflected in the choosing and retention of a faculty immeasurably stronger, and a student body whose members win laurels in every field far beyond their proportionate numbers. He has taken his place at the head of national educational organizations, on the boards of great philanthropic foundations, and on commissions of international import in the service of his government.
>
> He has brought to every task the integrity of a man unafraid to

battle for his conviction, unashamed of laughter or tears. He has infused among students, faculty, alumni, and citizens, the warmth of his spirit. He leaves with the heartfelt gratitude and best wishes of all who have known him, and are better for it.[18]

At his annual and final "State of the University" message, on June 5th, Murphy "broke into tears" at the surprise announcement by chancellor-designate Wescoe that "without your knowledge, administrative protocol has been broken." The Board of Regents had voted that day to name the music and arts building at KU in his honor. "Never has a violation been so sweet," Murphy said, visibly shaken.[19] No more fitting honor could have proved that his "man cannot live by bread alone" message had made an impact.

From the Board of Regents with the permanent honor, from students with 4,800 names on a petition begging him to stay,[20] from faculty, from newspapers all over the state came words in evidence of his followers' feelings for a leader. All were heartfelt and sincere, but public and crafted well.

For the truth, perhaps it's best to turn to a private source for evidence of Murphy's leadership and impact on those he led. On June 7th, Robert Talmadge wrote one of his long and detailed letters to Bob Vosper, in England on sabbatical. In it, he described the 1960 graduation weekend, just passed:

> It was a gala weekend, record-breaking crowd at the All-University Dinner (over 1,100,) cool weather, a beautiful Baccalaureate evening. Music-Dramatic Arts is now Murphy Hall. Senior Reception yesterday afternoon was pleasant. It was sprinkling lightly —pavement now damp, now dry— most of the day, right up to the moment that the procession started down the hill, but then it quit and Commencement went very nicely in the Stadium. As a final surprise (and I think it really was a complete surprise to Murphy) there was a Distinguished Alumni Citation.
>
> He leaves with every honor, I think, that KU can bestow. I have never witnessed such unanimous, unreserved expressions of affection and esteem, both official and non-official, as Murphy has had, beginning with the highly emotional student convocation less than twenty-four hours after his resignation was announced.[21]

Perhaps Raymond Nichols knew Murphy better than did any other colleague. They worked together every day that the chancellor was in Lawrence and kept in very close touch in the years that followed his resignation from KU. Nichols has worked with every senior administrator of the university since 1929. "Franklin Murphy was the man of the century for KU," Nichols said. "They broke the mold with Franklin. There's not another leader like him."[22]

The Patterns of Murphy's Career

Franklin Murphy's career reflects the successful balance of apparent contradictions. He was a young man in an era of aged leaders and an intellectual in an anti-intellectual age. He combined the leisurely 19th-century manners that he learned in his childhood with a 20th-century impatience for action. He loved history and its artifacts, but warned against relying too heavily on the past. When viewed as a whole, Franklin Murphy's career as a leader reveals the following obvious patterns—principles, lessons, and precepts—that underlay his actions.

* Avoid Second-rate in Anything. Expect Excellence

All of his life, Franklin Murphy wore confidence as if it were muscle: it was fundamental and tangible. Given great freedom by his aged and busy parents, he learned early to have confidence in his own instincts.[23] He rarely lost. He rarely came in second. With such constant reinforcement, Murphy came to expect excellence in himself and in those around him.

The teen-aged Dürer purchase and continuing conversations with Frank Glenn, the antiquarian bookseller, helped solidify and extend Murphy's interest in original art, instead of facsimiles. "We must have here in the Great Plains," he wrote, "the original documents that are primary records of our cultural and intellectual heritage. Our libraries cannot accept second-class status by virtue of possessing only utilitarian copies of copies."[24] Surrounded by excellence at home and among his close extended family, he demanded it of himself and others. In every way, his life vision centered on an expectation of excellence. "I never wanted to get into anything where I didn't at least try to be the best," he said. "Who the hell wants to be second?"[25]

* In Solving any Problem, First Look for Universals

Aristotle called it "art" (techne). Murphy called it "just my training; I am a scientist, you know."[26] Murphy's life-direction came into focus as the result of research. Although he preferred journalism as a college student, he wrote a zoology paper and decided to choose medicine as a career. His European research fellowship changed his life and his research during medical school extended to World War II, when he spent those years testing such vital wartime drugs such as penicillin and synthetic quinine. Furthermore, as a 31-year-old faculty member at the University of Kansas Medical Center, his research as leader of the "Young Turks" led directly to his appointment as dean and to his launching of the Kansas Rural Health Program. One might say that Murphy, at heart a scientist, merely translated the procedures of the laboratory into a wider world. The universals sought in the scientific method became not only the consensus he sought as chancellor, but also the life-long ability to think through a complicated problem or new idea, condense it, and then lay out a solution.

* If Something's Worth Having, You'll Always Find a Way to Pay for it

As a young man, he stood outside the financial devastation of his generation's catastrophic Great Depression, protected by the confidence of stable family wealth and the interlocking rings of social connections.[27] As money never constituted a problem for Murphy, he learned to view it as a tool. Without that perspective, he could not have turned his vision into reality. Even though young Franklin held part-time work from the age of 11 onward, he did not do so for reasons of need. Later, as an administrator, he quickly learned how to match people and their interests with projects he wanted to fund. In similar situations, many others simply did without. Franklin Murphy rarely failed to find the money for something he considered important. At his death, on June 16, 1994, the *Los Angeles Times'* obituary led its tribute with a first sentence as long and comprehensive as was Murphy's talent: "Franklin D. Murphy, the doctor, educator, administrator and business executive who helped lift Los Angeles onto the cultural, artistic and educational world stage through his uncanny ability to weave together people, projects and the means to pay for them, died Thursday."[28]

Share Your Vision with All
Share Complete Trust with Few

While acquainted with hundreds of people and charming to most, Murphy preferred to take full responsibility alone.[29] As his vision, at every stage, outstripped the energies of any one individual, the Murphy-team pattern developed time and again. Excellence seeks excellence; but only those few of perfect mental match were on the inside team. When the match is struck, the Murphy pattern gave total trust, total freedom to the partner. Such was the case with Robert Vosper, his bibliophilic partner and director of libraries at the University of Kansas. This pattern also translated into a perception of arrogance and unapproachability among those who were not on the Murphy inside team. The perception was apparent among the faculty and students. In fact, Murphy's contact with students appears to have been limited, and his correspondence with students often reflected the concerns of a parent.

Murphy also shared complete trust with Emily Taylor, hired as KU dean of women in 1956. Since the Depression, administrative cuts had resulted in the loss of deans of women positions at institutions of higher education around the country. Deans of women assumed other titles such as "counselor," as they moved on organizational charts from positions parallel to deans of men to posts supervised by them. Initially, Taylor turned down the KU offer because the proposed position would report administratively to dean of students Laurence C. Woodruff. When she insisted that she report directly to Murphy, the chancellor changed the chain of command in her case, even though the dean of men, Don Alderson, reported to the dean of students, not to the chancellor. While the organization chart showed the dean of women as subordinate to Woodruff, Murphy nevertheless continued to allow the dean of women direct access to the chancellor's office, as noted in the press release announcing the change: "This move in no way affects the right of direct access to the chancellor's office possessed by the dean of women," Murphy said. "She retains the primary responsibility for women's activities."[30]

* "Man Cannot Live by Bread Alone"

From his concert-pianist mother and his paternal Aunt Alice, a painter of the Ashcan School and a friend of Mary Cassatt, Murphy inherited an affinity for the fine arts.[31] Raised largely on his own, he turned early to books as his companions and was supported in this by his father, who collected rare books about the history of medicine.[32] During Murphy's pivotal year abroad, he began to collect antique medical books as well. There, of great lifetime importance, the young man spent six months discovering the cathedrals and museums of Europe. "My whole outlook on life changed," he said. "It was a mind-stretching, eye-opening experience for a little Midwestern boy who had never been anywhere...."[33] From that time onward, the aesthetic side of life as reflected in fine books, art and music stood for Murphy as an important element in his life. Many Murphy speeches contained a reminder that "man cannot live by bread alone."[34]

* Be Proud of Things Kansan, and Promote Them

Born in Kansas City in 1916 and graduated from the University of Kansas in 1936, Franklin Murphy had never lived and rarely traveled outside the Midwest until that time. He was proud of the region's culture and its people, and until age 20, had little need to defend either. During a year in Germany after college and in medical school at the University of Pennsylvania, Murphy realized that the Midwest and Kansas did not enjoy the high reputation he believed they deserved. If considered at all, Kansas was the object of ridicule more often than not.[35]

Murphy graduated first in his medical school class, "which pleased me very much," he said. "I was there with a lot of Ivy League types who had their undergraduate work at Princeton and Harvard and Yale. It pleased me that a little ol' Kansas boy could beat 'em to the wire."[36] Time and again, Franklin Murphy seemed driven to prove the inherent and created worth of Kansas. It even extended to his family. He said he was attracted to his future wife, Judy, for her brains and her beauty, but also because she was from Kansas City.[37]

* "Enjoy Yourself—or Do Something Different"[38]

Murphy enjoyed life thoroughly. He loved a hearty intellectual discussion—his curiosity seemed to know no bounds. He gained enormous pleasure in cornering an expert on taxes or tapestries or any other topic that caught his interest, which then sent him to books and to other experts. One finds in his correspondence evidence of a startling range of interests. From his earliest days to his last, he enjoyed life fully as his many friends attest in their stories of "Franklin's marvelously quick wit"—his excitement for living and for discovering new people and new ideas.[39] He seems to have understood Aristotle's ultimate admonition—the end of action is to live well.[40] As the history of his KU leadership proves, when he no longer enjoyed his work, he found something different to do.

The Puzzle of Franklin Murphy

Why should one study the career of a man—in spite of the heights he reached—who never held elected office, who spent most of his 78 years as an administrator, and whose name is not a household word, except among some professors in Kansas and California and in the comparatively rarified world of philanthropists, art-museum directors, and rare-book collectors? In an attempt to understand Murphy, it helps to picture a baseball-sized wooden puzzle, shaped like a globe. Perfectly round, the tight-but-obvious cracks on its smooth surface only suggest what lies within. Moving the puzzle from hand to hand, one looks for the unlocking clue: after all, a puzzle is made to take apart and put back together again. Finally, by chance, the clue becomes apparent. As the round, wooden structure loosens, one sees that it is not a perfect sphere at all, but instead is built from an intricate collection of interlocking shapes—some jagged, some smooth, but none simple. Inside, the pieces curve and turn into one another, fitting as tightly as the ancient cyclopean walls outside Mycenae and as precisely as the works inside Remington's repeating rifle. Slowly each piece slides away from the whole to reveal distinct and separate pieces, each constructed to fit tightly into the whole. If any piece is missing the puzzle doesn't work—it falls apart. Clearly, this tight object must be the perfect illustration of the whole comprising more than the sum of its parts.

It's an appropriate analogy for Franklin Murphy. Just like a wooden fit-together puzzle, Murphy the leader comprised a tight package—a puzzle that deserves examination. A man who thoroughly enjoyed such cunundra, Murphy would have attacked it for the fun of the effort and for the intellectual stimulation. Moreover, as was the result of many projects he undertook in his 78 years, Murphy would have learned something in the process.

The parts that comprise the Franklin Murphy puzzle include strengths and weaknesses. This book examines only a few of those puzzle pieces. If one laid out the pieces of the Franklin Murphy leadership puzzle, one might find *character* as a strong and central element. It is said that if a culture fails to teach a concept for two generations, that concept is lost. The old-fashioned notion called "character" was in danger of just such a fate, but educators now recognize that a nation cannot teach values or ethics or morality without defining the expected result, which we call "character." It is the evidence, the distinctive mark, the aggregate of all the mental and moral qualities that form and distinguish an individual. The English Cardinal Henry Edward Manning, in 1875, described character as "that intellectual and moral texture which all our life long we have been weaving up the inward life that is in us."[41]

Murphy's character developed from the standards of morality, ethics, courtesy and respect set and modeled by his parents and extended family. It developed with intelligence and curiosity. It strengthened in a life that often served as a model for others. But character alone does not make a leader. In an investigation of Murphy's career, one could construct a long list of traits and talents, including: a passion for excellence, a solid and unending education, practical experience, a strong affinity for history and the lessons it teaches, and an interest in people. Add to that a logical mind that sees solutions instead of problems, a physician's drive to find answers and a scientist's need to solve problems systematically and to recognize universals.

With Murphy, one would add the love of words in all their combinations and a talent for putting them together, and the ability to listen—to hear other's ideas and translate them into action. One would also find pride to the degree of arrogance and a loud voice. In him, one sees the ability to explain his vision, to draw others to it, to judge people quickly, to meld a team that shares the vision, and to persuade—with logic, enthusiasm, and passion. One sees enormous physical and mental energy, charm, an eye for detail, decisiveness, loyalty, a competitive nature, and a talent for convincing each individual involved that he or she is an important part of the enterprise. In Murphy, always, one perceives a longing for beauty and the honest enjoyment of it.

It is not a short list. In 1990, Murphy's own list was very short indeed. Leadership requires two things, he said: "the ability to identify the vision and the ability to get the people motivated."[42] Two-and-a-half years later, that definition hadn't changed. "My job," he said, reflecting on his entire career, "was to share the vision, find the talent, provide the freedom, and secure the funds."[43]

Throughout his career, Murphy articulated a vision similar to that he described in 1955 at the University of Pennsylvania. In his 1960 inaugural address as chancellor of the University of California at Los Angeles, he promised to lead the school to "major scholarly distinction in worldwide terms. To do less," he said, "would represent unimaginable lack of vision and inexcusable timidity."[44]

Even though followers choose freely to get involved, they do not do so for the same reasons. The leader must understand the widely varying personal interests of his or her followers in order to identify separate intermediate goals, all of which help achieve the ultimate vision. Murphy did not suggest to the director of the Solon Summerfield Foundation, for instance, that he fund a collection of economics books. He knew that Summerfield's interests had centered in the Renaissance and, concentrating on that, generated enormous sums from the estate.[45] He knew how to cause action.

"During the last 25 to 30 years," wrote Charles E. Young (the UCLA chancellor who followed Murphy in that role), "Franklin Murphy is probably the most seminal person across the board in terms of the growth and development of the Los Angeles community into a world leader."[46] Called a "fortuitous matchmaker," Murphy had a knack for fitting the perfect person to every project.[47] As a leader, people wanted to join him. "One reason he was asked to do so many things," one colleague noted, "is he was not egocentric. He was there for a purpose and that made people trust him. Finally, Murphy was a peppy person, and conversation with him was fun."[48]

APPENDIX

Franklin D. Murphy's Positions and Affiliations

EMPLOYMENT

1948-51	Dean of the School of Medicine and Associate Professor of Internal Medicine, University of Kansas
1951-60	Chancellor of the University of Kansas
1960-68	Chancellor of the University of California, Los Angeles
1968-81	Chairman of the Board and Chief Executive Officer, Times Mirror Company
1981-86	Chairman of the Executive Committee, Times Mirror Company
1986-94	Director Emeritus, Times Mirror Company

CORPORATE BOARD DIRECTORSHIPS
Bank of America
Ford Motor Company
Hallmark Cards, Inc.
McCall Corporation
Norton Simon Inc.
Times Mirror Company

CULTURAL FOUNDATIONS AND INSTITUTIONS
Chairman
Samuel H. Kress Foundation

Los Angeles County Museum, Board of Trustees
National Gallery of Art

President
Samuel H. Kress Foundation
Los Angeles County Museum, Board of Trustees

Trustee
The Ahmanson Foundation
California Museum of Science and Industry
The J. Paul Getty Trust
Los Angeles County Museum, Museum Associates
National Gallery of Art
Skirball Cultural Center, Honorary Posthumous

Fellow
Royal Society of Arts

Member
Kansas City Conservatory of Music
Kansas City Philharmonic Orchestra, Board
Museum of Archeology and Anthropology, University of Pennsylvania, Board of Overseers
Presidential Task Force on the Arts and Humanities
President's Committee on the Arts and Humanities

CIVIC, PUBLIC AFFAIRS, EDUCATINAL,
AND SCIENTIFIC ORGANIZATIONS

Chairman
American Council on Education
Carnegie Foundation for the Advancement of Teaching, Board of Trustees
Commission on Intergovernmental Relations, Study Committee on Federal Aid to Public Health
Council on Higher Education in the American Republics
President's Biomedical Research Panel

President
State Universities Association

Trustee
Carnegie Institution of Washington

Eisenhower Exchange Scholarship Program
Institute of International Education
Midwest Research Institute
Salk Institute
University of Pennsylvania

Fellow
American Academy of Arts and Sciences
American Association for the Advancement of Science

Member
Alpha Omega Alpha
American Board of Internal Medicine
American College of Physicians
American Council of Education, Committee on Institutional Research Policy and Committee on Problems and Policies
American Legion, Medical Advisory Commission
American Medical Association, Council on Medical Education and Hospitals
Association of American Medical Colleges, Vice-president
Beta Theta Pi
Boy Scouts of America, National Council
College of Physicians of Philadelphia
Federal Commission on Government Security
Foreign Intelligence Advisory Board
Institute of Medicine, National Academy of Sciences
National War College, Board of Consultants
Nu Sigma Nu
Peace Corps National Advisory Council
Phi Beta Kappa
President's Task Force on Private Sector Initiatives
Sigma Xi
United States Advisory Commission on International Educational Cultural Affairs
United States Air Force, Board of Visitors to the Air University
Urban Institute
Veterans Administration, Special Medical Advisory Group
Woodrow Wilson National Fellowship Foundation

Source: Margaret Leslie Davis, *The Culture Broker: Franklin D. Murphy and the Transformation of Los Angeles*, University of California Press, 2007, 451-53.

"The Meaning of University"

A speech written and delivered by Franklin D. Murphy Commencement, University of Pennsylvania June 15, 1955.

Although man has always sought to gratify his desire for knowledge, nothing closely paralleling the medieval university existed in the ancient world. Greece and Rome, as well as Egypt, the Near East, and the Orient, had, it is true, a kind of higher education, but it was essentially personal and unorganized—with no formal examinations, no degrees, no corporate entity. The medieval university stood out in contrast to its predecessors and was, in fact, nearly unique. It flamed into being almost *de novo,* and its spirit has powerfully influenced the course of human events for eight hundred years.

The soil from which it sprang was black indeed—the dark ages « centuries of anarchy, fear, superstition, and ignorance. The lamps of learning seemed to have been permanently extinguished (although we know they were still flickering in the Muslim, the Byzantine and Oriental worlds). Then in 11th-Century Europe a slight glow was again discernable, which in the 12th Century suddenly grew into a great flame. It was as though a subterranean fire had been burning through several hundred years of darkness, which had developed such intensity that its appearance, when it came, was explosive.

The prologue to this great epoch in European intellectual history is vividly, if not somewhat romantically, described by Schachner: "... when the twelfth century opened, the problems were set, the weapons forged. Men's minds were stirred by the winds of these great discussions. Learning became something combative and fascinating. All over Europe young men, and older ones too, became restless and dissatisfied. They wanted to be in the thick of things, to hear from the lips of the protagonists themselves the details, step by subtle step, of these strange new arguments. This was the beginning of a hegira unprecedented in the history of the world. There had been mass migrations before, greater in extent and area, but never a one in eager search for knowledge. From the ends of Europe, from northernmost Sweden, from the plains of Hungary, from the dour fastnesses of Scotland, from Germany and England, from Bohemia and Sicily, from Ireland, Italy, and France, they poured in an increasing flood to the centres where learning was to be had, where they could literally sit at the feet of the great teachers and absorb wisdom. Travel was hard and dangerous in those days; the roads were choked with dust in the hot dry summers, thigh-deep in mud in the wet season, breast-high with snow in the winters; brigands and cut-throat soldiery infested the highways; and every few miles was an alien land, to whose inhabitants the foreigner was fair game. Yet, undeterred, the students traversed the length and breadth of Europe; the poor man trudging wearily on foot, knapsack on back, begging his way from hamlet to hamlet; the rich youth on horseback, with an armed servant in attendance; the more elderly rich man in a great bouncing carriage with a retinue of clattering retainers." Clearly this was no pedestrian trade-school enterprise. This was exciting, intellectual adventure.

Yet despotism was abroad in that day, as it is today and as it has been in all periods of human history. To defend themselves from religious and civil tyranny, masters and scholars banded together in corporations, or universities, and thus the immediate ancestor of the modern university came into being.

To call the roll of those venerable European centers of learning is to stir up a vivid feeling of nostalgia and occasionally in these times a sense of envy: Salerno, Paris, Bologna — Oxford, Padua, Salamance — Prague, Cambridge, Montpelier — the power and influence of these institutions can but with difficulty be realized today. Cities vied for the honor of sheltering them. Kings quailed before the collective threats or anger of masters and students. Once a Pope apologized to the learned doctors of Paris for having differed with them on a theological point — and wondrous to behold (to present a reverse side of the record) the students at Bologna fined their professors for being absent, tardy, or failing to deliver their lectures properly, a tradition which seems to have disappeared, undoubtedly to the economic gain of the teaching profession.

But the example of political power is by no means the significant contribution of the universities of the Middle Ages. Such power only indicated their impact on medieval and Renaissance life. The basic strand which ties any modern university, worthy of bearing the designation, to early university tradition is the ferment of the "free market-place of ideas." One cannot forget the tragic Abelard reminding his students to "never use constraint to win your neighbor over to your belief. The human mind should reach its conclusions only by its own lights!" Or Roger Bacon, putting "questions to nature," regardless of consequences! Or John Fisher, Chancellor of Cambridge, suffering death for defying Henry VIII! Or the courageous Wycliff in the halls of Oxford, stoutly espousing his views on authority and privilege in an age in which the commoner was dramatically less than the King or Bishop!

To be sure, activity in the intellectual market place has not always been vigorous or fruitful as, for example, when in the medieval times disputation became sterile and pointless, or as in our time when gadgets tend to replace ideas as the major interest. The doors to this mart have not always remained wide open and even have been bolted closed from time to time, here and there. But always some doors have been open to some degree, and always some activity has been present, and to this fact in no small degree can be credited the cultural, political, technical and indeed spiritual advances of mankind. A strong case can be made for the view that the best yardstick with which to measure the real freedom of a people is the freedom which exists in their market places of ideas, their universities.

But the character of university has a significance far beyond its historic tradition. It even can be measured in very practical terms, if that is what we today demand.

In the first place, the complexity of the problems facing the twentieth century is such as to require for wise solution much more than the technically trained mind — the crucial need is the educated mind, implying powers of reason, analysis, synthesis, with sound historical perspective. This kind of mind can be fashioned, toughened and tempered only in the crucible of free and open discussion. This is the mind that denies man has ever reached the millenium, and that he must proceed through sound knowledge and the strength it creates.

Secondly, no thoughtful person can fail to recognize the practical role played by our present-day institutions of higher learning in expanding our economy and standard of life. Our economic frontier is no longer a geographic one—it is in the minds of men—men and women working in laboratories across the world, dedicatedly and undramatically, having one fundamental common denominator—curiosity; putting questions to nature, to man and to his institutions. There seems to be widespread misunderstanding concerning the meaning of research, and the simple analogy of a bank may help clarify the issue. Industry and medicine, for example, go to this intellectual bank to draw knowledge, which is then fashioned into tools with which to raise our standard of living and to increase our life expectancy. But if the bank account is not to be overdrawn, new fundamental knowledge must be deposited in proportion to that withdrawn. Over the centuries, it has been the universities where, in the main, this vital effort has been carried forward, by men and women who simply want to know more.

The American people must support in much larger measure this basic effort, for scientific leaders of our time in increasing chorus are telling us that this bank account is falling dangerously low. Yet any greater support will be in vain if the intellectual market place is not permitted to remain free and unsuspected.

Finally, we must acknowledge the importance of our universities and all they stand for to our national security. Sir Winston Churchill tells us that in his judgment the greatest force for peace and liberty in the Western World immediately following World War II was the possession of the atomic bomb by the United States. If this be true, the credit must go mainly to brilliant, often non-conforming minds, working in or products of university laboratories, whose genius created the weapon, — not to their latter day detractors. The market place, where ideas are traded, has always been and continues to be under assault. Would-be tyrants try to close its doors. Some trained but misguided and intolerant minds foul it with their denial of human dignity and with their conspiratorial and clandestine efforts to destroy it. Such persons do not deserve admission to it. But to confuse these evil efforts with non-conformity is both stupid and dangerous, leading to a denial of our national birthright, our constitution and the whole movement of western civilization for a thousand years.

Above all else, this unfettered intellectual market place is basic to the maintenance of freedom in all its aspects. Political democracy, as a device to promulgate human liberty, is a calculated risk—one worth taking, but nonetheless a risk. To consider it a sound risk, one must be essentially sanguine about mankind. One must believe that respect for human dignity, a desire to be free, and the quest for truth, are basic instincts of man. We must agree with Milton when he writes in *Areopagitica,* 'Though all the winds of doctrine were let loose to play upon the earth, so Truth be in the field, we do ingloriously, by licensing and prohibiting, to misdought her strength. Let her and Falsehood grapple; whoever knew Truth put to the worse in a free and open encounter?' Three hundred years later a distinguished jurist, Learned Hand, phrases the same thought in different words, saying "I believe the community is already in process of dissolution where faith in the eventual supremacy of reason has become so timid that we dare not enter our convictions in the open lists to win or lose.

The 'open lists' where "free and open encounter may take place" represent the fundamental significance of university. The existence of university makes possible the excitement of the intellectual chase and the search for truth, which we were told almost two thousand years ago would set us free.

The University of Pennsylvania has kept faith with those medieval and Renaissance heroes who fought and died to keep the marketplace of ideas free, for here the doors have remained upon. Through them have been urged all who would espouse or defend their ideas freely openly. Here then is the real reason for pride in bearing the degree you will momentarily receive. And herein lies your first obligation as a product of this tradition—to help guarantee that the market place of ideas will, in your time, remain free and therefore productive so that man may continue to proceed through reason as well as through faith.

Franklin Murphy, "The Meaning of University," Commencement Address, University of Pennsylvania, June 15, 1955. University of Kansas Alumni Association Archives.

Shelby Letter

November 20, 2013
Matt Bean
Managing Editor
SPORTS ILLUSTRATED
135 West 50th Street,
New York, N.Y. 10020-1393

Dear Mr. Bean,

In your October 14, 2013 Sports Illustrated article entitled, "The Freshman", there were several items reported regarding the desegregation of Lawrence, Kansas in the 1950's that were erroneous and a bit misleading. Taking into consideration the well-chronicled role that the City of Lawrence, Kansas played as a catalyst to the American Civil War, the historical value of recording the desegregation of Lawrence in 1957 with accuracy takes on monumental importance!

It is important for you to understand this letter is in no way intended to suggest that Sports Illustrated was deliberately attempting to misrepresent history… I just want to set the record straight.

But first, let me establish my credibility regarding this matter.

In 1958, on the campus of Kansas University, I was one of four occupants who shared the top floor and attic living quarters of the on-campus house of Kappa Alpha Psi, a collegiate fraternity with predominantly African-American membership. These four quartermates were Wilt Chamberlain, Charlie Tidwell, David Harris and myself, Ernie Shelby. Collectively, 1958 was our junior year at KU.

In your October 14, 2013 article it was written: "Chamberlain had been shielded from this kind of prejudice during two well-scripted campus visits, and he was furious when he discovered the reality of the region's racial climate. He sped off to Allen house in Lawrence and threatened to return to Philly if he ran into any more refusals of service." While it may well be true that such a threat by Wilt to leave campus might have occurred as a sudden furious outcry upon his arrival at KU… The meeting which actually resulted in the ultimate desegregation of Lawrence, Kansas was a group meeting between Chancellor Franklin D. Murphy and KU's top African-American athletes. This meeting did not occur until late 1957… Wilt's *THIRD* year at KU!

In correlation with any claims in your article which may have evolved from Wilt's personal memoirs, I feel obligated to mention the fact that, because Wilt was a man of such conspicuous and enormous celebrity, many doors were uniquely open to him before this meeting took place in 1957. However, these same doors were not open to others until after the momentous meeting with Dr. Murphy occurred.

Contrary to the report made in your article, the segregation which existed in 1955 was *NOT* immediately eradicated by a sudden emotional explosion upon wilt's arrival on campus! As a matter of fact, as late as 1957, African-Americans were still being forced to sit in the balcony at the movie theaters; were not allowed to dine in any restaurant and were compelled to wait (while standing) for food orders, which were brought to us in brown paper bags. In addition, we were not provided service in barber shops or beauty salons, or allowed in public swimming facilities, etc.

Our decision in 1957 to schedule an appointment to speak with Chancellor Murphy about our mutual frustration with the degree of segregation in Lawrence was well thought out and discussed at length between us all, *in advance*, in the presence of Shannon Bennett, a graduate Kappa member and KU Law School attendee.

It was decided that the meeting attendees would be:

1. Wilt Chamberlain, All-American basketball star & Captain of the '57-'58 KU Basketball Team

2. Homer Floyd, all-Conference football star & future Captain of the '58 KU Football Team

3. Charlie Tidwell, All-American track star & world record holder and

4. Ernie Shelby (myself) All-American track & future Captain of the '59 KU Track Team

*Most importantly, it was our collective agreement that we would **ALL leave KU** if the problem was not immediately addressed.*

During the meeting with Dr. Murphy, we established the areas of concern that we had, informed him of our collective decision to leave and suggested to him the myriad problems that would be derived from the perception of Kansas University losing its key African-American athletes due to Racial Discrimination. Dr. Murphy's reaction was extremely attentive, accompanied with great understanding and empathy.

In response, he shared his straightforward plans to declare the city "Off Limits" to all students if all retail establishments of Lawrence did not cooperate. At that point in time his plans were incomplete and still unvarnished. There were rumors that he also threatened to open a free, on-campus interracial movie theater, showing the same movies playing at the local theaters, to expand the menu of the campus cafeteria to compete with the local restaurants and to open an on-campus, interracial beauty salon/barber shop.

I am not in a position to verify any of his specific intimidations or how they were received by the local retail establishments. However, Dr. Murphy got back to us within a few days to inform us that the businessmen of Lawrence had almost immediately capitulated and agreed to desegregate, due to their heavy dependency on KU student patronage. We promptly check it out and found it to be true!

In your article, your phraseology was again erroneous when writing: "Lawrence establishments (were integrated) one by one by sitting down, daring anyone to ask them to leave." I'm sorry, but why would any of us "*dare anyone to ask us to leave*"? The truth is that, to the person, we all understood that being confrontational would have proven to be *counterproductive*... Besides, if anyone *DID* ask any of us to leave after the agreement with Chancellor Murphy, we were then able to simply report them to the Chancellor.

There was also another sports incident of historical importance connected with this eventful group meeting with Chancellor Murphy. Although the upcoming 1958 Football and 1959 Track seasons had not yet arrived, when they did, it would mark *the first time in American sports history*, that the captains of three major NCAA Division 1 sports programs in adjacent and contiguous years, were African-American. (Wilt Chamberlain, Homer Floyd & Ernie Shelby)

As a final note of record:

In 1959, Kansas University won the National Men's Outdoor Division 1 Track and Field Championship, with Tidwell and myself being the High-Point men. This category would not have occurred without the desegregation intervention of Chancellor Dr. Franklin D. Murphy, which prevented the exodus of KU's best known African-American athletes at that time.

In view of the spotlight being focused currently on today's racial conditions, the occurrence of this 1957 meeting may eventually become a historical gem!

In closing Dr. Murphy, Wilt Chamberlain and Charlie Tidwell (three of the five participants in that historic meeting) are now deceased. Everything written on these pages has been vetted with

Homer Floyd, Shannon Bennett and David Harris, the remaining KU alumni that took part in the discussions before the meeting and conversations afterwards. To the best of our collective recollections, we all have corroborated the statements made in this letter.

Sincerely,
Ernie Shelby
2062 Delrosa Drive
Los Angeles, CA 90041
Home-Office: 323.258.8449
Cell: 323-350.3433
eshelby@eathlink.net

cc:
Luke Wynn, Senior Writer, Sports Illustrated
Bernadette Gray-Little, Chancellor, Kansas University
Barbara G. Head, Assist. V.P., KU Endowment Association

Endnotes

Introduction

1. Chevrolet roadster. Advertisement. *Literary Digest* 95:1, Oct. 1, 1927: 37; Seven-Week Cruise. Advertisement. *Literary Digest* 95:1, Oct. 1, 1927: 47; Real Electric Range. Advertisement. *Building Age* 51:5, May, 1929: 144; Crosley radio. Advertisement. *Literary Digest*, Oct. 1, 1927: 51; Herald Tribune. Advertisement. *Literary Digest*, Oct. 1, 1927:77.

2. Franklin Murphy, telephone interview with author, April 18, 1990. In following references, this interview will appear as Murphy, interview with author, April 18, 1990; Bruce Cole and Adelheid Gealt, *Art of the Western World* (New York: Summit Books, 1989) 129; Murphy, interview with author, April 18, 1990; Funk and Wagnalls. Advertisement. *Literary Digest*, Oct. 1, 1927: 77.

3. Murphy, interview with author, April 18,1990; Franklin Murphy, "Family Background of FDM," unpublished manuscript, Murphy Scrapbook I, University of Kansas Archives, 174; Edwin C. McReynolds, *Missouri: A History of the Crossroads State.* (Norman: University of Oklahoma Press, 1962) 354.

4. Murphy, interview with author, April 18, 1990; Cole and Gealt, Art, 129.

5. Murphy, interview with author, April 18, 1990.

6. Cole and Gealt, Art, 130.

7. Murphy, interview with author, April 18, 1990.

8. Ibid.

9. Murphy, personal interview with author, Los Angeles, Oct. 5, 1992. Hereafter, this interview will appear as Murphy, Los Angeles interview with author, Oct. 5, 1992.

10. Bob Considine, Kenneth A. Spencer Memorial Lecture. Lawrence, Kansas, 1973. Chancellor's Correspondence. KU Archives.

11. Alexandra Mason, personal interview with author, Lawrence, Kansas, April 9, 1990.

12. Murphy, Los Angeles interview with author, Oct. 5, 1992.

13. Alexandra Mason, personal interview with author, Apr. 9, 1990. Hereafter referred to as Mason, interview with author, Apr. 9, 1990.

14. Raymond Nichols, personal interview with author, Mar. 24, 1990. Hereafter referred to as Nichols, interview with author, Mar. 24, 1990; George Baxter Smith, personal interview with author, Mar. 24, 1990. Hereafter referred to as Smith, interview with author, Mar. 24, 1990.

15. "Resolution," The University Senate, May 10, 1960. Senate Minutes. KU Archives.

16. Aristotle, *Metaphysics* II. 1 and V.2. *Aristotle on Man In the Universe.* Louise Ropes Loomis, ed. (New York: Walter J. Black, 1943).

17. Mortimer Adler, *Time*, June 15, 1974: 60.

18. Mortimer Adler, *Time*, June 15, 1974.

19. Aristotle, *Rhetoric* 1:2 1356b. W. Rhys Roberts, tr., (Chicago: William Benton, 1952) 595.

20. Clifford Griffin, *The University of Kansas: A History* (Lawrence: University of Kansas Press, 1974); Michael Fisher, *The Turbulent Years*, diss., University of

Kansas, 1979; Heidi Pitts, "Racism and Reformation with Franklin Murphy." May 13, 1992. Copy in author's possession.

Chapter I

1. Murphy, Speech at Special Convocation, Mar. 18, 1960: 4. KU Alumni Association; Murphy, Los Angeles interview with author, Oct. 5, 1992.
2. Murphy, University of Kansas School of Medicine Oral History Project interview with Deborah Hickle, Jan. 19, 1990. Hereafter, this source will be referred to as Murphy, interview with Hickle, Jan. 19, 1990.
3. Franklin Murphy, "Family Background of Franklin D. Murphy," May 3, 1956, Murphy Scrapbook, KU Archives. Hereafter, this biography will be referred to as Murphy, family biography, May 3, 1956.
4. Murphy, family biography, May 3, 1956.
5. Ibid.
6. Ibid.
7. "School receives endowed chair," *Lawrence Journal World*, Sept. 13, 1976: 1.
8. Richard B. Fowler, "Leaders in Our Town," *Kansas City Star*, Nov. 20, 1949: IE.
9. Murphy, family biography, May 3, 1956; *Lawrence Journal World*, Sep. 13, 1976: 1.
10. Murphy, family biography, May 3, 1956; Murphy, interview with author, Apr. 18, 1990.
11. Murphy, interview with author, Apr. 18, 1990.
12. Murphy, interview with Hickle, Jan. 19, 1990.
13. Murphy, interview with Hickle, Jan. 19, 1990: 4.
14. "Murphy Exhibition Coming to KU," *Lawrence Journal World*, May 8, 1972.
15. Ibid.
16. Ibid.
17. Ibid.
18. Murphy, interview with author, Apr. 18, 1990.
19. Charles W. Graham, "A Young Man Looks to New Goals in Kansas Medicine," *Kansas City Star*, April 18, 1948: 1C.
20. Murphy, interview with author, Apr. 18, 1990.
21. Graham, *Kansas City Star*, April 18, 1948: 1C.
22. "Franklin D. Murphy, The Man of the Month," *Swing*, December, 1950: 561-564. KU Alumni Association Archives.
23. Graham, *Kansas City Star*, April 18, 1948: 1C.
24. Ibid.
25. Fowler, *Kansas City Star*, Nov. 20, 1949: IE.
26. Murphy, Los Angeles interview with author, Oct. 5, 1992.
27. Graham, *Kansas City Star*, April 18, 1948: 1C.
28. Fowler, *Kansas City Star*, Nov. 20, 1949: IE.
29. Anna Mary Murphy, "Franklin Murphy Went From Graduate to Chancellor in 15 Years," *Topeka Daily Capital*, August 5, 1951.
30. Gray D. Boone, "Lawrence: A Dynamic Relationship Between the University and the Community Nurtures Art and Culture," *Horizon*, September, 1987: 18.
31. James Moeser, "School of Fine Arts receives two major bequests" *Endowment Digest*, October, 1976.
32. Archie Dykes to Murphy, Jan. 16, 1978. KU Alumni Association Archives.

33. Murphy, interview with author, Apr. 18, 1990.
34. Murphy, interview with Hickle, Jan. 19, 1990.
35. Susan Craig, personal interview with author, Apr. 9, 1990.
36. Murphy, interview with author, Apr. 18, 1990.
37. Fowler, *Kansas City Star*, Nov. 20, 1949: IE.
38. Ibid.
39. *Swing*, Dec. 1950: 563.
40. Murphy, interview with author, Apr. 18, 1990.
41. Fowler, *Kansas City Star*, Nov. 20, 1949: IE
42. Murphy, interview with author, Apr. 18, 1990.
43. John A. Scarffe, *From Vision to Reality: 100 Years of Private Support through the University of Kansas Endowment Association*. (Lawrence: The Kansas University Endowment Association, 1991) 26.
44. Murphy, family biography, May 3, 1956.
45. Murphy, interview with author, Apr. 18, 1990.
46. Fowler, *Kansas City Star*, Nov. 20, 1949: IE.
47. Betty Bond Prohodsky, personal interview with author, Oct. 2, 1993.
48. Murphy, interview with author, Apr. 18, 1990.
49. Fowler, *Kansas City Star*, Nov. 20, 1949: IE.
50. Graham, *Kansas City Star*, April 18, 1948: 1C.
51. Those plinths now stand in the Arthur Weaver Courtyard. The sculptures have been moved to the Spencer Museum of Art.
52. "Franklin D. Murphy," biography prepared by the KU Alumni Association as part of FDM's nomination for the Fred Ellsworth Medallion. KU Alumni Association Archives.
53. Donald F. Knapp, "The Fighting Irishman," *Beta Theta Pi*, May, 1962: 425. KU Alumni Association Archives.
54. Graham, *Kansas City Star*, Apr. 18, 1948: 1C.
55. Fowler, *Kansas City Star*, Nov. 20, 1949: IE.
56. Ibid.
57. Murphy, interview with author, Apr. 18, 1990.
58. Ibid.
59. Ibid.
60. Ibid.
61. Ibid.
62. Ibid.
63. Ibid.
64. Ibid.
65. *Swing*, December, 1950: 563.
66. Ibid.
67. Murphy, family biography, May 3, 1956; Murphy, interview with author, Apr. 18, 1990.
68. *Horizon*, Sept., 1987: 17.
69. "Beta Theta Pi," *The Jayhawker*, 1935: 36; *Swing*, December, 1950: 562.
70. *The Jayhawker*, Fall Number, 1935.
71. Knapp, *Beta Theta Pi*, May, 1962:426.
72. Richard Kane to KU Alumni Association, Dec. 30, 1982. KU Alumni Association Archives.
73. Fowler, *Kansas City Star*, Nov. 20, 1949: IE.
74. Franklin D. Murphy, "Rally, rally." *The Jayhawker*, December, 1935: 93.

75. Franklin D. Murphy, "Dictapators," *The Jayhawker*, October, 1935:40.

76. Murphy, *The Jayhawker*, Oct. 1935: 40.

77. Murphy, *The Jayhawker*, Oct. 1935: 40. Without questions, young men in the U.S. copied the clothing styles of British royalty. On p. 62, The 1935 *Jayhawker*, for example, advertises a popular suit in the "Duke of Kent model" with soft roll lapels, British stripes, and "side vents, of course."

78. Donahue cartoon, *The Jayhawker*, October, 1935:41.

79. George Baxter Smith, interview with author, Apr. 18, 1990.

80. Later, Murphy would urge the local school board chair to expand foreign language in the high school curriculum. Murphy to Ralph Pine, letter, Oct. 31, 1955. KU Archives.

81. Fowler, *Kansas City Star*, Nov. 20, 1949: 5E.

82. Anna Mary Murphy, *Topeka Daily Capital*, August 5, 1951.

83. John Keegan, ed., *The Times Atlas of the Second World War* (New York: Harper & Row, Publishers, 1989) 36.

84. C.L. Sulzberger, *American Heritage History of World War II* (New York: American Heritage Publishing Co. Inc., 1966) 19.

85. Graham, *Kansas City Star*, April 18, 1948: 1C.

86. Murphy, handwritten letter to Chancellor Lindley, Oct. 26, 1936, Göttinger, Germany.

87. Graham, *Kansas City Star*, Apr. 18, 1948: 1C.

88. *The Journal of Physicology*, July 15, 2014, 592, 2911-2914. Politics & Physiology: Herrman Rein and the Nobel Prize 1933-1953. Ils Hansson and Serve Dann "Rein nominated 12Y, 1933-1953. "Nazi prhohibited German scholars to accept Nobel.Hermann Klein active during 1933-1945 in Nazi orgs. Wikipedia. Notes 1, 2.

89. "Murphy Installed as Chancellor," *Lawrence Journal World*, Sep. 17, 1951: 1.

90. Graham, *Kansas City Star*, Apr. 18, 1948: 1C.

91. Ibid.

92. Fowler, *Kansas City Star*, Nov. 29, 1949: 5E.

93. Murphy, interview with Hickle, Jan. 19, 1990.

94. Fowler, *Kansas City Star*, Nov. 29, 1949: 5E.

95. Lyman Field, "Rambling around in Europe," *The Jayhawker*, May, 1936: 374.

96. Murphy, interview with Hickle, Jan. 19, 1990.

97. Ibid.

98. Prohodsky, interview with author, Oct. 2, 1993; Mary Martha Kellogg, interview with author, Feb. 1, 1990.

99. Murphy, family biography, May 3, 1956.

100. Fowler, *Kansas City Star*, Nov. 20, 1949: 5E.

101. Anna Mary Murphy, *The Topeka Daily Capital*, August 5, 1951.

102. Fowler, *Kansas City Star*, Nov. 20, 1949: 5E.

103. Ibid.

104. Mary Lou Loper, "Judy Murphy Pins Her Hopes for Future on Young People," *Lawrence Journal World*, May 16, 1967, reprinted from the *Los Angeles Times*.

105. Fowler, *Kansas City Star*, Nov. 20, 1949: 5E.

106. Loper, *Lawrence Journal World*, May 16, 1967.

107. Ibid.

108. Murphy, interview with Hickle, Jan. 19, 1990, 5; Murphy, interview with author, Apr. 18, 1990.
109. Franklin Murphy, unpublished biography, 1953, KU Alumni Association Archives.
110. Murphy, unpublished biography, 1953.
111. Graham, *Kansas City Star*, Apr. 18, 1948: 1C.
112. Murphy, interview with Hickle, Jan. 19, 1990.
113. Ibid.
114. Fowler, *Kansas City Star*, Nov. 20, 1949: 5E.
115. Graham, *Kansas City Star*, April 18, 1948: CI.
116. Tom Yoe, "Murphy Appointed as Med School Dean," news release, Feb. 28, 1948. K.U Alumni Association.
117. *Webster's New World Dictionary* (New York: The World Publishing Company, 1958). 263, 1195.
118. Murphy, interview with author, April 18, 1990.
119. Murphy, Los Angeles interview with author, Oct. 5, 1992.
120. Ibid.
121. Graham, *Kansas City Star*, April 18, 1948: CI.
122. Anna Mary Murphy, *Topeka Daily Capital*, Aug. 5, 1951.
123. Murphy, Los Angeles interview with author, Oct. 5, 1992.
124. Ibid.
125. Fowler, *Kansas City Star*, Nov. 20, 1949: 1E; Murphy, Los Angeles interview with author, Oct. 5, 1992.
126. Graham, *Kansas City Star*, Apr. 18, 1948: 1C; Fowler, *Kansas City Star*, Nov. 20, 1949, IE.
127. Graham, *Kansas City Star*, Apr. 18, 1948: 1C.
128. Ibid.
129. Ibid.
130. Murphy, Los Angeles interview with author, Oct. 5, 1992.
131. Fowler, *Kansas City Star*, Nov. 20, 1949: IE.
132. Ibid.
133. Loper, *Lawrence Journal World*, May 16, 1967.
134. Graham, *Kansas City Star*, Apr. 18, 1948: 1C.
135. Murphy, Los Angeles interview with author to author, Oct. 5, 1992; Graham, *Kansas City Star*, Apr. 18, 1948: 1C.
136. Fowler, *Kansas City Star*, Nov. 20, 1949: IE.
137. Graham, *Kansas City Star*, Apr. 18, 1948, 1C.
138. Ibid.
139. Murphy, interview with Hickle, Jan. 19, 1990.
140. Graham, *Kansas City Star*, Apr. 18, 1948, 1C.
141. Murphy, interview with Hickle, Jan. 19, 1990.
142. Ibid.
143. Ibid.
144. Ibid.
145. Ibid.

Chapter 2

1. Mary Anna Murphy, *Topeka Daily Capital*, Aug. 5, 1951.
2. Fowler, *Kansas City Star*, Nov. 20, 1949: IE.
3. Graham, *Kansas City Star*, Apr. 18, 1948: 1C.
4. Tom Yoe, "Murphy Appointed as Med School Dean," news release, Feb. 28, 1948. KU Alumni Association.
5. Franklin D.Murphy, "We Need More Doctors." *Saturday Evening Post*, May 26, 1951: 85. Hereafter, this source is referred to as Murphy, *Post*, May 16, 1951.
6. Fowler, *Kansas City Star*, Nov. 20, 1949: IE.
7. Graham, *Kansas City Star*, Apr. 18, 1948: 1C.
8. Ibid.
9. Murphy, interview with Hickle, Jan. 19, 1990.
10. Ibid.
11. Murphy, Los Angeles interview with author, Oct. 5, 1992.
12. Murphy, *Post*, May 26, 1951; Fowler, *Kansas City Star*, Nov. 20, 1949: IE.
13. Fowler, *Kansas City Star*, Nov. 20, 1949: IE.
14. Graham, *Kansas City Star*, Apr. 18, 1948:1C.
15. Fowler, *Kansas City Star*, Nov. 20, 1949: IE.
16. Murphy, Los Angeles interview with author, Oct. 5, 1992.
17. Murphy, interview with Hinkle, Jan. 19, 1990.
18. Murphy, interview with Hinkle, Jan. 19, 1990.
19. Fowler, *Kansas City Star*, Nov. 20, 1949: IE.
20. Ibid.
21. Murphy, interview with Hickle, Jan. 19, 1990.
22. Murphy, Los Angeles interview with author, Oct. 5, 1992.
23. Graham, *Kansas City Star*, Apr. 18, 1948: 1C.
24. Murphy, *Post*, May 26, 1951: 19.
25. Ibid.
26. Murphy, *Post*, May 26, 1951: 20.
27. Murphy, *Post*, May 26, 1951: 19.
28. Murphy, *Post*, May 26, 1951: 20.
29. Ibid.
30. Ibid.
31. Murphy, *Post*, May 26, 1951: 21.
32. Ibid.
33. "Dr. Franklin D. Murphy: The Man of the Month," *Swing*, Dec., 1950: 564. KU Alumni Association.
34. James E. Gunn, KU News Bureau release, Mar. 16, 1960. KU Alumni Association Archives. Hereafter referred to Gunn, release, Mar. 16, 1960.
35. Gunn, release, Mar. 16, 1960.
36. Murphy, *Post,* May 16, 1951: 21. (Note: 20 brand-new medical schools on the drawing board in 1949 included those at the University of Washington - Seattle, University of California - Los Angeles, University of Mississippi, The State University of New Jersey - Rutgers, the University of Connecticut, and the University of Florida.)
37. Murphy, *Post*, May 26, 1951: 21.
38. Murphy, *Post*, May 26, 1951: 87.
39. Ibid.

40. Murphy, *Post*, May 26, 1951: 82.
41. Fowler, *Kansas City Star*, Nov. 20, 1949: IE.
42. Ibid.
43. Murphy, *Post*, May 16, 1951: 85.
44. Ibid.
45. Ibid.
46. Murphy, interview with Hickle, Jan. 19, 1990.
47. Ibid.
48. Murphy, *Post*, May 16, 1951: 85-86.
49. Fowler, *Kansas City Star*, Nov. 20, 1949.
50. Murphy, *Post*, May 16, 1951: 87.
51. Fowler, *Kansas City Star*, Nov. 20, 1949: IE.
52. Murphy, *Post*, May 16, 1951: 87.
53. Fowler, *Kansas City Star*, Nov. 20, 1949: IE.
54. Ibid.
55. Murphy, interview with Hickle, Jan. 19, 1990.
56. "Students to View Operations by TV," *Milwaukee-Journal*, Sep. 26, 1949: 50.
57. Anna Mary Murphy, *Topeka Daily Capital*, Aug. 5, 1951.
58. "Murphy is Named KU Chancellor," *Lawrence Journal World*, July 2, 1951: 2.
59. *Swing*, December, 1950: 562.
60. Ibid.
61. Anna Mary Murphy, *Topeka Daily Capital*, August 5, 1951.
62. Fowler, *Kansas City Star*, Nov. 20, 1949: IE.
63. Ibid.
64. *Swing*, December, 1950: 562.
65. Murphy, *Post*, May 16, 1951: 87.
66. Murphy, *Post*, May 16, 1951: 86.
67. Gunn, release, Mar. 16, 1960.
68. *Swing*, December, 1950: 563.
69. *Swing*, December, 1950: 561.
70. Murphy, *Post*, May 16, 1951: 20.
71. *Swing*, December, 1951: 564.
72. "Murphy is Chancellor," *Lawrence Daily Journal World*, July 2, 1951.
73. Murphy, Los Angeles interview with author, Oct. 5, 1992.
74. "KU's New Chancellor," *St. Louis Globe Democrat*, March (n.d.) 1951. KU Alumni Association.
75. "Murphy is Chancellor," *Lawrence Daily Journal World*, July 2, 1951.
76. *St. Louis Globe Democrat*, March, (n.d.) 1951.
77. Robert Dunwell, telephone interview with author, April 19, 1994. Perhaps the preference was made easier by Dunwell's previous knowledge of Murphy. His wife, he said, had been the Murphy family babysitter when she was a nursing student at the KU Medical Center.
78. *Lawrence Daily Journal World,* July 2, 1951.
79. Ibid.
80. Murphy, Los Angeles interview with author, Oct. 5, 1992.
81. Ibid.
82. Murphy, interview with Hickle, January 19, 1990.
83. Murphy, Los Angeles interview with author, Oct. 5, 1992.

84. Murphy, interview with Hickle, January 19, 1990.
85. Ibid.
86. Ibid.
87. *Lawrence Journal World*, July 2, 1951.
88. Murphy, Los Angeles interview with author, Oct. 5, 1992.
89. Ibid.
90. Ibid.
91. Ibid.
92. Murphy to Deane Malott, September 10, 1951. KU Archives.

Chapter 3

1. Clifton Daniel, *Chronicle of the 20th Century* (Mount Kisco, N.Y.: Chronicle Publications, 1987).
2. "Expect River to Return to Banks," *Lawrence Journal World*, July 2, 1951.
3. "Murphy is Chancellor," *Lawrence Daily Journal World*, July 2, 1951: 1.
4. Anna Mary Murphy, "Franklin Murphy Went from Graduate to Chancellor in 15 years," *Topeka Daily Capital*, August 5, 1951.
5. The July 2, 1951, announcement was covered widely. The move date is reported in "Murphy Family to Take over Chancellor Home in August," *Lawrence Journal World*, July 3, 1951.
6. Murphy, Los Angeles interview with author, Oct. 5, 1992.
7. *Lawrence Journal World*, July 3, 1951.
8. Ibid.
9. Anna Mary Murphy, *Topeka Daily Capital*, August 5, 1951.
10. Ibid.
11. To Interim Post," *Lawrence Journal World*, July 2, 1951: 1.
12. Nichols to Malott, letter August 27, 1951, KU Archives.
13. Murphy to Dr. Donald Young, letter September 9, 1951, KU Archives.
14. Donald Young to Murphy, letter September 17, 1951, KU Archives.
15. Nichols to Malott, letter August 29, 1951, KU Archives.
16. Nichols, Interview with author, Mar. 24, 1990; G.B. Smith, Interview with author, Mar. 24, 1990.
17. Frank Burge, interview with author, May 1, 1990.
18. Murphy to Malott, letter September 10, 1951, KU Archives.
19. McCoy, Alvin, "Murphy Aim High," *Kansas City Star,* September 17, 1951: 1.
20. *Kansas City Star*, September 17, 1951: 2.
21. Ibid.
22. *Kansas City Star*, September, 17, 1951.
23. "Murphy Installed as KU Chancellor," *Lawrence Journal World*, September 17, 1951: 1.
24. *Lawrence Journal World*, September 17, 1951: 1.
25. Ibid.
26. Franklin Murphy, "The Meaning of University," University of Pennsylvania commencement address, June 15, 1955. KU Alumni Association Archives.
27. Jerry Waugh, personal interview with author, interview, Apr. 6, 1990.
28. David Awbrey, "Budig learned Murphy's lesson," *Wichita Eagle*, June 21, 1994.
29. Murphy, "The Meaning of University," Jun. 15, 1955; Murphy, Los Angeles interview with author, Oct. 5, 1992.

30. Murphy, "The Meaning of University," June 15, 1955. As Chancellor of the University of California at Los Angeles, he prohibited police from arresting student demonstrators who had engaged in the free marketplace of ideas. After they began to occupy university buildings, however, he changed his mind. "I believe that the university should be a marketplace of ideas," he said, "but we won't tolerate anything here that interferes with our operation." William H. Honan, New York *Times*, Jun. 17, 1994: Al 1.
31. Murphy to author, Los Angeles interview, Oct. 5, 1992.
32. *Topeka Capital Journal*, Mar. 18, 1960.

Chapter 4

1. *Webster's Biographical Dictionary* (Springfield, Mass.: G. & C. Merriam Co., 1961) 1261.
2. Charles Eldredge, *Handbook of the Collection* (Lawrence: The University of Kansas, 1978) 16.
3. Frank Burge, interview with author, May 1, 1990.
4. "Spencer Museum of Art," The Helen Foresman Spencer Museum of Art, University of Kansas. Undated brochure. Author's collection.
5. Eldredge, *Handbook* 16.
6. Murphy, interview with author, Apr. 18, 1990.
7. Bob Considine, Kenneth A. Spencer Memorial Lecture, Lawrence, Kansas, 1973. Chancellor's Correspondence KU Archives.
8. For a thorough and fascinating account of the 19th century Summerfield family, see David M. Katzman, "The Children of Abraham and Hannah: Grocer, Doctor, Entrepreneur: The Summerfields of Lawrence, Kansas," *Kansas History: A Journal of the Central Plains* 37 (Spring 2014): 2-19.
9. Scarfi", *Vision to Reality* 22.
10. Murphy to William Felstiner, letter, Dec. 19, 1957. KU Archives.
11. Murphy, interview with author, Apr. 18, 1990.
12. Ibid.
13. Murphy to William Felstiner, letter, Dec. 10, 1957. KU Archives.
14. William Felstiner to Irvin E. Youngberg, letter, Feb. 3, 1958. KU Archives.
15. Murphy to Sarah Shoner, letter, Feb. 25, 1958. KU Archives.
16. George Baxter Smith, interview with author, Mar. 24, 1990. Smith and Nichols both noted Murphy's love of "trans-Mississippi West" and "Man cannot live by bread alone" in his speeches, most of which both men read. They also agreed that his favorite word was "vigor." Vosper's favorite words were "vigor" and "vigorous." Alexandra Mason, written comments to author, July 5, 1995.
17. Murphy, speech, Great Plains Conference on Higher Education, Norman Oklahoma, Oct. 18, 1956. Reprinted in *Books and Libraries at the University of Kansas*, 1:14, Feb. 1957.
18. Murphy, speech, Great Plains, Oct. 18, 1956.
19. Murphy to George Cukor, letter, May 27, 1959. KU Archives.
20. James Maser to Samuel Berke, letter, May 23, 1959. KU Archives.
21. Murphy to George Cukor, letter, May 27, 1959. KU Archives.
22. Eldredge, *Collection* 113.
23. Murphy to Thomas Hart Benton, letter, May 12, 1958, KU Archives; Edward A. Maser to Murphy, letter, Nov. 23, 1957. KU Archives.

24. *Webster's Biographical Dictionary*. 138, notes the "grand-nephew" status. As the earlier T. H. Benton lived from 1782 -1858 and as his daughter, Jessie Benton Fremont, lived 1824-1902, it seems clear that T. H. Benton, the painter, born 1889, was the senator's great grand-nephew.

25. James Maser to Murphy, letter, Apr. 25, 1958. KU Archives.
26. James Maser to Murphy, letter, Apr. 25, 1958, KU Archives.
27. Murphy to Thomas Hart Benton, letter, May 12, 1958. KU Archives.
28. Eldredge, *Collection*.
29. Susan Craig, interview with author, Apr. 11, 1990.
30. "Franklin Murphy dedicates Library of Art History in Spencer Museum of Art, *Kansas Alumni, Hilltopics Alumni,* Dec. 1980: 4.
31. Boone, *Horizon*, Sep. 1987. Ibid., 18.
32. Margaret Leslie Davis, *The Culture Broker: Franklin D. Murphy, and the Transformation of Los Angeles*. University of California Press, 2007, 451-53.
33. *Horizon*, Sep. 1987: 18.
34. G. B. Smith, interview with author, Mar. 24, 1990.
35. Ibid.
36. Ibid.
37. Laurie Mackey, "Memo for the record," The Kansas University Endowment Association, Oct. 7, 1980.
38. Raymond Nichols, Interview with author, Mar. 24, 1990.
39. Murphy, quoted in C. Heiskel, "The Book Collector's Ephemeron," 4:2, Nov. 1989, Los Angeles.
40. Murphy to Sarah Shoner, letter, Feb. 25, 1958. KU Archives.
41. Murphy to Robert Vosper, letter, June 1, 1955, KU Archives.
42. Murphy to George Matthew Adams, Nov. 3, 1954, KU Archives.
43. Graham. *Kansas City Star*, Apr. 18, 1948.
44. Alexandra Mason, interview with author, Apr. 10, 1990.
45. University of Kansas Library Annual Reports 1951-1960, University of Kansas Archives; Robert Vosper, University of Kansas Library Final Report, Manuscript with correspondence; W.P. Albrecht to T.R. Buckman, letter, May 23, 1961, University of Kansas Library Correspondence, Archives.
46. J. L. Wortham to Dr. Lawrence Clark Powell, letter, February 5, 1952, Chancellor's Correspondence (Vosper), University of Kansas Archives.
47. *Topeka Capital Journal*, Mar. 11, 1955. KU Alumni Association archives.
48. University of Kansas Library Annual Reports 1951-1960, University of Kansas Archives; Robert Vosper, University of Kansas Library final report, Manuscript with correspondence W.P. Albrecht to T.R. Buckman, May 23, 1961, University of Kansas Library Correspondence, Archives.
49. Murphy to Great Plains Conference on Higher Education, speech at Norman, Oklahoma, Oct. 18, 1956. Abstracted in *Books and Libraries at the University of Kansas*, 1:14, Feb. 1957. KU Archives.
50. Jacques Barzun, *The House of Intellect* (New York: Harper, 1959) 38.
51. Alexandra Mason, "Golden Years," *Kansas Alumni*, Feb, 1982: 2.
52. Murphy, Los Angeles interview with author, Oct. 5, 1992.
53. Murphy, interview with Hickle, Jan. 19, 1990; Murphy Scrapbook Vol. I, KU Archives.
54. Robert Vosper, Interview with Betty Milum, American Library Association Oral History Project, May 17, 1989.

55. Robert Vosper, Telephone interview by author, 17 April, 1990, 6. Description verified by L. E. James Helyar, Interview with author, March 27, 1990; John Nugent, Interview with author April 19, 1990; Alexandra Mason, Interview with author, Lawrence, Kansas , April 9,1990; John Glinka, Interview with author, April 9, 1990; and Franklin Murphy, interview by author, April 18, 1990.

56. Chancellor Malott ordered Baker to stop asking for additional staff funds. Glinka, comments, July 5, 1995.

57. For wartime library staff, see Nichols, Interview by author, Ibid. Baker's budget problems are described in University Senate Committee Reports, 1950-51, University of Kansas Archives 3.0, 2. NOTE: Mr. Baker is said to have turned down $65,000 for book purchases, offered by the new Chancellor Murphy, in 1951. Baker reportedly responded that he had enough books already. (Nichols, Interview with author, Mar. 24, 1990; and G. B. Smith, Interview with author, Mar. 24, 1990.)

58. John Glinka, interview with author, Apr. 9, 1990.

59. John Glinka to Jerry Harper, interview, June 23, 1995.

60. "Report of the Special Committee on the University Library," W.H. Shoemaker, Chairman, College of Liberal Arts and Sciences. (Lawrence: University of Kansas, March, 1951), 1,4, 12,13. (NOTE: Hereafter cited as LAS Library Report).

61. Robert Vosper, "A Pair of Bibliomanes for Kansas: Ralph Ellis and Thomas Jefferson Fitzpatrick," reprinted from *Papers of the Bibliographical Society of America*, Vol. 55, Third Quarter, 1961, 1.

62. Vosper, "Pair of Bibliomanes," 1, 9.

63. LAS Library Report, 5.

64. Ambrose Saricks, interview with author, April 2, 1990. Glinka interview July 5, 1995. Saricks was hired to replace Professor Melvin, who died after hitting his head in the stacks on a low concrete beam and door.

65. Saricks, interview with author, April 2, 1990.

66. Ibid.

67. Ibid.

68. Saricks, interview with author, Apr. 2, 1990. Although the committee cited "favorable" reading room facilities, in fact no undergraduate reading room existed for two years to come. Glinka, Interview with author, Apr. 9, 1990. Ibid.

69. Glinka, Interview with author, Apr. 9, 1990. Ibid.

70. J. L. Wortham to L.C. Powell, letter, Feb. 5, 1952. KU Archives.

71. LAS Library Report: 6.

72. Ibid.

73. Murphy, Interview with author, Apr. 18, 1990.

74. LAS Library Report: 3.

75. LAS Library Report: 1.

76. LAS Library Report: 6.

77. Ibid.

78. Ibid.

79. Ibid.

80. David Riesman, "Bookworms and the Social Soil," *Individualism Reconsidered* (Glencoe, Illinois: The Free Press, 1954) 258-65.

81. LAS Library Report: 6-7.

82. Vosper, interview with author, Apr. 17, 1990; Murphy, interview with author, Apr. 18, 1990.

83. Glinka, interview with author, Apr. 9, 1990.

84. Ibid.

85. LAS Library Report: 2.

86. G.B. Smith, interview with author, Mar. 24, 1990.

87. Franklin D. Murphy, "Cultural and Intellectual Growth in the Great Plains Area," Abstract of remarks at the Great Plains Conference on Higher Education; Norman, Oklahoma., Oct. 18, 1956. Reprinted in *Books and Libraries*, 1:14, Feb, 1957:2.

88. Vosper, interview with author, Apr. 17, 1990.

89. Committee Reports, 1950-51, University Senate, 1, University of Kansas Archives 3/0 - University Senate Artificial Records; Murphy, interview with author, Apr. 18, 1990; Vosper, interview with author, Apr. 17, 1990; Glinka, interview with author, Apr. 9, 1990. Actually, Baker remained longer and was given the title "University Bibliographer" by Vosper.

90. Committee Reports, 1950-51, 1951-52, 1952-53, University Senate, 1. KU Archives.

91. Griffin, *History*.

92. Chancellor's Correspondence, 1950-51, Archives, Ibid.

93. Chancellor's Correspondence, 1951-52, Archives (Vosper); Vosper, interview with author, Apr. 17, 1990.; Vosper, interview with Milum, May 17, 1989; Murphy, interview with author, Apr. 18, 1990.

94. Vosper, interview with author, Apr. 17, 1990.

95. Chancellor's Correspondence, 1951-52, Archives (Vosper).NOTE: At no time in his career did Vosper earn a Ph.D. or M.S. in Library Science.

96. Chancellor's Correspondence, 1951-52, Archives (Vosper), KU Archives.

97. Chancellor's Correspondence, 1951-52 (Vosper). KU Archives. "Library Experience"; Vosper's formal application of January 7, 1952 (misdated as 1951 on the original) is addressed to James L. Wortham and is located with the other Vosper-hiring correspondence in University of Kansas Archives 3/0 as cited.

98. Wortham to Lawrence Clark Powell, UCLA Librarian, letter, January 30, 1952, KU Archives.

99. Chancellor's Correspondence, 1951-52 (Vosper). KU Archives.

100. Lawrence Clark Powell to J. L. Wortham, letter, January 30, 1952. KU Archives.

101. Vosper, interview with author, Apr. 17, 1990; Vosper to J. L. Wortham, letter, February 19, 1952, KU Archives; Vosper to Murphy, letter, March 4, 1952, KU Archives.

102. Vosper, interview with author, Apr. 17, 1990.

103. Murphy, interview with author, Apr. 18, 1990.

104. Murphy, interview with author, Apr. 18, 1990; Vosper, interview with author, Apr. 17, 1990.

105. Murphy, interview with author, Apr. 18, 1990; Vosper, interview with author, Apr. 17, 1990; Nichols, interview with author, Mar. 24, 1990.

106. Murphy, interview with author, Apr. 18, 1990.

107. Vosper, interview with author, Apr. 17, 1990.

108. John Glinka, interview with author, Apr. 9, 1990.

109. Alexandra Mason, interview with author, Apr. 9, 1990.

110. Glinka, interview with author, Apr. 9, 1990.

111. Mason, telephone interview with author, Apr. 7, 1990.

112. Glinka, interview with author, Apr. 9, 1990; Mason, interview with author, Apr. 9, 1990.

113. Burge, interview with author, May 1, 1990.
114. Ibid.
115. Murphy to Vosper, letter, Apr. 8, 1952. KU Archives.
116. Murphy, Los Angeles interview with author, Oct. 5, 1992.
117. Vosper to Murphy, letter, March 4, 1952, KU Archives.
118. Vosper to James Wortham, letter, March 5, 1952. KU Archives.
119. Mason, interview with author, Apr. 9, 1990.
120. Murphy, interview with author, Apr. 18, 1990.
121. Murphy, interview with author, Apr. 18, 1990; Nichols, interview with author, Mar. 24, 1990; Mason, interview with author, Apr. 9, 1990; Helyar, interview with author, Mar. 27, 1990.
122. Murphy to Vosper, letter, Apr. 19, 1952. KU Archives.
123. J. H. Nelson to F. Thomas Heller, letter, July 22, 1952. KU Archives.
124. W. H. Shoemaker to Frank Glenn, letter, July 22, 1952. KU Archives.
125. Nichols to Vosper, letter, August 1, 1952. KU Archives.
126. Vosper to Murphy, letter, April 22, 1952. KU Archives.
127. Vosper to Murphy, letter, May 5, 1952. KU Archives.
128. Murphy to Vosper, letter, May 7, 1952. KU Archives.
129. Ibid.
130. Mason, "Golden Years," *Kansas Alumni*, Feb., 1982.
131. Ray Nichols, interview with author, Mar. 24, 1990.
132. Vosper to Murphy, letter, May 5, 1952, KU Archives.
133. Vosper, interview with author, Apr. 17, 1990.
134. Ibid.
135. Vosper to Murphy, letter, Nov. 6, 1952. KU Archives.
136. Murphy, interview with author, Apr. 18, 1990.
137. Nichols, interview with author, Mar. 24, 1990; G. B. Smith, interview with author, Mar. 24, 1990.
138. Vosper, interview with author, Apr. 17, 1990.
139. B.J. Pattee, interview with author, Mar. 9, 1994.
140. Ambrose Saricks, interview with author, Apr. 12, 1990. In April, 1960, Saricks would deliver the Faculty Senate's statement in praise of Murphy on his resignation.
141. Griffin, *History* 518.
142. On June 30, 1960, Franklin Murphy had left KU and Bob Vosper was completing his sabbatical year in England. Acting Director Robert Talmadge wrote to Vosper that he had learned "at Rotary on Monday that Clarke Wescoe *(the new chancellor)* has directed a return to the Malott *modus operandi:* all requests for funds are to go initially to the Budget Committee." Talmadge to Vosper, letter, June 30, 1960. KU Archives.
143. Griffin, *History* 573.
144. Ibid..
145. Griffin, *History* 574.
146. Calder Pickett, "Murphy, Wescoe stir old memories," *Lawrence Journal World*, Oct. 29, 1990.
147. Pickett, *Lawrence Journal World*, Oct. 29, 1990.
148. Glinka, interview with author, Apr. 9, 1990.
149. Vosper, interview with author, Apr. 17, 1990.
150. Glinka, interview with author, Apr. 9, 1990.
151. Mason, interview with author, Apr. 9, 1990.

152. *Biblo-Tracks*, the first in-house library newsletter, announced a party in honor of John Glinka's birthday and asked "Don't those people ever work?" *Biblo-Tracks*, May, 1953. KU Archives.
153. Glinka, interview with author, Apr. 9, 1990, July 5, 1995.
154. Mason, interview with author, Apr. 9, 1990.
155. Mason, interview with author, Apr. 9, 1990.
156. Murphy, interview with author, Apr. 18, 1990.
157. Ibid.
158. Murphy, interview with Hickle, Jan. 19, 1990: 17.
159. Ibid.
160. Murphy, interview with Hickle, Jan. 19, 1990, 27.
161. Murphy to Irvin Youngberg, letter, Oct. 21, 1958. KU Archives.
162. Mason, written comments to author, Jul. 5, 1995.
163. Mason, interview with author, Apr. 9, 1990.
164. Mason, "Golden Years," *Kansas Alumni*, Feb. 1982: 3.
165. *Kansas Alumni*, Feb. 1982: 3.
166. Ibid.
167. Ibid.
168. "KU Gets Rare Books," *University Daily Kansan*, Apr. 28, 1958.
169. Murphy to Vosper, letter, Feb. 5, 1958. KU Archives.
170. Murphy to Vosper, letter, Dec. 8, 1958. KU Archives.
171. Murphy to Vosper, letter, Feb. 5, 1958. KU Archives.
172. Form-letter from Chancellor's Office to an attached list, Mar. 12, 1953. KU Archives.
173. Murphy in *Books and Libraries at the University of Kansas*, 1:3, Apr. 1953; Tom Yoe, news release, Mar. 5, 1953; form-letter invitation from the Chancellor's Office, Mar. 12, 1953. KU Archives.
174. Form-letter from Chancellor's Office to an attached list, Mar. 12, 1953. KU Archives.
175. Vosper, "Another Report from Kansas," *Hoja Volante*, University of California at Los Angeles, May, 1953. A. Mason files.
176. In itself, *Books and Libraries* constitutes a fascinating history of the Vosper years.
177. *Books and Libraries at the University of Kansas*, Feb. 1958. KU Archives.
178. Glinka, interview with author, Apr. 9, 1990.
179. Now called the Center for Research Libraries. Mason, written comments to author, July 5, 1995.
180. *Biblo-Tracks*, May, 1953. KU Archives.
181. G. B. Smith, interview with author, Mar. 24, 1990.
182. Murphy, Los Angeles interview with author, Oct. 5, 1992.
183. Nichols, interview with author, Mar. 24, 1990.
184. Ibid.
185. G. B. Smith, interview with author, Mar. 24, 1990. Nichols, interview with author, Mar. 24, 1990. In Murphy's references to trans-Mississippi West, Smith said, half the time people didn't know what he meant, and he rarely stopped to explain.
186. Nichols, interview with author, Mar. 24, 1990.
187. Dwight Eisenhower to Murphy, letter, Oct. 23, 1957. KU Archives.
188. Harry S. Truman to Murphy, letter, May 12, 1955. KU Archives.
189. Robert Vosper, "A Report on Books and Libraries in Kansas," *California Librarian*, 14:3, Mar. 1953. KU Archives.

190. "Director on the Move," *JayhawkBiblo-Tracks*, 1:5, May, 1953. KU Archives.

191. Robert Vosper, "Acquisition Policy - Fact or Fancy?" *College and University Libraries*, Oct. 1953, 367-370. KU Archives.

192. Vosper, interview with author, Apr. 17, 1990.

193. Ibid.

194. Ibid.

195. In 1982, the group celebrated its 50th anniversary. To honor the occasion, Harry Kurdian wrote "Some Reminiscences," which was published at the Sign of the Four Ducks, Bill Jackson, prop. Author's collection.

196. Vosper, interview with author, Apr. 17, 1990.

197. No alcohol was served on university property, including in the Chancellor's house. Often, according to Vosper, Burge, Glinka, and Smith, special occasions began at a private home with wine or cocktails.

198. Harry Kurdian, *Some Reminiscences* (Wichita: Sign of the Four Ducks, 1982).

199. Vosper, University of Kansas Library Annual Report, July 1955 - June 1956: 3. KU Archives.

200. Vosper, interview with Milum, May 17, 1989.

201. *Kansas Alumni*, Feb. 1982.

202. "Library Staff Increased by 11," *University Daily Kansan*, Sep. 25, 1953. In addition to Talmadge and Rubinstein, the new employees included G.S.T. Cavanaugh, medical librarian; Alec Ross, head of the acquisitions department; Earl Farley, assistant to Rubinstein; Charles Sargent, head of the Kansas Collection; William Martin Jr., stack supervisor, Patricia Turner and William Shore, acquisitions department; Mrs. Richard Wilkie, preparations department; and Mrs. Melvin Heckt, circulation department. Mrs. Heckt, a graduate of the University of Minnesota Library School, had been the command librarian with the U.S. forces in Austria.

203. *Biblo-Tracks*, May, 1953. KU Archives. Although she did not address Vosper as "Bob," Mason later referred to the staff as "a somewhat confusing bunch of Bobs." Mason, written comments to author, July 5, 1995. Glinka told of the mid-'50s library joke, always told with tongue in cheek, that the only way to join the administrative staff is to be named Bob. Glinka, interview with author, July 5, 1995.

204. L. E. James Helyar, interview with author, Mar. 27, 1990.

205. "A 22-Mile High Book Store Grow A Mile A Year," *University Daily Kansan*, Feb. 26, 1957.

206. "Everything's Up To Date in Kansas City," London *Times Literary Supplement*, July 6, 1956: 416. KU Archives.

207. Vosper, interview with Milum, May 17, 1989.

208. Glinka, interview with author, Apr. 9, 1990.

209. Vosper, interview with Milum, May 17, 1989.

210. London *Times Literary Supplement*, July 6, 1956.

211. Glinka, interview with author, Apr. 9, 1990.

212. Ibid.

213. "Librarian to Close the Book on Watson," *Lawrence Journal-World*, Mar. 29, 1994.

214. Sharon Lambert, "KU librarian doesn't fit the stereotype," *Lawrence Journal-World*, Apr. 2, 1990: 3A.

215. Vosper, interview with Milum, May 17, 1989.

216. Vosper, interview with author, Apr. 17, 1990.

217. Vosper, interview with Milum, May 17, 1989.
218. Mason, interview with author, Apr. 19, 1990.
219. "Anything You Can Do…," London *Times Literary Supplement*, May 30,1958.
220. Glinka, interview with author, Apr. 9, 1990.
221. Robert Vosper, "Another Report From Kansas," *Hoja Volante*, May and August, 1953. A. Mason files.
222. "NU Offered Much of Late Teacher's Book Collection," *Lincoln Evening Journal and Nebraska State Journal*, Feb. 20, 1953. KU Archives.
223. Marvin Cruse, "Scientific Rarities From Nebraska." n.d., 1953 Libraries files, KU Archives. Thomas Jefferson Fitzpatrick descended from U.S. President Thomas Jefferson. Cruse was a University of Nebraska librarian.
224. *Lincoln Evening Journal and Nebraska State Journal*, Feb. 20, 1953. KU Archives.
225. Cruse, "Scientific Rarities From Nebraska.
226. *Lincoln Evening Journal and Nebraska State Journal*, Feb. 20, 1953. KU Archives.
227. Ibid.
228. Cruse, "Scientific Rarities in Nebraska." KU Archives.
229. Ibid.
230. He might have been wise to purchase the "Mormon stuff" as it has increased in value geometrically.
231. Murphy, interview with author, Apr. 18, 1990.
232. Frank Glenn to Murphy, letter, Mar. 5, 1953. KU Archives.
233. Ibid.
234. Robert Vosper, *A Pair of Bibliomanes for Kansas: Ralph Ellis and Thomas Jefferson Fitzpatrick* (Lawrence: University of Kansas Libraries, 1982): 13.
235. Robert Vosper, "Another Report From Kansas," *Hoja Volante*, May and August, 1953. A. Mason files.
236. Cruse, "Scientific Rarities in Nebraska." KU Archives; Vosper, *Hoja Volante*, May and August, 1953.
237. Vosper, *Hoja Volante*, May and August, 1953.
238. Cruse, "Scientific Rarities in Nebraska," KU Archives.
239. Ibid.
240. Vosper, *Hoja Volante*, May, 1953.
241. Vosper, interview with author, Apr. 17, 1990.; Vosper, *A Pair of Bibliomanes*. KU Archives.
242. Vosper to Murphy, letter, Mar. 31, 1953. KU Archives.
243. Six KU men went to Nebraska for a weekend of book selection, including Vosper, Howey, Glenn, Quinsey, Aaron Polansky, and Glinka. Glinka to author, Interview July 5, 1995.
244. Vosper, interview with author, Apr. 17, 1990.
245. Murphy to Vosper, letter, Apr. 8,1952. KU Archives.
246. Vosper to Murphy, letter, May 23, 1953. KU Archives. The letter stands as Vosper's official request to hire Robert Talmadge, who would serve as Acting Director during Vosper's 1959-60 sabbatical.
247. Robert Mengel to Ray Nichols, letter, Aug. 16,1953. Chancellor's correspondence, KU Archives.
248. Murphy to Hubert Brighton, letter, Mar. 27, 1953. KU Archives.

249. Vosper, *Hoja Volante*, August, 1953. KU Archives.

250. Vosper to Murphy, letter, Mar. 4, 1952, KU Archives.

251. Glinka, interview with author, Apr. 9, 1990.; Mason, interview with author, Apr. 9, 1990.

252. R.S. Howey to Vosper, letter, Apr. 13, 1953. KU Archives.

253. Ibid.

254. Vosper to Murphy, letter, Apr. 14, 1953. KU Archives.

255. Ibid.

256. Vosper to Murphy, letter, Dec. 2, 1953. KU Archives.

257. Departmental Book Allocation Report, 1953-54, Vosper to department chairs, June 10, 1953. KU Archives. This document illustrates the relative importance, in one respect, of all university departments in 1953. In 1960-61, none of the following departments received more than $200 in annual book-buying allocations: Geology, German, Physics, Law, Pharmacy, English. Talmadge to Vosper, letter, Apr. 8, 1960. KU Archives.

258. Department Book Allocation Report, KU Libraries, 1954. KU Archives.

259. Ibid.

260. Robert Talmadge to Eugene Hiatt, State Purchasing Director letter, Aug. 25, 1953. KU Archives.

261. For a fascinating report on the potential value and use of a collection, see Joseph Rubenstein's Report of George Catlin Material, Nov. 2, 1953, Libraries Correspondence. KU Archives. In it, Rubenstein provides detailed evaluation and history of the material and the reports of faculty members who commented on it.

262. See Report on Stack Storage Space, Robert L. Quinsey, Chief of Reader Services, May 19, 1953. KU Archives.

263. Murphy to Frank Glenn, letter, Nov. 11, 1953. KU Archives.

264. Vosper, *Books and Libraries*, May, 1960. KU Archives.

265. Talmadge to Vosper, letter, April 18, 1960. KU Archives.

266. Robert Talmadge to Vosper, letter, June 14, 1960. KU Archives.

267. Vosper, interview with Betty Milum, May 17, 1989. For a complete account of Vosper's years at the University of Kansas, see *Nine Eventful Years*, an Index to *Books and Libraries at the University of Kansas*, Numbers 1-16, Dec. 1952-May 1961. The publication includes a tribute to Vosper, written by Thomas R. Buckman, and the index, compiled by Alexandra Mason. *Nine Eventful Years* (Lawrence: University of Kansas Libraries, 1961).

268. Murphy, interview with author, April 18, 1990.

Chapter 5

1. Pitts, "Racism and Reformation," quoting Lavonnes Squires in interview, 13.

2. Kansas historian Bliss Isely writes that the crates were labelled as "Bibles," and that 600 arrived from the church contributions of Henry Ward Beecher, in New York. Richard Cordley, in his 1895 history of Lawrence, differs: he wrote that the crates were marked as "books," that they came from Boston, and that they numbered 100. Without question, however, the crates contained Sharp's rifles. Bliss Isely. *The Kansas Story*. (Oklahoma City: Harlow Publishing Corporation, 1961), and Richard Cordley, *A History of Lawrence*. (Lawrence: Lawrence Journal Press, 1895) 37. Sharps rifles were created by Christian Sharps. Alexandra Mason to author, written comments, July 5, 1995.

3. Isely, *The Kansas Story*. 125. Again, Cordley disagrees: he wrote that the rifles were funded, in one hour, after a desperate pleas from the Lawrence settlers. They were sent, he wrote, 24 hours later. Being labelled "books," they attracted no attention from the "illiterate Missourians" who watched for more dangerous parcels. Cordley, *A History of Kansas*. 37.

4. Cordley, *A History of Lawrence*. 28.

5. Isely, *The Kansas Story*. 125.

6. Cordley, *A History of Lawrence*. 7.

7. Isely, *The Kansas Story*.

8. Cordley, *A History of Lawrence*. 244.

9. The Sharps rifles and Beecher's Bibles prompted the founding of other communities as well. Wabaunsee, Kansas, for example, grew from a group of abolitionists in New Haven, Conn., who organized a Connecticut Kansas Colony. Group members were to come to Kansas, each carrying a Bible and a rifle, to help the anti-slavery effort. Some of the rifles were pledged by Henry Ward Beecher. In thanks, the Wabaunsee group re-named itself the Beecher Bible and Rifle Colony. In 1995, the original Beecher Bible and Rifle Church continued to hold weekly services, with about a dozen parishioners. "Kansas church has rich past." *Lawrence Journal World*, June 2, 1995.

10. Cordley, *A History of Lawrence*, 163.

11. Cordley, *A History of Lawrence*, 269.

12. William M. Tuttle Jr. "Introduction," *Embattled Lawrence, Conflict and Community*, Dennis Domer & Barbara Watkins, eds., The University of Kansas Continuing Education, 2001, 139.

13. Tuttle, William M., Jr., "Separate but Not Equal: African Americans and the 100-year Struggle for Equality in Lawrence and at The University of Kansas, 1850s–1960," as cited in *Embattled Lawrence*, 142, notes 12, 13, 14, 17.

14. As cited by Tuttle in "Separate But Not Equal," 143, note 19.

15. Ibid.,144.

16. Ibid. 145, notes 28, 29.

17. As cited by Tuttle in "Separate But Not Equal," 146, notes 31, 32, 33.

18. As cited by Tuttle in "Separate But Not Equal," 147, notes 37, 38, 39.

19. As cited by Tuttle in "Separate But Not Equal, 148, note 43.

20. Robert Vosper to author, letter Apr. 23, 1990; Raymond Nichols, interview with author, Feb. 11, 1987; "Phelps to receive Distinguished Service Award," *University Daily Kansan*, Feb. 11, 1987.

21. Heidi Pitts, *"Racism and Reformation with Franklin Murphy,"* unpublished manuscript, May 13, 1992. The author is indebted to Ms. Pitts, whose research is quoted often in this work. Ms. Pitts pointed out that infant nurseries were not desegregated until 1960.

22. Jerry L. Harper, interview with author, June 1, 1995.

23. Murphy, Los Angeles interview with author, Oct. 5, 1992.

24. *University Daily Kansan*, Sep. 17, 1951.

25. Robert Vosper to author, letter, April 23, 1990.

26. Mike Fisher, *Deaner* (Kansas City: The Lowell Press, 1986) 205.

27. Murphy, Los Angeles interview with author, Oct. 5, 1992.

28. Murphy, "Untitled." Unpublished speech, Sep. 28, 1951. KU Alumni Association Archives.

29. Pitts, "Racism and Reformation," 12, quoting Murphy to Fred Hall, letter, Dec. 29, 1954, KU Archives.

30. Pitts, "Racism and Reformation," 12, quoting Murphy to Mrs. Glen Smith, letter, Oct. 31, 1958, KU Archives.

31. Murphy, Los Angeles interview with author, Oct. 5, 1992; Murphy, interview with Heidi Pitts, Apr. 7, 1992.

32. Murphy, Los Angeles interview with author, Oct. 5, 1992.

33. "Murphy Speaks to Science Clubs," *University Daily Kansan*, Oct. 25, 1954.

34. In response to an enquiry about his decision to remove Rock Chalk Revue from KU-YMCA, Murphy wrote: "I have taken the position that if I believe what I keep preaching about student responsibility for their own affairs I must implement this philosophy with action, and I have now taken the position that the matter of the Rock Chalk Revue must be in the hands of the Student Council." Murphy to G. Irvin Gaston, letter, Nov. 4, 1953. KU Archives.

35. "Chancellor Tells AWS of Goals of University," *University Daily Kansan*, Oct. 22, 1954. In spite of his advice to challenge new ideas, for Murphy *propriety* reigned often. In one speech, Murphy responded to the Dean of Women's policy against wearing the very-popular Bermuda shorts in public. He said he thought the same rules of good taste and common sense applied. He doubted, he said, that he would attend a club meeting or go to the office in either "jeans" or Bermudas, but that he saw no objection to wearing such clothing around the house. Therefore, no Bermudas on campus.

36. Murphy, Los Angeles interview with author, Oct. 5, 1992.

37. "10 Young Men Rated at Top," *Milwaukee Journal*, Feb. 18, 1950, 22.

38. "Ike Sat at His Feet," *Time* Magazine, Oct. 22, 1952: 60; *University Daily Kansan*, Oct. 23, 1952.

39. "Murphy Denies FSA Job Offer," *University Daily Kansan*, Nov. 25, 1952. Such rumors continued: on March 16, 1953, he denied having been asked to serve as FSA head Oveta Culp Hobby's assistant.

40. Murphy, Los Angeles interview with author, Oct. 5, 1992.

41. "Murphy, Glueck Stress Need for Human Dignity," *University Daily Kansan*, June 12, 1953.

42. Murphy, Los Angeles interview with author, Oct. 5, 1992.

43. Ray Nichols recalled the instance of Marian Anderson being forced to stay overnight with the principal of the Negro school for the same reason: Raymond Nichols, "50 Years at KU," unpublished speech, Lawrence Unitarian Fellowship, 1992. Nichols also said that Sinclair Lewis almost cancelled his KU speech because he didn't like the wallpaper in his hotel room.

44. Pitts, "Racism and Reformation," 12. Pitts' interview of Lavannes Squires suggests that Fitzgerald had no place to stay. Murphy recalled that she stayed in the guest house.

45. John Hope Franklin and Alfred A. Moss, Jr., *From Slavery to Freedom*, sixth ed., (New York: Alfred A. Knopf, 1988).

46. Franklin and Moss, *From Slavery to Freedom*. 439.

47. From Osborne's 1956 novel *Look Back in Anger*.

48. Jack Kerouac's *On the Road* was published in 1957.

49. J.D. Salinger's *Catcher in the Rye* was published in 1951.

50. *Time* Magazine, "Why Haven't We Heard From Them," special issue, Nov. 6, 1951.

51. "25,000-a-Month To Be Drafted," *University Daily Kansan*, Mar. 15, 1954.

52. *University Daily Kansan*, Oct. 6, 1952.

53. Murphy, Los Angeles interview with author, Oct. 5, 1992.

54. Murphy to President A. Whitney Griswold, Yale University, letter, Nov. 29, 1952. KU Archives.

55. *University Daily Kansan,* June 12, 1953.

56. Clifford S. Griffin, *The University of Kansas: A History* (Lawrence: The University of Kansas Press, 1974) 519.

57. Murphy was joined on the committee by the presidents of Stanford, Brown, Washington University, and Yale.

58. "Communism and the Colleges," *Time* Magazine, Apr. 6, 1953.

59. "Teachers Divided in Feelings About Loyalty Investigations," *University Daily Kansan*, March 18, 1953; "AAU Report Upholds Academic Freedom," *University Daily Kansan*, March 31, 1953.

60. Teachers Union news release, Mar. 31, 1953. Chancellor's Correspondence 52-53, KU Archives.

61. R.H. Garvey to Murphy, letter, Feb. 17, 1953, KU Archives.

62. Murphy to R.H. Garvey, letter, Feb. 24, 1953, KU Archives.

63. Ted Schweiter to Murphy, letter, May 17, 1952, KU Archives.

64. Murphy to Ted Schweiter, letter, June 2, 1952, KU Archives.

65. In 1950, only 1.5 million American families owned a television set. By the end of 1951, the number had exploded to 15 million. Daniel, *Chronicle of the 20th Century*.

66. "The Man They Nominated," *The Milwaukee Journal*, Sep. 19, 1952. KU Archives.

67. Paul G. Hoffman, "Freedom is For the Brave," Commencement Address, Jun. Hoffman quoted Benjamin Franklin.

68. Arnold Rampersad, ed. *The Collected Poems of Langston Hughes*. (New York: Alfred A. Knopf, 1994) 15.

69. Robert H. Lynn to Murphy, letter, Oct. 27, 1953. KU Archives.

70. Thomas Median, "Must We Be Nostalgic About the Fifties?" *Horizon,* Vo. DC, No. 1, Winter, 1972: 7.

71. As the daughter and sibling of polio victims, I write of the fear from personal experience. My mother's polio left her mobile, but disabled. I did not enter a public movie theater until 1954, when I was 11. The entire family napped from noon until 3:00 every day in the summer.

72. *University Daily Kansan*, Oct. 21, 1952.

73. *University Daily Kansan*, Oct. 9, 1952.

74. *University Daily Kansan*, Jan. 31. 1952.

75. "We Must Accept Brotherhood, Murphy Says," *University Daily Kansan,* Feb. 27, 1952.

76. Rampersad, *Poems of Langston Hughes*: 14. "Hughes is attacked by the influential book *Red Channels: The Report of Communist Influence in Radio and Television*." Arnold Rampersad, *The Life of Langston Hughes*, Vol. 1: 1902-1941, Vol. 2: 1941-1967 (Oxford University Press: London).

77. Rampersad, *Poems of Langston Hughes*: 15.

78. Rampersad, *Poems of Langston Hughes*: 16.

79. U.S. Census, 1900, as explained in Lizzie E. Goodnight, "Negroes of Lawrence," Master's Thesis 1903. Kansas Room, Lawrence Public Library.

80. Isely , *The Kansas Story*: 209.

81. Langston Hughes, *The Big Sea* (New York & London: Alfred A. Knopf, 1940) 16.

82. Hughes, *The Big Sea*: 21.

83. Ibid.

84. Hughes, *The Big Sea*: 22.

85. Hughes, *The Big Sea*: 23. Hughes' uncle Nat had taught music to the famous performer, who was known professionally as George Walker. He returned to Lawrence to die.

86. Pitts, "Racism and Reformation."

87. Pitts, "Racism and Reformation," 10.

88. Pitts, "Racism and Reformation" quoting Paul Gilles, letter to the editor, *University Daily Kansan*, April 8, 1943. Gilles would later join the University of Kansas faculty in the chemistry department.

89. Pitts, "Racism and Reformation," 10, quoting Deane Malott to Governor Andrew Schoeppel, Mar. 19, 1943, in Griffin, *The University of Kansas. A History*.

90. Robert Vosper to author, letter, Apr. 23, 1990; Raymond Nichols, interview with author, Feb. 11, 1987; "Phelps to receive Distinguished Service Award," *University Daily Kansan*, Feb. 11, 1987.

91. Pitts, "Racism and Reformation," 4, quoting Lavannes Squires.

92. Squires. Pitts, "Racism and Reformation," 5.

93. Deane W. Malott, *Statement for Journal-World*, June 6, 1950, folder "Athlete Office, 1949-50," box 1, series 2/10/5, Chancellor's Office Libraries. See for a full history of this issue, S. Zebulon Baker, "To Help Foster Athletic Equality Here in the Midwest": Defeating Jim Crow in the Big Seven Conference," *Kansas History: A Journal of the Central Plains*, 39, Summer 2016, 74-93.

94. Murphy, Los Angeles interview with author, Oct. 5, 1992.

95. William Scheinman, *University Daily Kansan*, Jan. 17, 1947.

96. Pitts, "Racism and Reformation," 5.

97. Amanda Bollier, "Kansan Comments ... Race Prejudice," *University Daily Kansan*, Mar. 5, 1947.

98. Fisher, Deaner: 205.

99. Pitts, "Racism and Reformation," 7, quoting "Fine Arts Faculty Denies Barring of Negroes from Participation in Campus Musical Organizations," *University Daily Kansan*, Nov. 26, 1943.

100. Pitts, "Racism and Reformation," 8.

101. Pitts, "Racism and Reformation," quoting Deane Malott to Governor Andrew Schoeppel, letter, Mar. 19, 1943, in Griffin, *The University of Kansas. A History*.

102. Pitts, "Racism and Reformation," 8.

103. Pitts, "Racism and Reformation," 8. At its June 6, 1995, meeting, the Lawrence City Commission set a public hearing for August 1 to demand demolition of the 1014 Mississippi Street structure, formerly the Alpha Phi Alpha house. The fraternity owed unpaid property taxes on the structure, which had been vacant for some time. "Fraternity razing considered," Lawrence City Commission agenda highlights, *Lawrence Journal World*, June 5, 1995.

104. Shelby, Ernie. Letter to *Sports Illustrated*, Nov. 20, 2013.

105. A full-page feature describing life at the Jayhawk Coop appeared in the *University Daily Kansan*, Oct. 3, 1952.

106. October and November, 1952, were months of intense student interest in the Chancellor's efforts to provide university housing. See *University Daily Kansan*, Oct. 14, 1952, Oct. 17, 1952, Oct. 30, 1952, Nov. 7, 1952, Nov. 14, 1952, and Nov. 25, 1952.

107. Pitts, "Racism and Reformation," 11, quoting "CORE Protests Card Labeling," *University Daily Kansan*, Oct. 23, 1947.

108. "CORE Trying to Get Four Hill Cafeterias to Desegregate," *University Daily Kansan*, Feb. 27, 1948.

109. "We Must Accept Brotherhood, Murphy Says," *University Daily Kansan*, Feb. 27, 1952.

110. "4 Hill Cafe Owners Ignore Petition, Refuse to Serve KU Negro Students," *Daily Kansan*, May 13, 1952.

111. Pitts, "Racism and Reformation," quoting LaVannes Squires in interview, 13.

112. Murphy, Los Angeles interview with author, Oct. 5, 1992.

113. Murphy, Los Angeles interview with author, Oct. 5, 1992; Pitts, "Racism and Reformation," 13.

114. Murphy, Los Angeles interview with author, Oct. 5, 1992; Nichols, interview with author, Feb. 11, 1987; Pitts, "Racism and Reformation," 13.

115. Murphy, Los Angeles interview with author, Oct. 5, 1992.

116. Ibid.

117. Murphy to J.D. King, letter, Feb. 28, 1952. KU Archives.

118. Pitts, "Racism and Reformation," 13.

119. Murphy, Los Angeles interview with author, Oct. 5, 1992.

120. Murphy to J.D. King, letter, Jan. 29, 1954. KU Archives.

121. Murphy, Los Angeles interview with author, Oct. 5, 1992.

122. Pitts, "Racism and Reformation, "citing "Negro Students View Local Discriminations," *University Daily Kansan.* May 11, 1954.

123. Franklin and Moss, *From Freedom to Slavery*: 439.

124. "Cafes Weigh Racial Discrimination," *University Daily Kansan*, May 12, 1952.

125. "First Step Taken in Movement to Bring End to Racial Discrimination," *University Daily Kansan*, May 13, 1952.

126. *University Daily Kansan*, May 12, 1952.

127. Ibid.

128. "Restaurant Employe Quits Job Over Negro Segregation Issue, *University Daily Kansan*, May 15, 1952.

129. "Students Oppose Cafe Race Barrier," *University Daily Kansan*, May 16, 1952.

130. "Boycott Urged to End Discrimination," *University Daily Kansan*, May 16, 1952.

131. "NAACP Leader to Address Public Forum on Brotherhood," *University Daily Kansan*, May 16, 1952.

132. Mrs. F. Garrett to Murphy, letter, May 13, 1952. KU Archives.

133. Murphy to Mrs. F. Garrett, letter, May 15, 1952. KU Archives.

134. "Negro GI Cited for Korean Heroism," *University Daily Kansan*, Mar. 17, 1953.

135. "Student Hits Town Segregation Policy," *University Daily Kansan*, Oct. 5, 1953.

136. *University Daily Kansan,* Oct. 31, 1952, 1.

137. "Supreme Court Hears School Racial Problem," *University Daily Kansan*, Dec. 5, 1952.

138. "Group Gone—Not Forgotten, *University Daily Kansan*, Sep. 29, 1953.

139. Advertisement, *University Daily Kansas*, Oct. 14, 1953.

140. "Two More Reply On Discrimination," letter to editor, *University Daily Kansan*, Oct. 14, 1953.

141. "Student Group to Fight Against Discrimination," *University Daily Kansan*, Nov. 5, 1953.

142. "Group Fights Intolerance—Cautiously," *University Daily Kansan*, Feb. 12, 1954.

143. "Civil Rights Law Nil, Group Told," *University Daily Kansan*, Mar. 8, 1954.

144. "Students Resent Race Bias, Poll Shows," *University Daily Kansan*, Mar. 15, 1954.

145. "How Does It Feel to Be a Negro?" *University Daily Kansan*, Mar. 22, 1954.

146. Murphy, Los Angeles interview with author, Oct. 5, 1992; Murphy, interview with Pitts, Apr. 7, 1992.

147. Pitts, "Racism and Reformation," 14.

148. In an editorial entitled "The Land of the Free," *University Daily Kansan*, Sep. 26, 1958, the author wrote that "we know at least one restaurant that has served Negroes for the past two years without incident. None of the holdouts is in danger of being the first."

149. Nancy Simons to Chancellor Franklin D. Murphy, letter, Jan. 28, 1954. KU Archives.

150. Murphy to Nancy Simons, Feb. 19, 1954, KU Archives.

151. Pitts, Ibid., 14, citing Oct. 17,1956 letter found in Box 22, notes of Clifford S. Griffin. *The University of Kansas. A History*. Ibid., KU Archives.

152. "Integration Ball is Rolling," *University Daily Kansan*, Mar. 20, 1957.

153. Lloyd Kerford to Murphy, letter, Jan. 6, 1955. KU Archives.

154. Murphy to Lloyd Kerford, letter, Jan. 8, 1955. KU Archives.

155. "Polio Shots Available at Watkins Hospital," *University Daily Kansan*, Oct. 19, 1956.

156. The new field house was dedicated on Mar. 1, 1954, and named in honor of Coach Forrest "Phog" Allen on Dec. 17, 1954. Many opposed the honor, one seldom accorded a living individual.

157. Mike Fisher, Deaner: 205.

158. Murphy, Los Angeles interview with author, Oct. 5, 1992.

159. Dr. Forrest "Phog" Allen was a Doctor of Osteopathy. Fisher, Deaner.: 195.

160. Brady Prauser, "Waiting for Wilt," *University Daily Kansan*, May 3, 1993.

161. Fisher, Deaner: 198.

162. Fisher, Deaner. 202.

163. In his autobiography, Chamberlain explained his skill in many sports, including the shot put and arm wrestling. In fact, he won the national championship in the shot put during his freshman year at KU. Wilt Chamberlain's ego matched Allen's: "I could tell you hundreds of stories about the unbelievable amounts of weight I've lifted," he wrote. Wilt Chamberlain, *A View From Above* (New York: Signet, 1992) 31.

164. Murphy, Los Angeles interview with author, Oct. 5, 1992.

165. Dale Morsch, "Quote By Wilt In Magazine Brings Protest," *University Daily Kansan*, Nov. 29, 1956. Apparently it was quite a collection at the airport, even though Oklahoma A&M's coach, Hank Iba, and Bruce Drake of Oklahoma University denied having "been with half-a-mile of the place."

166. Chamberlain and David Shaw, *Wilt Chamberlain*. 1973, as quoted in "Waiting for Wilt," *University Daily Kansan*, May 3, 1993.

167. Chamberlain. *View from Above*: 160.
168. Chamberlain, *View from Above*: 156.
169. Murphy, Los Angeles interview with author, Oct. 5, 1992.
170. Ibid.
171. Minutes of the University of Kansas Physical Education Corporation Board Meeting, Mar. 29, 1956. KU Archives.
172. Clarence P. Houston to Murphy, telegram, May 1, 1956. KU Archives.
173. Murphy, Los Angeles interview with author, Oct. 5, 1992.
174. Chamberlain, *View from Above*: 144.
175. Photo, *University Daily Kansan*, Oct. 28, 1957.
176. Murphy to Wilton Chamberlain, 1134 Mississippi, letter, Oct. 29, 1957. KU Archives.
177. Shelby, Ernie. Letter to *Sports Illustrated*, November 20, 2013.
178. UPI Bulletin, *University Daily Kansan*, May 6, 1957.
179. Chamberlain, *View from Above*: 143.
180. "Wilt Tells Kansan He Has No Regrets," *University Daily Kansan*, Jan. 15, 1958.
181. "Waiting for Wilt," *University Daily Kansan*, May 3, 1993.
182. *University Daily Kansan*, May 3, 1993: 9.
183. Ibid.
184. Toleration Called Need in Religion," *University Daily Kansan*, Feb. 23, 1956.
185. "Has Integration Interest Died?," *University Daily Kansan,* Mar. 8, 1957.
186. "Women Have No Place in the KU Band," *University Daily Kansan*, Oct. 23, 1957.
187. *University Daily Kansan*, Dec. 3, 1957.
188. Dale Morsch, "Integration Ball is Rolling," *University Daily Kansan*, Mar. 29, 1957.
189. "Discrimination Problem Set For Future Study," *University Daily Kansan*, Sep. 24, 1957.
190. "Faubus Prepares To Face Judge," *University Daily Kansan,* Sep. 18, 1957.
191. "Murphy, Must Have Free Idea Exchange," *University Daily Kansan*, Sep. 20, 1957.
192. "8 of 20 See Ike Deliver Telecast," *University Daily Kansan*, Sep. 25, 1957.
193. "Bayonets Protect Negro Students," *University Daily Kansan*, Sep. 25, 1957.
194. "Negroes Are Not Integrated," *University Daily Kansan*, Feb. 12, 1958.
195. "ASC Urged to Study Local Discrimination," *University Daily Kansan*, Sep. 25, 1958.
196. "Enough Confusion On Discrimination," *University Daily Kansan*, Sep. 25, 1958.
197. *University Daily Kansan*, Sep. 25, 1958.
198. "Murphy Distressed at Discrimination," *University Daily Kansan*, Sep. 26, 1958.
199. "Mixed Races Eat in 10 Cafes Only," *University Daily Kansan*, Sep. 26, 1958.
200. "Mayor Favors Integration," *University Daily Kansan*, Sep. 29, 1958.
201. "ASC Sanctions Racial Study," *University Daily Kansan,* Oct. 1, 1958.
202. "The Land of the Free," *University Daily Kansan*, Sep. 26, 1958.

203. "Letters," *University Daily Kansan*, Oct. 1, 1958.

204. "Faubus Acts Called Venal," *Topeka Capital Journal*, Oct. 2, 1958.

205. *Topeka Capital Journal*, Oct. 2, 1958; "Chancellor Murphy Criticizes Faubus," *University Daily Kansan*, Oct. 2, 1958.

206. Mrs. Glen Smith to Murphy, letter, Oct. 31. 1958.

207. The only apparent evidence of "form" letters appears in the chapter on Kansas politics.

208. Murphy to Mrs. Glen Smith, letter, Oct. 31, 1958.

209. "Civil Rights, Making It a Misdemeanor To Deny Certain Rights On Account of Race, Color, Religion, National Origin Or Ancestry," House Bill No. 467, Kansas Session 1959, found in the Dean of Men's files 1957-1964, KU Archives, as quoted by Pitts.

210. Pitts, "Racism and Reformation," 15, quoting a memo on discrimination, Dec. 14,1959, found in the Dean of Men's Files, 1957-1964, KU Archives. Lawrence taverns included Dine-A-Mite, Stables, Rockchalk, and The Wheel.

211. See Pitts, "Racism and Reformation" for a detailed account.

212. "Housing Bias Unintentional, Woodruff Says," *University Daily Kansan*, Feb. 18, 1959.

213. "Murphy Slams Greeks' Bias," *University Daily Kansan*, Mar. 16, 1959.

214. *University Daily Kansan*, Mar. 16, 1959.

215. Pitts, "Racism and Reformation," 2, quoting personal interview with Murphy.

216. Murphy, Los Angeles interview with author, Oct. 5, 1992.

217. "Report on Discriminatory Clauses," found in box 3.0, University Senate Records, 1959-60, KU Archives.

218. Yale Dolginou, interview with Karen Gallagher, Jan. 20, 1995.

219. Ibid.

Chapter 6

1. "Gubernatorial Sketch," *University Daily Kansan*, April 17, 1958.

2. "Gov. Hall Vetoes Right-to-Work Bill," *University Daily Kansan*, Mar. 28, 1955:1.

3. Governor Fred Hall's exit from office resulted in one of the three 1958 campaign's proposed amendments—that to appoint justices to the State Supreme Court on a non-partisan basis. Amendment No. 1 passed as voters remembered the 1956 "triple-play" that put Fred Hall on the Supreme Court. Just 11 days before his tenure as governor was to end, Hall's plan went into action: Chief Justice William Smith resigned from the court, Hall resigned from the governor's office and left that seat to Lt. Governor John McCuish, and McCuish appointed Hall to the court. "While there was actually no illegality in the move, citizens throughout the state felt that his action was morally reprehensible." "Voters Give All Three Amendments Big Yes Vote," *Topeka Capital Journal*, Nov. 4, 1958.

4. Clifford Griffin, *The University of Kansas: A History* (Lawrence: University of Kansas Press, 1979) 530-531.

5. Isely, *The Kansas Story* 395.

6. "State Survey Shows Reed is Sprinting," *Topeka Capital Journal*, Oct. 21, 1955:7.

7. Isely, *The Kansas Story* 394. Interestingly, in the majority of years after Docking, there were more Democratic governors than Republican. This might be the result of a change from two-year gubernatorial terms to four-year terms.

8. "Parties View Amendment," *University Daily Kansan*, Oct. 15, 1958.

9. Murphy, Los Angeles interview with author, October 5, 1992.

10. Griffin, *History* 527.

11. "Kansas U. Chancellor Thanks Legislature," *Omaha World Herald*, Apr. 11, 1953: 4 and "Killing TV Fund Bill 'Distresses' KU Head," *Omaha World Herald*, Mar. 25, 1953: 26.

12. Griffin, *History* 543. See Griffin's chapter 27 for a thorough explanation of Murphy's attempts to increase the state income for the university.

13. Griffin, *History*.

14. Griffin, *History* 530.

15. Ibid.

16. Murphy to James A. McCain, letter, Jan. 26, 1955. KU Archives.

17. Dwight Eisenhower to Murphy, letter, Feb. 4, 1955. KU Archives. That traditional view, Eisenhower wrote, "creates a serious problem for an old war horse that looks longingly toward the green fields and fat cattle of a small farm."

18. No evidence exists of Murphy having courted a female legislator.

19. Griffin, *History* 517.

20. Griffin, *History* 522.

21. Ibid.

22. Murphy, Los Angeles interview with author, Oct. 5, 1992.

23. "Communism and the Colleges," *Time*, Apr. 6, 1953; A. Whitney Griswold to Murphy, letter, Nov. 18, 1952; Murphy to A. Whitney Griswold, letter, Nov. 29, 1952. KU Archives. KU Archives.

24. Murphy, Los Angeles interview with author, Oct. 5, 1992.

25. Dwight D. Eisenhower to Murphy, letter, Jan. 12, 1954. KU Archives.

26. See "Eisenhower correspondence" file, Chancellor's Correspondence, KU Archives.

27. Dwight D. Eisenhower to The Right Honorable Sir Winston Churchill, letter, Apr. 16, 1957.

28. Murphy, Los Angeles interview with author, Oct. 5, 1992.

29. Griffin. *History* 519.

30. Murphy, Los Angeles interview with author, Oct. 5, 1992.

31. Ibid.

32. Griffin, *History* 525.

33. Murphy to A. John T. Ford, letter, Oct. 7, 1953. KU Archives.

34. "Murphy Trustee of Carnegie Group," *University Daily Kansan*, Nov. 17, 1955.

35. Griffin, *History*. Griffin.

36. *History* 517-18.

37. Murphy, Los Angeles interview with author, Oct. 5, 1992.

38. Ibid.

39. Murphy to George Docking, letter, Nov. 8, 1956, KU Archives.

40. Docking's initiatives and responses, over the next years, are limited to their sources. We have only newspaper accounts and letters and memories of those involved, as Docking's papers were destroyed at his death.

41. Raymond Nichols, "Four Tumultuous Years," unpublished speech. Old and New Club, Jan. 26, 1990.

42. Nichols, "Four Tumultuous Years."
43. Ibid.
44. Ibid.
45. Ibid.
46. Ibid.
47. "Kansas Needs Money - Docking," *University Daily Kansan*, Nov. 30, 1956.
48. Bill Mayer reported the governor's comments in the *Lawrence Journal World*, Feb. 4, 1957, and generated an angry "I never comment on anything that self-styled newspaper ever says" response from Docking. "Loaded Story Unfair," *University Daily Kansan*, Feb. 6, 1957. "Athletic Funds Eyed for State Revenue" *University Daily Kansan*, Feb. 6, 1957.
49. His efforts to bring newly elected legislator Joe Warren, of Arkansas City, into the KU fold stand as a case in point. A series of letters between Murphy and Kirke Dale, owner of the Home National Bank Building in Arkansas City, outline those efforts. Kirke Dale to Murphy, letter, Nov. 13, 1956, and Murphy to Kirke Dale, Jan. 14, 1957, KU Archives.
50. "Ticket Used for Lobbying,' *Omaha Word-Herald* Jan. 16, 1960: 6.
51. Leroy Zimmerman, "Right-to-work Bill Valid," *University Daily Kansan*, Mar. 11, 1957: 2.
52. "Right-to-work Debated Tuesday," University Daily Kansan, Dec. 4, 1957:4.
53. Murphy to Merl L. Lemert, letter, Nov. 4, 1958. KU Archives.
54. "Living Cost Up for The Month," *University Daily Kansan*, Apr. 23, 1957.
55. "115 at KU Get At Least $750 Monthly, Gov. Docking Says," *University Daily Kansan*, March 6, 1957.
56. Nichols, "Four Tumultuous Years."
57. Murphy to Tom L. Kiene, letter, Nov. 30, 1953. KU Archives.
58. Griffin, *History* 531.
59. "Docking's Travel Charge Answered by Chancellor," *University Daily Kansan*, Mar. 21, 1957.
60. Griffin, *History* 531.
61. Griffin, *History* 532.
62. "Docking Asks Survey of College Budgets," *University Daily Kansan*, Sep. 27, 1957.
63. "Economy Short Course," *University Daily Kansan*, Sept. 30, 1957.
64. *University Daily Kansan*, Sept. 30, 1957. "Budget Talk Up To Regents."
65. *University Daily Kansan*, Oct. 3, 1957.
66. Griffin. *History* 521.
67. "Clean Out 'Course Clutter,'" Docking Says," *University Daily Kansan*, Jan. 13, 1958.
68. *University Daily Kansan*, Jan. 13, 1958.
69. Murphy to Frank Theis, letter, Jan. 15, 1958. KU Archives.
70. "Dr. Murphy Seeks Honor for Egghead," *Kansas City Times*, Jan. 16, 1958.
71. Murphy to Tom L. Kiene, letter, Nov. 30, 1953. KU Archives.
72. Nichols, "Four Tumultuous Years."
73. "Disagreements 'Not Personal,'" *University Daily Kansan*, Jan. 17, 1958.
74. Murphy, Los Angeles interview with author, Oct. 5, 1992.
75. Frank Burge, interview with author, May 1, 1990.
76. Murphy to John McCormally, letter, April 23, 1958. KU Archives.
77. Marcellus M. Murdock to Murphy, letter, Oct. 3, 1958.
78. Murphy to Marcellus M. Murdock, letter, Oct. 7, 1958.

79. Murphy, Los Angeles interview with author, Oct. 5, 1992.
80. A. Lewis Oswald to Murphy, letter, November 6, 1957. KU Archives.
81. Murphy to A. Lewis Oswald, letter, Nov. 12, 1957, KU Archives.
82. Murphy to Oswald, letter, Nov. 12, 1957.
83. Frank Burge, interview with author, May 1,1990.
84. George Baxter Smith, interview with author, Mar. 24, 1990. When Smith asked what Murphy would do, in that case, Murphy said that he'd take his wife and kids and go to Europe for a year.
85. Griffin, *History* 534.
86. Murphy, Los Angeles interview with author, Oct. 5, 1992.
87. "Disagreements Not Personal," *University Daily Kansan*, Jan. 17, 1958.
88. Nichols, interview with author, Mar. 24, 1990; Nichols, "Four Tumultuous Years." Griffin, *History* 534.
89. "Docking 'Faults' Listed," *Topeka Capital Journal*, May 25, 1958.
90. "Oswald Talk is Attacked," *Topeka Capital Journal*, May 26, 1958.
91. "Docking to Seek Second Term," *University Daily Kansan*, May 7, 1958.
92. "Prairie Politics," *University Daily Kansan*, Nov. 20, 1957.
93. Murphy to Clyde M. Reed, Jr., letter, Mar. 28, 1958. KU Archives. In a postscript, Murphy wrote to Reed: "The material on the Severance Tax is also enclosed. This was prepared by Ethan Allen at my request. He did not know who was seeking the information. He says this is the best he can do. When you are finished with the monograph on Oil and Gas, would you mind returning it? No rush, but some day it ought to get back into the library."
94. "Docking Forgets Schools, Says Reed," *University Daily Kansan*, April 28, 1958.
95. *University Daily Kansan*, April 28, 1958.
96. "Parties View Amendment," *University Daily Kansan*, Oct. 15, 1958: 4.
97. "State Survey Shows Reed is Sprinting," *Topeka Capital Journal*, October 21, 1955: 3.
98. *Topeka Capital Journal*, October 21, 1955: 3.
99. "Editors give nod to Reed in Home Area," *Topeka Capital Journal*, Oct. 17, 1958.
100. "Chancellor Calls Russian Sputnik A 'Pearl Harbor,'" *University Daily Kansan*, Oct. 29, 1957.
101. "Intellectuals Key to U.S. Supremacy," *University Daily Kansan*, Jan. 16, 1958. In 1990, Murphy reflected on the intervening 32 years, when asked whether he believed that America's attitude toward intellectuals had changed, "... we still do not honor our intellectuals the way the French, the Italians, the Europeans generally do, and the way the Chinese do,... the Orientals. We are still a nation of Yankee toolmakers," he said. "But I think we're improving." Murphy, interview with author, April 18, 1990.
102. Murphy, Los Angeles interview with author, October 5, 1992.
103. George Docking's personal papers as governor were destroyed at his death, according to the archivist of the Kansas State Historical Society.
104. "Loaded Story Unfair," *University Daily Kansan*, Feb. 6, 1957.
105. "Prairie Politics," *University Daily Kansan*, Nov. 20, 1957.
106. David L. Blair to Murphy, letter, Dec. 7, 1957, and Murphy to David L. Blair, letter, Dec. 13, 1957. KU Archives. In his response to Blair's request to run against Docking, Murphy replied: "I have, from time to time, in the past three or four

years, had to consider the matter of entering public life in terms of elective office. I have consistently refused to think of such a move for a number of reasons..."

107. Murphy to David L. Blair, letter, Dec. 13, 1957.

108 Murphy, Los Angeles interview with author, Oct. 5, 1992. In fact, when asked why he had never accepted a federal appointment, Murphy grimaced and replied instantly: "I'd have to move to Washington!."

109. Raymond Nichols, interview with author, Mar. 24, 1990.

110. George Baxter Smith, interview with author, Mar. 24, 1990.

111. Murphy, Los Angeles interview with author, Oct. 5, 1992.

112. Murphy to C. O. Wright, letter, Oct. 2, 1958.

113. "KU Students Invade Democratic Rally," *University Daily Kansan*, Sep. 30, 1958.

114. "Political Pranks," *University Daily Kansan*, Oct. 1, 1958.

115. KU young GOP Denies Damage at Demo Rally," *Topeka Capital Journal*, Oct. 1, 1958. The student who identified himself to Docking as Joe Reed was actually Steve Newcomer, a KU student from Omaha.

116. *University Daily Kansan*, Sep. 30, 1958.

117. Ibid.

118. Even the KU student newspaper called the student picketers "brainless." "Kansas Picket Parties," *University Daily Kansan*, Oct. 10, 1958.

119. William Clarke Wescoe to Harold W. Dodds, letter, Sept. 28, 1959, University Archives, as quoted in Michael P. Fisher, "The Turbulent Years: The University of Kansas, 1960-1975," diss., University of Kansas, 1979:28.

120. "Straw Vote Indicates Close Governor's Race," *Topeka Capital Journal*, Oct. 26, 1955.

121. Murphy, Los Angeles interview with author, Oct. 5, 1992.

122. *YOUR Government*, XTV, 1, September 15, 1958. KU Archives. As a university-sponsored publication, *YOUR Government* was printed by the state printer, which office affixed the union label to all its work.

123. "Student Straw Poll Okays Bill for 'Right-to-work'," *University Daily Kansan*, Oct. 3, 1958: 6.

124. "Grumm says work bill would punish unions," *University Daily Kansan*, Oct. 15, 1958: 4.

125. "Oldfather, Titus Blast Amendment 3," *University Daily Kansan*, Oct. 30, 1958: 1.

126. "Will you let Reuther get away with it?" *Topeka Capital Journal*, Oct. 26, 1958; "Labor's answer to the 'Right to (Wreck) Work' Amendment," *Topeka Capital Journal*, Nov. 1, 1958; and "We are Americans but we are strenuously opposed," *Topeka Capital Journal*, Nov. 2, 1958.

127. George D. Bell to J. E. Schaefer, letter, Oct. 6, 1958, KU Archives.

128. J. E. Schaefer to George D. Bell, letter, Oct. 8, 1958, KU Archives.

129. Ibid.

130. Schaefer included in his letter to Murphy a long paragraph describing his recent trip to Arizona, where "the unions.. are going all out to defeat" Goldwater, "who has done so much on the McClellan Committee to expose racketeering in labor circles" and who is "a delightful person to meet and know." Schaefer to Murphy, letter, October 31, 1958, KU Archives.

131. Schaefer sent copies to Harry Darby, Willard Breidenthal, C. C. Kilker, Kenneth Spencer, Gerald Gordon, Reed Larson, and H. M. Van Auken. List typed onto copy of J.E. Schaefer to George D. Bell, letter, Oct. 8, 1958, KU Archives.

132. Dwight Eisenhower to J. Earl Schaefer, letter, Jan. 22, 1952. KU Archives.

133. Dwight Eisenhower to J. Earl Schaefer, letter, Jan. 24, 1952. KU Archives.

134. See the correspondence on the Wichita State issue in KU Archives: Jan.-Apr. 1955.

135. "Boeing Official to Speak Today," *University Daily Kansan*, Nov. 5, 1955.

136. Lynn Whiteside to Murphy, letter, Mar. 24, 1955. KU Archives.

137. *Kansas Alumni*, Sept./Oct., 1991. 36.

138. John A. Sarffe, *From Vision to Reality: 100 Years of Private Support through The Kansas University Endowment Association*. (Lawrence: The University of Kansas Endowment Association, 1991) 89.

139. Griffin, *History* 524, as quoted in Fisher, *The Turbulent Years* 28.

140. "Private Funds Vital for Growth, Murphy Says," *University Daily Kansan*, Mar. 11, 1957.

141. Kenneth A. Spencer to F.D. Murphy, letter, Oct. 27, 1958, KU Archives.

142. The ad appeared first in the *Wichita Eagle*, on Oct. 23, 1958. John E. Boyer to Murphy, letter, Oct. 23, 1958, KU Archives.

143. Political advertisement, Oct. 1958, KU Archives; *Topeka Capital Journal*, Oct. 28, 1958.

144. Murphy, Los Angeles interview with author, Oct. 5, 1992.

145. John Boyer to Murphy, letter, October 23, 1958, KU Archives.

146. "Letter and policy paper of The Voluntary Committee of Kansas Clergy and Educators Opposed to Amendment No. 3," n.d., 1958. Chancellor's correspondence 1958. KU Archives.

147. Ibid.

148. Ambrose Saricks, interview with author, Apr. 2,1990; John Boyer to Murphy, letter, Oct. 23,1958; Murphy to, form letter sent from Chancellor's office, Nov. 3, 1958, KU Archives.

149. Murphy. Los Angeles interview with author, Oct. 5, 1992.

150. In fact, several of 25 did not identify themselves as faculty members of the University of Kansas, but rather as "associate professor, Lawrence" or "Prof. of Chemistry, Lawrence."

151. Murphy to John E. Boyer, letter, Oct. 25, 1958, KU Archives.

152. Murphy relied most often on Whitley Austin of the Salina *Journal*, Alvin McCoy of the *Kansas City Star*, Marsh Murdock of the *Wichita Eagle*, John McCormally of the *Hutchinson News*, and Clyde Reed, Jr. of *The Parsons Sun*.

153. Murphy, Los Angeles interview with author, Oct. 5, 1992.

154. Murphy, Statement Oct. 30, 1958, KU Archives.

155. Partial list of addressees added to the letter from F.D. Murphy to Senator James B. Pearson, letter, Nov. 4, 1958, KU Archives.

156. Reed cancelled because Vice President Nixon was to appear in Wichita. *Topeka Capital Journal*, Oct. 18. 1958:20.

157. "50 hear senators split on Docking's education policy," *University Daily Kansan*, Oct. 31, 1958: 1.

158. Murphy, Los Angeles interview with author, Oct. 5, 1992.

159. Ambrose Saricks, interview with author, Apr. 2, 1990.

160. Paul Wilson, interview with author, Apr. 10, 1994.

161. Murphy had occasion for verbal spankings later at UCLA, he said, with faculty there who used the same strategy. Murphy, Los Angeles interview with author, Oct. 5, 1992.

162. "Murphy Wanted Only Facts in Talk With Faculty," *University Daily Kansan*, Nov. 10, 1958: 1.

163. "A Job Well Done," *University Daily Kansan*, Nov. 19, 1958: 2.

164. Saricks, interview with author, Apr. 2, 1990.

165. Smith, interview with author, Mar. 24, 1990.

166. Ibid.

167. Nichols, interview with author, Mar. 24, 1990.

168. Wilson, interview with author, Apr. 19, 1994. Youngberg was executive secretary of the Kansas University Endowment Association.

169. Saricks, interview with author, Apr. 2, 1990.

170. "Big Glamour of Show Business to Attack Right-to-Work Laws," *New York Times*, Oct., 1958, KU Archives.

171. "Murphy Wanted Only Facts in Talk With Faculty," *University Daily Kansan*, Nov. 10, 1958: 1.

172. "KU Professors Agree With Regents' Stand," *University Daily Kansan*, Nov. 11, 1958: 1.

173. *University Daily Kansan*, Nov. 11, 1958: 1.

174. Ibid.

175. Form letter, Chancellor's Office, Nov. 3, 1958, KU Archives.

176. The Associated Press carried Murphy's statement. "K.U. Neutral in Politics, Says Murphy," *Topeka Capital Journal*, Oct. 31, 1958.

177. "Governor's Race Viewed by Counties," *Topeka Capital Journal*, Nov. 5, 1958.

178. "Right-Work Vote Viewed by Counties," *Topeka Capital Journal*, Nov. 5, 1958.

179. A view of the future suggests that this might have been the overriding reason for Docking's success in 1958: George Docking did not raise taxes. His successor, William Avery, raised taxes and lost after one term to George Docking's son, Robert.

180. Robert Campbell, tr., *Seneca. Letters From A Stoic*. Letter XVI, (London: Penguin Books, 1969).

181. "Decision on Hall List Postponed," *University Daily Kansan*, Jan. 10, 1957.

182. Murphy to Senator Merl L. Lemert, letter, Nov. 4, 1958, KU Archives.

183. Griffin. *History* 518.

184. B. L. Humphreys to Murphy, letter, Nov. 6, 1958.

185. Murphy to B.L. Humphreys, letter, Nov. 10, 1958.

186. George Baxter Smith, interview with author, Mar. 24, 1990.

187. Murphy to John Conard, letter, Nov. 10, 1958, KU Archives.

188. Ibid.

189. Ibid.

190. "Docking Brands KU a Trouble Spot," *University Daily Kansan*, Feb. 20, 1959.

191. The description of the Governor's manner appeared in the article. *University Daily Kansan*, Feb. 20, 1959.

192. *University Daily Kansan*, Feb. 20, 1959.

193. *University Daily Kansan*, Feb. 20, 1959. On the same page of the newspaper, Docking put down a rumor that he would move from Lawrence to Arkansas City (which he did). "I think that was a rumor put out by one of the Lawrence newspapers," he said, referring to the *Lawrence Journal World*. "I haven't spoken to them for about four years, so they can't possibly have much direct knowledge."

194. "Docking Says Kansan Accurate but Amateur," *University Daily Kansan*, Feb. 23, 1959.

195. "GOP Hits Docking," *University Daily Kansan*, Feb. 24, 1959.

196. "Writer Says Murphy Will Stay Here If Politicians 'Let Him Run a School'." *University Daily Kansan*, Mar. 6, 1959.

197. News release in 1958/59 file, KU Archives; "Docking Says Kansan Accurate but Amateur," *University Daily Kansan*, Feb. 23, 1959.

198. Murphy, Los Angeles interview with author, Oct. 5, 1992.

199. Murphy to Alvin McCoy, letter, Sep. 8, 1959. KU Archives.

200. Murphy to Robert Vosper, letter, Jan. 6, 1960, KU Archives, as quoted in Fisher, *The Turbulent Years*: 29.

201. Murphy to Robert Vosper, letter, Jan. 6, 1960.

202. The Hoisington plan is laid out in chronological detail in an undated letter to Murphy, written during the one-month-long session, in January, 1960. Hoisington to Murphy, u.d. letter, January, 1960, Chancellor's Correspondence. KU Archives.

203. Murphy to Verne Hoisington, letter, Jul. 13, 1959. KU Archives.

204. Murphy to A. W. Lauterbach, letter, Oct. 15, 1959. KU Archives.

205. Ibid.

206. Murphy to Verne Hoisington, letter, Dec. 2, 1959. KU Archives.

207. Ibid.

208. Ibid.

209. Murphy to John E. King, letter, Jan. 5, 1960. KU Archives.

210. Statement of Murphy, and Murphy to Lauterbach, letter, Feb. 11, 1960. KU Archives.

211. Murphy to J. Mayone Stycos, letter, Jan. 14, 1960. KU Archives.

212. Murphy to Oscar S. Stauffer, letter, Jan. 14, 1960. KU Archives.

213. Murphy to J. Mayone Stycos, letter, Jan. 14, 1960. KU Archives; Murphy, Los Angeles interview with author, Oct. 5, 1992.

214. Murphy to Ray Evans, letter, Mar. 12, 1960. KU Archives.

215. Murphy, Los Angeles interview with author, Oct. 5, 1992.

216. "Docking Jabs at Murphy," Great Bend *Tribune*, Feb. 28, 1960; Nichols, "The Tumultuous Years," Griffin, *History*. 541: Fisher, *The Turbulent Years* 29.

217. Nichols, *Four Tumultuous Years*.

218. Murphy to Ray Evans, letter, Mar. 12, 1960. KU Archives.

219. Ibid.

220. Griffin, *History* 536.

221. Raymond Nichols to Glee Smith, letter, Mar. 14, 1960. KU Archives.

222. "Faculty 'Mourning' Greets Resignation," *University Daily Kansan*, Mar. 17, 1960.

223. "Kansas Loses Murphy," *University Daily Kansan Extra*, Mar. 17, 1960.

224. *University Daily Kansan*, Mar. 17, 1960.

225. See *Topeka Capitol Journal*, *University Daily Kansan. Lawrence Journal World*, *Kansas City Star*, Mar. 17 and 18, 1960.

226. "Two Committees Asked in Canvass for New KU Head," *Topeka Capital Journal*, Mar. 18, 1960.

227. "F ive Mentioned for KU Post," *Topeka Capital Journal*, Mar. 18, 1960.

228. Nichols, interview with author, Mar. 24, 1990; Nichols, "Four Tumultuous Years," Jan. 16, 1990.

229. Murphy, Los Angeles interview with author, Oct. 5, 1992.

Conclusion

1. Minutes of the University Senate, May 10, 1960, KU Archives; "Smooth Wescoe Path Sought," *Lawrence Journal World*, May 11, 1960.
2. "Two Regents Cite Docking Feuds For Resignation," *University Daily Kansas Extra*, Mar. 17, 1960.
3. Statement of the Chancellor, Mar. 17, 1960. KU Archives; "Chancellor Gives His Statement," *University Daily Kansan, Mar.* 17, 1960.
4. "Chancellor Goes to UCLA July 1," *University Daily Kansan Extra*, Mar. 17, 1960.
5. *University Daily Kansan Extra*, Mar. 17, 1960.
6. Vosper to Talmadge, letter, Mar. 27, 1960. KU Archives.
7. "Kansas Loses Murphy," *University Daily Kansan Extra*, Mar. 17, 1960.
8. Petition by KU students, Mar. 18, 1960.Chancellor's Correspondence. KU Archives.
9. "KU Chancellor Says He Is Not Being Chased Away," *Kansas City Star*, May 18, 1960.
10. Murphy, Los Angeles interview with author, Oct. 5, 1992.
11. Murphy, Los Angeles interview with author, Oct. 5, 1992. "Regents cite Docking Feuds For Resignation," University Daily Kansan, Mar. 17, 1960.
12. Griffin, *History*.
13. Fisher. *The Turbulent Years*.
14. Murphy, interview with Hickle, Jan. 19, 1990: 35.
15. Murphy, Los Angeles interview with author, Oct. 5, 1992.
16. *University Daily Kansan*, Mar. 17, 1960.
17. Resolution, The University Senate, May 10, 1960. Senate Minutes. KU Archives.
18. Franklin D. Murphy Distinguished Service Citation, June, 1960. KU Alumni Association Archives.
19. "Honor Moves Chancellor," *Topeka Capital Journal*, June 6, 1960.
20. *University Daily Kansan.* Mar. 17, 1960.
21. Talmadge to Vosper, letter, June 7, 1960. KU Archives.
22. Nichols, interview with author, Apr. 17, 1990.
23. Murphy, telephone interview with author, Mar. 24, 1990: Murphy, interview with Hickle, Jan. 19, 1990.
24. Murphy to Great Plains Conference on Higher Education, speech at Norman, Okla., Oct. 18,1956. Abstracted in *Books and Libraries at the University of Kansas*, 1:14, Feb., 1957. KU Archives.
25. Murphy, interview with author, Apr. 18, 1990.
26. Murphy, Los Angeles interview with author, Oct. 5, 1992.
27. Murphy interview with author, April. 18, 1990; Raymond Nichols, interview with author, March 24, 1990; George Baxter Smith, interview with author, March 24, 1990.
28. Myrna Oliver, "Franklin Murphy dies," *Los Angeles Times*, June 17, 1994: 1A.
29. Frank Burge, Interview with author, May 1, 1990; George Baxter Smith, Interview with author, Mar. 24, 1990; Raymond Nichols, interview with author, Mar. 24, 1990; Robert B. Vosper, Telephone interview with author, April 17, 1990; Robert

Vosper, Transcribed interview by Betty Milum, American Library Association Oral History Project, 1975.

30. Important research on the changes in deans of women's responsibilities appear in Kelly C. Sartorius, "Experimental Autonomy: Dean Emily Taylor and the Women's Movement at the University of Kansas," *Kansas History: A Journal of the Central Plains*, 33, Spring 2010, 2-21, and Kathryn Nemeth Tuttle, "What Became of the Dean of Women?: Changing Rules for Women Administrators in American Higher Education, 1940-1980" (Ph.D. diss., University of Kansas, 1996).

31. Nichols interview with author, Mar. 24, 1990.; Murphy interview with author, Apr. 18, 1990.; Murphy interview by Hickle; C. Heiskel, "The Book Collectors Ephemeron," (Los Angeles, November, 1989) 4:2.

32. Murphy interview with author, Apr. 18, 1990; Murphy, interview with Hickle, Jan. 19, 1990.

33. Franklin Murphy, 'Family Background of FDM," Scrapbook, KU Archives; Murphy interview with author, Apr. 18, 1990; Murphy interview by Hickle, Jan. 19, 1990.

34. George Baxter Smith, Interview with author, Mar. 24, 1990.

35. Franklin Murphy, 'Family Background of Franklin David Murphy," Scrapbook. KU Archives; Murphy, interview with author, Apr. 18, 1990; Murphy interview with Hickle, Jan. 19, 1990.

36. Murphy interview with Hickle, Jan. 19, 1990.

37. Murphy, Los Angeles interview with author, Oct. 5, 1992.

38. Murphy, interview with author, Apr. 18, 1990.

39. Nichols, interview with author, Mar. 24, 1990.

40. Aristotle, *Metaphysics* 1:1.

41. Henry Edward Manning, *The Temporal Mission of the Holy Ghost*, ii., 52. *Oxford English Dictionary* (New York: Oxford University Press, 1971), 280, definition 11.

42. Murphy, interview with Hickle, Jan. 19, 1990, 35.

43. Murphy to author, Los Angeles interview, Oct. 5, 1992.

44. Oliver, Myrna, "Franklin D. Murphy dies," Los Angeles *Times*, June 17, 1994, 1A.

45. For a full explanation of the Summerfield Foundations contributions to the University of Kansas, see the libraries chapter of this research.

46. Young, Charles E., quoted in Oliver, "Franklin Murphy Dies," Los Angeles *Times*, June 17, 1994, 1A.

47. Oliver, Ibid.

48. Roger Heyns, former University of California at Berkeley chancellor, as quoted in Oliver, Ibid.

Works Cited

Correspondence:
Murphy, Franklin D., Chancellor's Office General Correspondence 1951-1960. University of Kansas Archives.
_____. Correspondence and clippings. University of Kansas Alumni Association Archives.
Eisenhower, Dwight David. Correspondence with Franklin D. Murphy. University of Kansas Archives. Libraries, University of Kansas, General Files 1948-1961. University of Kansas Archives.
Vosper, Robert. Correspondence with author. April 23, 1990. Author's possession.

Interviews:
Burge, Frank., personal interview by author, Lawrence, Kansas. 1 May, 1990.
Craig, Susan, personal interview by author, Lawrence, Kansas. 11 April, 1990.
Dineen, Margaret, personal interview by author, Lawrence, Kansas. 5 December, 1993.
Dolginou, Yale, personal interview by Karen Gallagher. Lawrence, Kansas. 20 January, 1995.
Dunwell, Robert, telephone interview by author. Lawrence, Kansas. 19 April, 1994.
Glinka, John., personal interview by author, Lawrence, Kansas. 9 April, 1990.
_____, telephone interview by author, Lawrence, Kansas. 13 April, 1990.
_____, personal interview by author, Lawrence, Kansas. 28 June, 1995.
_____, personal interview by author, Lawrence, Kansas. 5 July, 1995.
Haugh, Oscar, personal interview by author, Lawrence, Kansas. 7 March, 1994.
Harper, Jerry, personal interview by author, Lawrence, Kansas. 1 June, 1995.
Helyar, L. E. James, personal interview by author, Lawrence, Kansas. 27 March, 1990.

Kellogg, Mary Martha, personal interview by author, Wichita, Kansas. 1 February, 1990.
Mason, Alexandra, personal interview by author, Lawrence, Kansas. 9 April, 1990.
_____, telephone interview by author, Lawrence, Kansas. 10 April, 1990.
_____, written corrections on library chapter, Lawrence, Kansas, 5 July, 1995.
Murphy, Franklin D., transcribed interview by Deborah HickJe, University of Kansas School of Medicine Oral History Project, 19 January, 1990.
_____, telephone interview by author, 24 March, 1990. Murphy, Franklin D., telephone interview by author, 18 April, 1990.
_____, personal interview by author, Los Angeles, California. 5 October, 1992.
Nichols, Raymond, personal interview by author, Lawrence, Kansas. 24 March, 1990.
Nugent, John, personal interview by author, Lawrence, Kansas. 19 April, 1990.
Pattee, B.J., personal interview by author, Lawrence, Kansas. 9 March, 1994.
Prohodsky, Betty Bond, personal interview by author, El Dorado, Kansas. 2 October, 1993.
Saricks, Ambrose, personal interview by author, Lawrence, Kansas. 2 April, 1990.
_____, personal interview by author, Lawrence, Kansas. 12 April, 1990.
Saur, Gordon, personal interview by author, Lawrence, Kansas, 23 March, 1990.
Shankel, Delbert, personal interview by author, Lawrence, Kansas, 5 December, 1993.
Smith, George Baxter, personal interview by author, Lawrence, Kansas. 24 March, 1990.
Tidwell, John Edgar, personal interview by author, Lawrence, Kansas, August, 2016.
Vosper, Robert, transcribed interview by Betty Milum, American Library Association Oral History Project, 17 May, 1989.
_____, telephone interview by author, 17 April, 1990.
Waugh, Jerry, personal interview by author, Lawrence, Kansas. 6 April, 1990.
Wiklund, Ann Fothergill, personal interview by author, Lawrence, Kansas. March 11, 1994.
Wilson, Paul E, personal interview by author, Lawrence, Kansas, 10 April, 1994.

Annual Reports: "University of Kansas Library Annual Reports," 1951-1960. University of Kansas Archives.

Books:
Ackrill, J. L.ed:, *A New Aristotle Reader*. Princeton: Princeton University Press, 1987.
Ackrill, J.L., *Aristotle, the Philosopher*. Oxford: Oxford University Press, 1981.
Adams, Virginia. *On The Hill*. Lawrence: University of Kansas Press, 1983. 128-143.
Adler, Mortimer and Carl Van Doren. *Great Treasury of Western Thought*. New York & London: R.R. Bowker Company, 1977. 497-499.
Adler, Mortimer J. *Ten Philosophical Mistakes*. New York: Macmillan Publishing Company, 1985. 195-198.
Bacon, Francis. Peter Urbach and John Gibson, tr. *Novum Orgamim*. 1:43. Chicago and La Salle, Illinois: Open Court Publishing Corporation, 1994. 55.
Barzun, Jacques. *The House of Intellect*. New York: Harper, 1959. 38
Blumenthal, Sidney. *The Rise of the Counter-establishment: From Conservative Ideology to Political Power*. New York: Times Books, 1986.
Burke, James. *Connections*. Boston: Little, Brown and Company, 1978. 98-100.
Campbell, Robin, tr.:, *Seneca: Letters From A Stoic*. London: Penguin Books, Inc., 1969.
Chamberlain, Wilt. *A View From Above*. New York: Signet, Penguin Books, Inc., 1992. 31-160.
Charles, David. *Aristotle's Philosophy of Action*. Ithaca: Cornell University Press, 1984.
Charleton, W. *Aristotle's Physics I. II*. Oxford: Oxford University Press, 1971.
Cole, Bruce and Adelheid Gealt. *Art of the Western World*. New York: Summit Books, 1989. 129.
Cordley, Richard. *A History of Lawrence*. Lawrence: Lawrence Journal Press, 1895.
Daniel, Clifton. *Chronicle of the 20th Century*. Mount Kisco, NY.: Chronicle Publications, 1987. 708.
Davis, Margaret Leslie. Positions and Affiliations, 2007. *The Culture Broker & Franklin D. Murphy and the Transformation of Los Angeles*, University of California Press, 2007 451-53.
Eldredge, Charles. *Handbook of the Collection*. Lawrence: The Helen Foresman Spencer Museum of Art, 1978.
Fisher, Mike. *Deaner*. Kansas City: The Lowell Press, 1986.
Flew, Antony. *A Dictionary of Philosophy*. New York: St. Martin's Press, 1984.
Franklin, John Hope and Alfred A. Moss, Jr. *From Slavery to Freedom*. 6th ed. New York: Alfred A. Knopf, 1988.
Gilbert, James. *Another Chance: Postwar America 1945-1985*. 2nd ed. Chicago: The Dorsey Press, 1986. 1-25.

Griffin, Clifford S. *The University of Kansas: A History*. Lawrence: The University Press of Kansas, 1974.

Haskell, Henry C. Jr. and Richard B. Fowler. *City of the Future, a Narrative History of Kansas City. 1850-1950*. Kansas City: Frank Glenn Publishing Co., Inc., 1950.

Heffels, Monika, ed.:, *Albrecht Purer: The Complete Woodcuts*. Kirchdorf: Berghaus Verlag, 1990.

Hughes, Langston. *The Big Sea*. New York & London: Alfred A. Knopf, 1940. 16-23.

Hutchins, Robert Maynard, ed:, *Great Books of the Western World: IX - Aristotle II*. Chicago: Encyclopaedia Brittanica, Inc., 1952. 593 ff.

Isely, Bliss. *The Kansas Story*. Oklahoma City: Harlow Publishing Corporation, 1961.

Kaplan, Justin, ed.:, *The Pocket Aristotle*. New York: Washington Square Press, 1958.

Keegan, John, ed. *The Times Atlas of the Second World War*. New York: Harper & Row Publishers, 1989.

Lee, Desmond, tr. Plato: *The Republic*. London: Penguin Books, 1987.

Loomis, Louise Ropes, ed:, *Aristotle. On Man in the Universe*. Roslyn, NY.: Walter J. Black, 1943.

Mason, Alexandra and Thomas R. Buckman. *Nine Eventful Years: An Index to Books and Libraries at the University of Kansas. Numbers 1-16. Dec. 1952 - May. 1961*. Lawrence: University of Kansas Libraries, 1961.

McReynolds, Edwin C. Missouri: *A History of the Crossroads State*. Norman: University of Oklahoma Press, 1962.

Morris, Van Cleve and Young Pai. *Philosophy and the American School*. Boston: Houghton Mifflin Company, 1976.

Organ, Troy Wilson. *An Index to Aristotle*. New York: Gordian Press, Inc., 1966.

Owens, Joseph . *The Doctrine of Being in the Aristotelian Metaphysics*. Toronto: Pontifical Institute of Mediaeval Studies, 1978.

Oxford English Dictionary. The Compact Edition. New York: Oxford University Press, 1971.

Rampersad, Arnold, ed.: *The Collected Poems of Langston Hughes*. New York: Alfred A. Knopf, 1994.

_____. *The Life of Langston Hughes*. Vol. 1: 1902-1941. London: Oxford University Press, 2002.

_____. *The Life of Langston Hughes*. Vol. 2: 1941-1967. London: Oxford University Press, 2002.

Reale, Giovanni. *The Concept of First Philosophy and the Unity of the Metaphysics of Aristotle*. Albany: State University of New York Press, 1980.

Riesman, David. *The Lonely Crowd*. New Haven: Yale University Press, 1950.

_____. *Abundance for What?* New York: Doubleday & Company, Inc., 1964.
Russell, Bertrand. *Wisdom of the West.* Garden City, NY.: Doubleday & Co., 1959.
Sartorius, Kelly C., D*eans of Women and the Feminist Movement: Emily Taylor's Activism.* Palgrave Macmillan, 2014.
Scarffe, John A. *From Vision to Reality: 100 Years of Private Support through the University of Kansas Endowment Association.* Lawrence: The Kansas University Endowment Association, 1991.
Stegner, Wallace. *The Letters of Bernard DeVoto.* Garden City, New York: Doubleday & Company, 1975.
Stegner, Wallace. *Angle of Repose.* New York: Ballantine Books, 1971. 423.
Sulzberger, C.L. *American Heritage History of World War II.* New York: American Heritage Publishing Co., Inc., 1966.
Van Doren, Carl. *Benjamin Franklin.* New York: The Viking Press, 1938.
Webster's Biographical Dictionary. Springfield, Mass.: G. & C. Merriam Co., 1961.
Webster's New World Dictionary. New York: The World Publishing Company, 1958.
Wills, Garry. *Certain Trumpets.* New York: Simon & Schuster, 1994.
Witt, Charlotte. *Substance and Essence in Aristotle: An Interpretation of Metaphysics VII-IX.* Ithaca: Cornell University Press, 1989.

Chapters in Books:
Bacon, Francis. "Franciscus de Verulamio sic cogitavit." *Novum Organum.* chapter in *Practical Cogitator.* Boston: Houghton Mifflin Company, 1945. 16-20.
Gunn, James E., ed.; *Man and the Future.* Murphy, Franklin D. "The Changed and Changing University." Lawrence and London: The University Press of Kansas, 1968. 279-296.
Mele, Alfred R. "Aristotle on the Proximate Efficient Cause of Action." *New Essays on Aristotle.* Guelph, Ontario: Canadian Association for Publishing in Philosophy, 1984.
de Montaigne, Michel E. "Of the Education of Children," *Selected Essays.* Donald W. Frame, trans. Roslyn, New York: Walter J. Black, 1943. 10.
Riesman, David. "Bookworms and the Social Soil." *Individualism Reconsidered.* Glencoe, Illinois: The Free Press, 1954. 258-65.
Tuttle, William M., Jr. "Introduction," *Embattled Lawrence Conflict and Community,* Dennis Domer & Barbara Watkins, eds., The University Continuing Education, 2001.
_____. "Separate But Not Equal: African-Americans and the 100-year Struggle for Equality in Lawrence and at The University of Kansas, 1850s-1960," *Embattled Lawrence, Conflict and Community,* Dennis Domer & Barbara Watkins, eds., The University of Kansas Continuing Education, 2001. 139-151.

Brochures and Pamphlets:

"A Symposium in Honor of Franklin D. Murphy." Co-sponsored by UCLA and the J. Paul Getty Trust, October 15-17, 1992.

C. Heiskel, "The Book Collectors' Ephemeron," 4:2. (Los Angeles, November, 1989.)

Collection of John C. Carson, La Jolla, California. "From Birth to Maturity in 200 Years — An Oversimplified Analogy." Kenneth Aldred Spencer Memorial Lecture Series, University of Kansas, 14 March, 1973.

University of Kansas Alumni Association Archives. Kurdian, Harry. "Some Reminiscences." Wichita: Sign of the Four Ducks, 1982. "Opening Convocation and the Installation of Franklin D. Murphy." University of Kansas, 17 September, 1951.

University of Kansas Alumni Association Archives. "Spencer Museum of Art." The Helen Foresman Spencer Museum of Art, University of Kansas. Undated brochure. Author's collection. "The Wanderings of Odysseus," Program Notes for *Odyssey,* sponsored by the J. Paul Getty Museum, September and October, 1992.

"YOUR Government" XIV:1. September 15, 1958. University of Kansas Archives.

Journals:

Annas, Julia. "Aristotle on Inefficient Causes." *The Philosophy Quarterly.* 32:129 (October, 1982), 311-26.

Axtelle, George E. "The Philosophy of Organism Applied to Democratic Theory and Strategy." *The Educational Forum.* 15:2 ((January, 1951), 231-48.

Brumbaugh, Robert S. and Nathaniel M. Lawrence, Jr. "Aristotle's Philosophy of Education." *Educational Theory* IX: 1 (January, 1959), 1-15.

Hocutt, Max. "Aristotle's Four Becauses." *Philosophy* 49:190 (October, 1974), 385-399.

Mason, Alexandra. "Rare Books in the Great American Desert." *American Bookman* (March, 1982), 1603-17.

Moeser, James. "School of Fine Arts Receives 2 Major Bequests." *Endowment Digest* (October, 1976). University of Kansas Alumni Association Archives.

Murphy, Franklin D. "A Message to the Schoolmen of Kansas." *University of Kansas Bulletin of Education* 7, (November, 1952), 1-2.

_____. "The Chancellor's Response." *University of Kansas Bulletin of Education* 11. (November, 1956), 25-26.

_____. "The Purpose of the Program." *University of Kansas Bulletin of Education* 13. (February, 1959), 33-34.

Hermann, Rein. *The Journal of Physiology*, July 15, 2014, 592, 2911-2914. Politics & Physiology: Herrman Rein and the Nobel Prize 1933-1953. Ils Hansson and Serve Dann "Rein nominated 12Y, 1933-1953. "Nazi prhohibited German scholars to accept Nobel. Hermann Klein active during 1933-1945 in Nazi orgs. Wikipedia. Notes 1, 2.

Katzman, David M. "The Children of Abraham and Hannah: Grocer, Doctor, Entrepreneur: The Summerfields of Lawrence, Kansas." *(Kansas History: Journal of the Central Plains* 37. (Spring 2014), 2-19.

Seymour, Todd. "Endowment Book Value Reaches $51,110,905." *Endowment Digest* (October, 1976). University of Kansas Alumni Association Archives.

Sartorius, Kelly C. "Experimental Autonomy: Dean Emily Taylor and the Women's Movement at the University of Kansas," *Kansas History: A Journal of the Central Plains* 33 (Spring 2010): 2-21.

Sprague, Rosamund Kent. "The Four Causes: Aristotle's Exposition and Ours." *The Monist* 52:1, (January, 1968), 298-300.

Vosper, Robert. "A Report on Books and Libraries in Kansas." *California Librarian* 14:3, (March, 1953). Vosper, Robert. "Another Report from Kansas." *Hoja Volante*. University of California at Los Angeles. (May, 1953).

_____. "Another Report from Kansas." *Hoja Volante*. University of California at Los Angeles. (August, 1953). Vosper, Robert. "Acquisition Policy - Fact or Fancy?" *College and University Libraries*. (October, 1953) 367-370.

_____. "A Pair of Bibliomanes for Kansas: Ralph Ellis and Thomas Jefferson Fitzpatrick." *Papers of the Bibliographical Society of America*. 55 (Third Quarter, 1961).

Series:
Books and Libraries at the University of Kansas. 1: 1-25s:1 (1952-1960).
Library Collections. University of Kansas Archives. *Biblio-Tracks*. (1952-1954).
Library Collections. University of Kansas Archives. *The Gamut*. 1:1 - VII: 1 (1954-1960).
Library Collections. University of Kansas Archives.

Magazines and Periodicals:
Baker, S. Zebulon, "'To Help Foster Athletic Equality Here in the Midwest': Defeating Jim Crow in the Big Seven Conference," *Kansas History: A Journal of the Central Plains,* 39, 2. (Summer, 2016).

Barnett, Chris. "Chatting with Franklin Murphy in the Executive Suite at The Los Angeles Times." *Flightime* (May, 1974), 17-19. University of Kansas Alumni Association Archives.

Beatty, Jerome. "More and Better Doctors for Your Town." *American Magazine*. (June, 1955), 18-19. University of Kansas Alumni Association Archives. *Building Age*. 51:5 (May, 1929): 14. *Books in Print*. (January 13, 1995): R.R. Bowker. Boone, Gray D., "Lawrence:

A dynamic relationship between the university and the community nurtures art and culture." *Horizon.* (September, 1987), 18. "A Day in the Life of K.U.'s First Lady." *Kansas Alumni.* (November, 1956), 4-5. *Kansas Alumni.* (Sept./Oct. 1991), 36.

Knapp, Donald F. "The Fighting Irishman." *Beta Theta Pi.* (May, 1962), 425-426. *Literary Digest.* 95:1 (1 October, 1927): 36-77.

Mason, Alexandra. "Golden Years: Dr. Murphy Brought Mr. Vosper to KU as 'Grand Acquisitor." *Kansas Alumni* (February, 1982), 2-4.

Meehan, Thomas. "Must We Be Nostalgic About the Fifties?" *Horizon.* IX (Winter, 1972), 7. "Franklin Murphy Leaves Kansas; W. Clarke Wescoe to be Chancellor." *Kansas Alumni* (May, 1960). University of Kansas Alumni Association Archives. "Franklin Murphy Becomes Dean of Medicine." *Grad Magazine* (February 23, 1948). University of Kansas Alumni Archives.

Murphy, Franklin D. "We Need More Doctors." *Saturday Evening Post.* (May 26, 1951), 19-87.

_____. "International Situation Makes Scientific Research Crucial For Our Times." *Kansas Alumni.* (October, 1954). University of Kansas Alumni Association Archives.

_____. "The Opening of the Building for Music." *Kansas Alumni.* (October, 1957). "Dr. Franklin D. Murphy: The Man of the Month." *Swing Magazine.* (Dec, 1950), 561-564. University of Kansas Alumni Association Archives. "Speed Up." *Time.* 28:3. (July 16, 1951). *Time.* (June 15, 1974.) "Ike Sat at His Feet," *Time.* (October 22, 1952.) 60. "Why Haven't We Heard From Them?" *Time.* (Nov. 6, 1951.) "Communism and the Colleges." *Time.* (April 6, 1953)

Manuscripts

Cruse, Marvin. "Scientific Rarities from Nebraska." Undated manuscript. University of Kansas Library, 1953 files. University of Kansas Archives.

Fisher, Michael P. "The Turbulent Years: The University of Kansas, 1960-1975." Doctoral Dissertation, University of Kansas, 1979.

Goodnight, Lizzie E. "Negroes in Lawrence." Master's Thesis, University of Kansas, 1903. Kansas Room, Lawrence Public Library.

Murphy, Franklin. "Family Background of FDM," unpublished manuscript, Murphy Scrapbook, University of Kansas Archives.

Pitts, Heidi. "Racism and Reformation with Franklin Murphy." May 13, 1992.

Tuttle, Kathryn Nemeth, "What Became of the Dean of Women?: Changing Roles for Women Administrators in American Higher Education, 1940-1980" (Ph.D. diss., University of Kansas, 1996).

Newspapers:

Independence (Kansas) *Reporter,* (Oct. 14, 1955).

Great Bend (Kansas) *Tribune,* (February 28, 1960).
Kansas City *Star,* (1948-1960).
Kansas City *Times,* (Jan. 16, 1958).
Lawrence (Kansas) *Journal World,* (1948-1960).
London *Times Literary Supplement.* (July 6, 1956, 416; July 18, 1957, 39; May 30, 1958).
Los Angeles *Times,* (June 17, 1994).
The Milwaukee Journal. (Sept. 19, 1952).
New York Times, (June 17, 1994).
Parsons (Kansas) *Sun.* (1951-1960)
St. Louis *Globe Democrat.*
Topeka Capital Journal. (1951-1960).
University Daily Kansan. (1948-1960).
Wichita *Eagle,* (1948 - 1960).

Press Releases and Announcements:
"Dean of Libraries, University of Kansas." Position announcement, University of Kansas. May, 1990. Author's collection.
Gunn, James E., "Murphy Resigns." K.U. News Bureau, March 16, 1960. University of Kansas Archives. "Teachers' Union News Release." March 31, 1953. Chancellor's Correspondence 1952-53. University of Kansas Archives.
Yoe, Tom, "Murphy Appointed as Medical School Dean." Feb. 28, 1948. University of Kansas Alumni Association Archives. "Franklin Murphy: General View of His KU Years." K.U. News Bureau, Lawrence, 16 March, 1960. University of Kansas Alumni Association Archives. "Statement of the Chancellor." Chancellor's Office, University of Kansas, Mar. 17, 1960. "Franklin Murphy Awarded Citation for Distinguished Service." K.U. News Bureau, 6 June, 1960. University of Kansas Alumni Association Archives. Reports: "Minutes of the University Senate, May 10, 1960." University of Kansas. University of Kansas Archives.
Quinsey, Robert L., "Report on Stack Storage Space." University of Kansas Library. May 19, 1953. University of Kansas Archives.
Shoemaker, W.H., chairman. "Report of the Special Committee on the University Library." College of Liberal Arts and Sciences, University of Kansas, March, 1951.
Vosper, Robert. "Departmental Book Allocation Report, 1953-54. University of Kansas Library. June 10, 1953. University of Kansas Archives.

Published Speeches:
Hoffman, Paul G., "Freedom is For the Brave." Commencement Address. (14 June, 1953). University of Kansas Archives.

Milton, John, "Areopagitica: A Speech for the Liberty of Unlicensed Printing, to the Parliament of England." *British Poetry and Prose.* (Boston: Houghton Mifflin Company. 1950)

Murphy, Franklin D., "The Meaning of University," Commencement Address, University of Pennsylvania, June 15, 1955. University of Kansas Alumni Association Archives.

_____, "Inaugural Remarks," 17 September, 1951. University of Kansas Archives.

_____, "A Proven Investment for the State of Kansas: Farewell Greeting to the Class of '52." Published speech, University of Kansas. University of Kansas Alumni Association Archives.

_____, "Cultural and Intellectual Growth in the Great Plains Area." Great Plains Conference on Higher Education, University of Oklahoma, Norman, Oklahoma, October 18, 1956.

_____. "KU at Mid-Century: A Record of Achievement." *K.U. Today Newsletter*. Published speech, Hutchinson, Kansas, 21 December, 1957. University of Kansas Alumni Association Archives.

Unpublished Speeches:

Murphy, Franklin D., "Report to Alumni." Unpublished speech, University of Kansas, 1 June, 1952. University of Kansas Alumni Association Archives.

_____. "Farewell to the Graduates — June 1955." Unpublished speech, University of Kansas, June, 1955. University of Kansas Alumni Association Archives.

_____. "Remarks of the Retiring Chairman." Unpublished speech, Washington, D.C. 11 October, 1957. University of Kansas Alumni Association Archives.

_____. "Statement of Dr. Franklin D. Murphy at Annual Meeting of the K.U. Alumni Association of Greater Kansas City." Unpublished speech, Kansas City. 21 November, 1957. University of Kansas Alumni Association Archives.

_____. "The Goal at Stake in Kansas." Unpublished speech, Lawrence, Kansas. Undated. University of Kansas Alumni Association Archives.

_____. "Dr. Murphy's Speech at Special Convocation." 18 March, 1960. University of Kansas Alumni Association Archives.

Murphy, Franklin D. "untitled." Speech, 28 September, 1951. KU Archives.

Nichols, Raymond. "Four Tumultuous Years." unpublished speech, The Old and New Club, Lawrence, Kansas. 26 January, 1990.

_____. "50 Years at KU." Lawrence Unitarian Fellowship, 1992.

Yearbooks:

Field, Lyman. "Rambling around in Europe." *The Jayhawker*. (May, 1936) 374.

Murphy, Franklin D. "Rally, rally." *The Javhawker*. (Dec, 1935) 93.
Murphy, Franklin D. "Dictapators." *The Javhawker*. (Oct., 1935) 40.

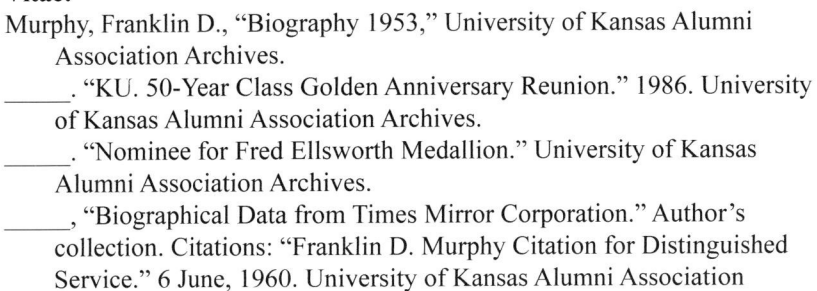

Vitae:
Murphy, Franklin D., "Biography 1953," University of Kansas Alumni Association Archives.
_____. "KU. 50-Year Class Golden Anniversary Reunion." 1986. University of Kansas Alumni Association Archives.
_____. "Nominee for Fred Ellsworth Medallion." University of Kansas Alumni Association Archives.
_____, "Biographical Data from Times Mirror Corporation." Author's collection. Citations: "Franklin D. Murphy Citation for Distinguished Service." 6 June, 1960. University of Kansas Alumni Association Archives.

Letters
Murphy, handwritten letter to Chancellor Lindley, Oct. 26, 1936, Göttinger, Germany.
Shelby, Ernie. Letter to *Sports Illustrated*, Nov. 20, 2013.

Index

abolitionists, 109, 110
Adams, George Mathew, 73
Adler, Elmer, 92
Adler, Mortimer, 6
AFL-CIO, 192
African Americans, 110-12, 117, 122, 125-126, 134, 140, 143-45, 212
Ahmanson Foundation, 72, 224
Aid Company, New England Emigrant, 108
Aitchison, R.T., 95
Alderson, Don, 150, 217
Allen Field House, 135
Allen, Dr. Forrest 'Phog,' 60, 111, 113, 126-27, 135-36, 138-39, 141, 153, 155
Alpha Omega Alpha, 9, 26, 225
Alpha Phi Alpha, 128, 131
Alumni Association, KU, 166, 213, 231
American Association of Retired Persons, 125
American Association of Universities, 60, 119, 164
American Council of Education, 225
American Library Association, 97
Anderson, John, 176
Appeal to Reason, 124
Areopagitica, 58, 230
Argersinger, W.J. Jr., 185
Aristotelian, 6-7, 55, 93, 116, 165
Aristotle, 6, 117, 216, 219
Army Medical Corps, 27
Arn, Governor Ed, 46, 54, 132
Art of the Western World, 2
Atkins, Mary McAfee, 12
Austin, Whitley, 171, 204, 206
Axe, Leonard, 204
Baker, Charles W., 75-76
Baker, S. Zebulon, 126
Baldwin, DeWitt, 142
Barton Salt Company, President of the, 199
Battenfeld, J.R., 18, 44
Baumgartel, Harold, 185
Baumgartner, Dr. W. J., 21
Baur, E.J., 185, 193
Beecher, Henry Ward, 108
Bell, George D., 183

Bennett, Shannon, 234-35
Benton, Thomas Hart, 66, 69-71
Beta Theta Pi, 18, 149, 225
bibliomania, galloping, 76, 100
Big Six Conference, 126
Blair, James L., 132
Blythe, Lawrence, 42
Board of Regents, 36, 40, 42, 46-47, 50, 54, 60, 77, 86, 89, 99-101, 104, 112, 134, 161, 163, 167, 169-72, 175, 181, 191, 193-94, 203-04, 206-07, 210-12, 214
Books and Libraries, 92-93
Books and Libraries at the University of Kansas, 92
books, love of, 73
Boyd, McDill "Huck," 171, 181, 193
Boyer, John, 154, 186-87, 194, 199
brain drain, 27, 164
Breidenthal, Maurice, 166, 184
Breslin, Jimmy, 137
Brighton, Hubert, Secretary of the Kansas Board of Regents, 101
Brotherhood Dinner, 123
Brotherhood, Jayhawk, 132-34
Brown vs. Topeka Board of Education, 113, 132
Brown, Cordelia, 10-11, 13, 70-72, 113, 117, 132, 143, 203
Brown, John, 70, 109, 112, 124
Burge, Frank, 53, 83, 173
Carlson, Governor Frank, 33, 42
Carnegie Foundation for the Advancement of Teaching, 38, 166, 224
Cervantes, 90, 91
Chair in Music, Cordelia Brown Murphy, 72
Chamber of Commerce, Lawrence, 144, 169, 179
Chamber of Commerce, U.S. Junior, 45, 144
Chamberlain, Wilt, 111, 127-28, 135-42, 155, 233-35
Chase, William Merritt, 12
Churchill, Winston, 52, 73, 164, 180, 230
Citation for Distinguished Service, 213

Clark, John W., 110
closed shop, 160-61, 196
Clymer, Rolla, 176
Cole, Bruce, 2, 3
College of Liberal Arts and Sciences, 77, 78, 212
Commencement Speech, University of Pennsylvania, June 15, 1955, 57
Commission, National Security, 143
Communists, 146, 147
Conard, John, 201
Conference, Missouri Valley, 125
Congress of Racial Equality, 128, 131
Congress of Racial Equality (CORE), 117
Considine, Bob, 1, 4
Constitution, Kansas, 169
Cook, Martha Jane, 10
Cordley, Richard, 109
Courtyard, Judith Harris Murphy, 71
Crerar, John Library of Economics, 103
Cukor, George, 69
culture, 23, 69, 125, 128, 199, 213, 218-19
Curry, John Steuart, 69-71, 88
Darby, Harry, 184, 205, 211
Davis, Dowdell, 136
Davis, George, 44
Davis, Margaret Leslie, 72, 225
Democrats, 160, 175, 176, 179, 191, 206
desegregate Lawrence, 128
Dick, Elliot C., 185
discriminatory clause, 150
Docking, George, 5, 71, 149, 156, 16-62, 167-81, 185, 191, 196-97, 199, 201-03, 206-08, 210-11
doctor shortage, 38, 40
Doliginou, Yale, 150
Dresden, Max, 77
Du Bois, W.E.B., 112, 122
Dunwell, Robert, 46
Dürer, Albrecht, 2-4, 17, 66, 86, 98, 151, 215
Education Committee, Senate, 202
egghead, 172, 196
Eisenhower, Milton, 126
Eisenhower, President Dwight D., 5, 52, 94, 116, 135, 142-43, 159, 163-65, 180, 184, 206, 225
El Dorado, 176
Eldredge, Charles, 12, 71
Ellis Collection, 76, 96

Ellis, Ralph N., Jr., 76
Ellsworth, Fred, 166, 202
Emerson, Ralph Waldo, 65-66
Emery-Bird-Thayer department store, 17
Endowment Association, 73, 165, 184
ethical citizenship, 115, 212
Evans, Ray, 206, 212
extraordinary meeting with Chancellor Murphy, 140
Eyes on the Prize, 117
Faubus, Orval, 5, 114, 142-43, 145
Federation of Labor, Kansas, 192
Fees, Walter S., 46-47
Fellowship of Reconciliation, 112
Felstiner, William, 68, 90
Field, Gertrude, 25
Field, J. Elden, 185
Field, Lyman, 16, 18-20, 23-25, 70
Field, Russell, 11, 11-17
find the money, 85, 89, 103, 216
Fisher, Michael, 7, 135-36, 228
Fisher, Mike, 135
Fitzgerald, Ella, 117
Fitzpatrick Collection, 85, 98-99, 101
Fitzpatrick, Professor, 85, 98-104
Fitzpatrick, Thomas Jefferson, 98
Flanagin, Martha, 10
Flexner Report, 38
Flood of 1951, 50, 76
Ford Foundation, 162, 166
Ford, A. John T., 166
foreign students, 107, 123, 128-29
Franklin, Ben, 121
free expression, 115-16, 118-19, 188-89, 212
free market-place of ideas, 7, 57, 189, 228
fund raising, 91, 165
G.I. Bill, 117, 128
Garvey, Ray, 120
Geological Survey, Kansas, 168
Gilles, Paul W., 125
Gleason, Gregory, 131
Glenn, Frank, 2-3, 10, 66, 73, 86, 98, 99-100, 104, 215
Glinka, John, 76, 83, 89, 97
Goettingen University, 21
Gorton, Thomas, 4
Governmental Research Center, University of Kansas, 182
Granada Theatre, 130

Index   285

Grand Tour, 23
Great Plains, 69, 74, 215
Greater University Fund, 67, 91, 166, 168, 184-85
Grier, Edward, 185
Griffin, Clifford, 7, 88, 163, 166, 170, 199
Grumm, John G., 182, 185, 193
Gunn, James, 61, 91
Gutenberg, Johann, 66, 69
Haines, Lacy, 36
Hall, E. Raymond, 76
Hall, Governor Fred, 54, 71, 87, 101, 115, 151, 161, 176, 179, 197, 214
Hall, Joyce, 44, 52, 165
Hallmark Card Company, 52
Harder, Marvin, 185
Harlem Globetrotters, 141
Harp, Dick, 139, 141
Harris, David, 128, 233, 235
Harvey family, 110
Heller, Francis, 77
Helyar, L.E. James, 96
Hibbard, Blaine, 18
Hibbs, Ben, 135
Hinman, Charlton, 98
hiring procedures, 59
Hitler, Adolph, 20-22
Hoisington, Verne, 202, 204-05
Home Management House, 127
Hopson, Dan Jr., 169, 185
Howey, Richard, 76-78, 95, 103
Hoyt, Palmer, 120
Hughes, Langston, 123-25, 127, 129
Hults, Donald S., 191
Human Relations, Group for the Improvement of, 134, 142
Huntington Library, 72
Hutchinson News, 17-74, 182
inaugural address, 23, 54, 220
infantile paralysis, 122
International Club, 143
Ise, John, 51, 60, 138, 169, 198
J. Paul Getty Museum, 72
Jayhawk Biblio-Tracks, 93
Jayhawk Coop, 128
Jayhawker, 19-20, 23
Jeans, Sam, 110
Jewish presence, 150
John Birch Society, 120
Jones, Al, 145
Jotham Meeker Club, 92

Judith Harris Murphy Courtyard, 71
Kansas Board of Regents, 46-47, 62, 75, 85, 100-01, 103, 163, 167-69, 171, 184, 191-94, 204-08
Kansas City, 2-3, 10-12, 17-18, 24-26, 28-31, 34, 36, 44-45, 50, 59, 66, 82-83, 91, 94, 98-99, 102, 122, 131-32, 136-37, 150, 166, 168, 172, 174, 179-80, 184-85, 197, 203, 211, 213, 218, 224
Kansas Clergy and Educators Opposed to Amendment No. 3, Voluntary Committee of, 182, 187
Kansas Rural Health Plan, 33, 41, 42, 163
Kansas State Teachers College, 204, 208
Kansas State University, 62, 110, 126, 138, 162-63, 165, 179-80, 204, 208
Kansas Technical Institute, 134, 136
Kansas Union, 133, 154
Kappa Alpha Psi, 128, 140, 233
Katzman, David M., 68
Kay, Morris, 123
Kelly, William A., 185
Kemp, Harry, 124
Kennedy, John Fitzgerald, 143
Kenyon, Bob, 18
Kerford, Lloyd, 134, 136
Kerr, Clark, 207, 210
Ketzel, Clifford, 182, 185
Kiene, Tom, 172
King Jr., Martin Luther, 113
King, J.D., 130
King, John E., 204-05, 208
King, Maurice, 111, 136
Kleinberg, Jacob, 185
Korean War, 60, 132, 135, 160
KU Endowment Association, 90, 95, 192, 245
Ku Klux Klan, 111
KU School of Medicine, 4, 13, 18, 39-40, 44, 58-59, 208
Kurdian, Harry, 95
KU-Y, 131
labor unions, 160, 186, 192
Laird, Roy D., 185, 193
Landon, Alfred M., 21
Lane, James, 112
LAS Report, 77, 78
Lauterbach, Senator A.W., 169, 204-05
Lawrence League for the Practice of Democracy, 123, 134

Lawrence, Amos, 109
Lawton, Keith, 61
leader, 3, 5-6, 24, 35, 41, 45, 59, 61-62, 113-14, 117, 125, 149, 162-63, 173, 176, 186, 192, 197, 209, 211-12, 214-16, 219-21
leadership style, 7, 36
Leadership Team, 85
Lemert, Merl L., 197
Library Committee, University Senate, 79
Lindley, Ernest H., 111
Linnaeus, 98-99
TLS, 96-97
Logan, James K., 185
London *Times Literary Supplement*, 96-97
LOOK Magazine, 45, 180
Los Angeles County Museum, 72, 224
Los Angeles Times, 67, 216
Lovellette, Clyde, 136
loyalty oath, 116, 119
Luck Tiger Manufacturing company, 25
Mag, Arthur, 44
Malott, Deane, Chancellor of the University of Kansas, 30-31, 34, 45-48, 50, 52-53, 75, 77, 79, 112, 125, 127
Man shall not live by bread alone, 65
Marshall, Thurgood, 123, 134, 143, 154
Maser, Ed, 67, 69-72
Mason, Alexandra, 59, 74, 83, 89-90, 97
McCain, James A., 62, 163, 204-05
McCarthy, Joseph, 5, 114, 116, 118, 121, 123, 164
McCormally, John, 173
McCoy, Alvin, 36, 91, 174, 203
McCoy, Lester, 47, 54
McDowell, Joseph, 191
McNair, John, 42
McWilliams, Robert B., 110
Melvin, Frank, 76
Mendel, Robert, 96
Midwest Inter-Library Center, 93
Midwest Research Institute, 45, 52, 225
Millay Collection, Edna St. Vincent, 71
Miller, Herb, 30, 111
Miller, Loren, 111
Minneola, 37, 44
Moeser, James, 13
Moreau, F.J., 185

Mount Oread, 18
Murphy, Chancellor, 4-6, 11, 21-22, 30, 34, 45, 47, 49, 50-54, 69, 75, 77-80, 82, 84, 87, 89, 92, 95-96, 111-14, 122-23, 125, 127-29, 131, 133-36, 138-42, 145-46, 149, 151, 154, 156, 158, 166, 173, 175, 180, 183-84, 190-91, 193, 196, 199, 201-02, 207, 213, 223, 228, 233-36
Murphy, Judith Joyce, 25-26, 29, 51
Murphy, Patrick, 12, 217
Museum of Art, Helen Foresman Spencer, 71
National Association for the Advancement of Colored People (NAACP), 111-12, 117, 131, 134, 143, 146
National Collegiate Athletic Association, 139
National Gallery of Art, 72, 224
National Research Council, 27
Nazi Germany, 22-23
Nehring, Earl, 185
Nelson, Edward G., 185
Nelson, John, 12, 51
Nelson, William Rockhill, 12, 51
Nesmith, Dean 'Deaner,' 135-36
New Republic, 121
Newell, Charles B., 35
Nichols, Clyde, 18, 51-52, 61, 85-86, 93, 167, 176, 180, 192, 207, 209, 215
Nichols, Raymond, 18, 51-52, 61, 85-86, 93, 167, 176, 180, 192, 207, 209, 215
Null, Harold, 95
Oldfather, Charles Jr., 182, 185, 192
Orel, Harold, 98
Parsons Sun, 177
Peck, Dr. J.H. Haddon, 35, 42
Pembroke School, 2, 16
penicillin, 27, 216
Phelps, Kermit, 125
picketers, 181
Pickett, Calder, 88
Pierce, Don, 127
Pitts, Heidi, 7, 149
Pittsburg State, 168, 204
Platonist, 116
polio, 122-23, 135
Pollack, Harvey, 141
Positions and Affiliations, 223

Powell, Lawrence Clark, 82
Professorship in Art History, Judith Harris Murphy, 72
"Purpose of University," 115
Quantrill, William, 109
Quinsey, Robert, 96
Rafinesque, Constantin F., 99
rare books, 2-3, 5, 74, 89, 95, 97-98, 100-01, 166, 218
Reed, Clyde, 71, 176-78, 181-82, 191, 196-97
Rein, Professor Hermann, 22
Renaissance, 2, 4-5, 24, 58, 66-69, 73-74, 90-91, 221, 228, 231
Report on the University Library, 77
Report to the University Senate's Library Committee, 75
Republican, 70, 119, 143, 159, 160-61, 163, 167, 169, 177-78, 179, 181, 184, 191, 196, 202
Republicans, KU Young, 181
Research Libraries, Association of, 60, 74, 77
Riemenschneider, Tilmann, 66-67
"right to work," 160-62, 169, 177-78, 182-83, 185-92, 194, 196-98, 212
Right-to-Work Amendment, 160-61, 169, 182-83, 186, 188, 190, 194, 196-97
Roberts, Roy, 44
Robinson, Harold, 126
Rubinstein, Joseph, 90-92, 96, 104
Rublee, Miss, 51-52, 61-62
Rural Health Plan, Kansas, 41-46
Russell Sage Foundation, 52
Salina *Journal*, 171, 182, 206
Samuel H. Kress Foundation, 72, 223-24
Saricks, Ambrose, 76, 88, 185, 192
Saturday Evening Post, 37, 41, 45, 124, 135, 137
Schaefer, J. Earl, 89, 183-84, 191
Schoeppel, Andrew, 125
School of Medicine, University of Kansas, 10, 14-15, 25, 29, 34, 38, 44, 53, 75, 213, 223
Seaver, James E., 77, 185
Shaeffer, Paul, 30
Shankel, Del, 72
Sharps rifle, 70, 108-09
Shaw, David, 137
Shaw, Warren, 161, 179

Shelby, Ernie, 128, 140-41, 154, 233-36
Shoemaker, W. H., 77, 80
slavery, 108-10
Smith, George Baxter, 52, 61, 72, 110, 175, 191-92
Smith, Senator Glee, 207
Socialism, 120-22
"Song of the Kansas Emigrant," 108
Spencer Chemical Company, 183, 185
Spencer Foundation, 71
Spencer Museum of Art, University of Kansas, 12, 66, 71, 73, 185
Spencer Research Library, 185
Spencer, Kenneth, 151-58, 183-85, 191
SPORTS ILLUSTRATED, 233
Sputnik, 85, 143, 146, 178
Squires, LaVannes, 111, 127-29
Staley, Charles E., 185
Star, Kansas City, 12, 30, 36, 91, 122, 138, 174, 203
Stirling-Maxwell collection, 91
Stirling-Maxwell, Sir William, 90
Stoic, 197
Stouffer, Oscar, 47
Stowel, Bob, 30
Student Council, All, 133, 144
students, dean of, 142, 217
Summerfield Foundation, 68, 90-91, 221
Summerfield, Solon E., 67-68, 90-91, 120-21
Symons, Eleanor, 97
Talmadge, Robert, 61, 96, 214
Taylor, Dean of Women Emily, 149, 217
Teacher's Association, Kansas State, 180
The Ballad of the Jealous Lover, 66, 70
The Crisis, 111-12
The Culture Broker: Franklin D. Murphy and the Transformation of Los Angeles, 72, 225
Theis, Frank, 172
Thurnau, the estate of Myrtle Elliott, 66
Tidwell, Charlie, 128, 140, 233-35
Till, Emmett, 118
Time Magazine, 116, 118
Times Literary Supplement, 96-97
Titus, James E., 185
Topeka State Journal, 172
"trans-Mississippi West," 69, 71, 93
Truman, Harry, 50, 53, 94, 152
Turnpike, Kansas, 138, 156
Tuttle, Jr., William M., 110

University of California Los Angeles
  (UCLA), 3, 5, 74, 81-82, 92, 104-05,
  149, 206-07, 210-11, 221
University of Kansas (KU), 3-7, 10, 12-
  13, 15, 17-18, 21-24, 26, 29-30, 34,
  39-41, 43-47, 49-54, 56-59, 61-63,
  66-81, 84, 89-91, 93-100, 102, 104,
  109-19, 123, 125-27, 129-32, 134-43,
  145, 148-58, 162-71, 173-87, 189-94,
  196-97, 199, 201-03, 205-19, 223,
  231, 233-36
University of Kansas Library, 73, 84
University of Pennsylvania, 9, 11, 15,
  21, 25-26, 28, 57, 164, 211, 218, 220,
  224-25, 227, 231
Valentine, Harry, 211
Vosper, Robert, 59, 61, 73, 80-105, 114,
  118, 157, 185, 203, 214, 217
Wahl, Dr. Harry, 30-31, 34
Walker, Nash, 124
wall of men, 108-09
War, Korean, 60, 132, 135, 160
Watson Library, 74-76, 79, 96-97, 203
Waugh, Jerry, 56, 136
Wescoe, Clarke, 45-47, 59, 149, 208,
  214
Wesley Foundation, 131
Western Civilization Program, 90
Whittier, John Greenleaf, 108
Whitworth, Roger, 126
Wichita Beacon, 202
Wichita Bibliophiles, 95
Wiley, Russell, 142
Williams, Skipper, 136
Wilson, Paul E., 185
Wood, Grant, 69-70
Woodward, C. Vann, 110
World War II, 26, 39, 117-18, 216, 230
Worth, George G., 185
Wortham, James, 77, 80-82, 84
Wright, C.O., 180
Yoe, Tom, 61, 91
"Young Turks," 30-31, 216
Young, Charles E., 221
Youngberg, Irvin, 90, 166, 192
Zook, E.R., 144-45, 169